THE EPIC OF JUAN LATINO

Dilemmas of Race and Religion in Renaissance Spain

The Epic of Juan Latino

Dilemmas of Race and Religion in Renaissance Spain

ELIZABETH R. WRIGHT

UNIVERSITY OF TORONTO PRESS
Toronto Buffalo London

Toronto Buffalo London
www.utppublishing.com

ISBN 978-1-4426-3752-8 (cloth)

Library and Archives Canada Cataloguing in Publication

Wright, Elizabeth R., 1963–, author
The epic of Juan Latino : dilemmas of race and religion in Renaissance Spain/ Elizabeth R. Wright.

(Toronto Iberic ; 22)
Includes bibliographical references and index.
ISBN 978-1-4426-3752-8 (cloth)

1. Latino, Juan, 1518?–. 2. Latino, Juan, 1518?– – Criticism and interpretation. 3. Epic poetry, Latin (Medieval and modern) – History and criticism. 4. Naval battles in literature. 5. Poets, Black – Spain – Biography. 6. Blacks – Spain – History – 16th century. 7. Race discrimination – Spain – History – 16th century. 8. Renaissance – Spain. 9. Spain – Race relations – History – 16th century. 10. Spain – Religion – 16th century. I. Title. II. Series: Toronto Iberic ; 22

PA8540.L615Z86 2016 871'.04 C2016-902983-2

University of Toronto Press acknowledges the financial assistance to its publishing program of the Canada Council for the Arts and the Ontario Arts Council, an agency of the Government of Ontario.

Canada Council for the Arts Conseil des Arts du Canada

Funded by the Government of Canada Financé par le gouvernement du Canada

Contents

For AQ

Acknowledgments

An essential question within *The Epic of Juan Latino* is how the educator-and-poet of Granada navigated the labyrinthine channels of power at court to publish his literary works. It seems appropriate, for my part, to recognize those who made this journey to publication edifying and pleasant. I thank Suzanne Rancourt of the University of Toronto Press for making this process meaningful and smooth. Miriam Skey and Barb Porter guided me in the editing and production. I owe profound gratitude to two rigorous and incisive anonymous readers. Maria Antonia Garcés gave numerous valuable suggestions, while sharing insights and references from her wide-ranging research on the early modern Mediterranean.

In the decade in which this project unfolded, I benefited from access to Spain's constellation of magnificent research libraries. I send a heartfelt thanks to the librarians and staff of the Biblioteca Histórica of the Universidad Complutense de Madrid, Casa de Velázquez, Real Biblioteca in Madrid's Royal Palace, Archivo General de Simancas, Archivo Universitario de Granada, and Biblioteca Nacional de España. Funding for work in these collections was provided by the Renaissance Society of America's Senior Scholar Research Grant, University of Georgia Provost's Summer Research Grant, and American Philosophical Society's Franklin Research Grant. Research leave time from University of Georgia's Willson Center for the Humanities and Arts was crucial for an early phase of work. A fellowship from the Gilder Lehrman Center for the Study of Slavery, Resistance, and Abolition at Yale University provided essential support for final revisions and also a context in which to debate lingering questions. Throughout, I have benefited from the scholarly communities that the Newberry Library and the John Carter Brown Library nurture, both on-site and beyond. Financial support for publication has come from the University of Georgia through the Department of Romance Languages, the Franklin College of Arts and Sciences, the Willson Center for the Humanities and Arts, and the President's Venture Fund.

It would take a long chapter to detail the ideas and inspirations I gained from Sarah Spence and Andrew Lemons, with whom I collaborated on the translation and edition of Juan Latino's Lepanto epic, the *Song of John of Austria*, a major part of the larger editorial project that became *The Battle of Lepanto* (2014), published as volume 61 of the I Tatti Renaissance Library. Their acuity as readers and interpreters of Latin poetry, senses of humour, and unfailing punctuality made a long-running and complex collaborative venture a pleasure from start to finish. Here too, I thank Leah Whittington, Associate Editor of the I Tatti Renaissance Library, who sacrificed evenings and weekends during a summer research trip to Rome to see our project through to completion. James Hankins, General Editor, gave unstinting support. His commitment to publishing Juan Latino's Lepanto epic within the ground-breaking I Tatti series was crucial for our collaborative edition, but also critical for my work on this monograph. This inclusion of Latino's epic in a series that is drawing new attention and giving wide access to neo-Latin literature of the Renaissance is also a boon to early modern Spanish studies as it expands from a long-standing focus on Castilian literature to take into account the full range of literary production in the realms of the Spanish Monarchy. Support from the National Endowment for the Humanities's Scholarly Edition and Translation Grant and from the Rockefeller Foundation's Bellagio Center Residency program – while specifically used to prepare *The Battle of Lepanto* – paid substantial added dividends in my work on *The Epic of Juan Latino*. I thank both agencies for support that was doubly useful.

Thoughtful interlocutors and cherished friends commented on sections-in-progress and debated central ideas. Thank you to Michael Armstrong-Roche, Laura Bass, Margaret Greer, A. Katie Harris, Aurelia Martín Casares, Ricardo Padrón, Sarah Pearsall, María José del Río Barredo, Tanya Tiffany, and my brother, Edward Wright-Ríos. As this project unfolded, it was of enormous help to work with Rodrigo Cacho Casal, Barbara Fuchs, Leah Middlebrook, and Emily Weissbourd in their capacity as editors of articles I prepared on Juan Latino. I thank them for the insights and suggestions I used to prepare those earlier examinations of this topic, which, in turn, helped me develop ideas here. Here too, I am indebted to José María Anguita, with whom I collaborated on an article for *Criticón* that explored Latino's interpretation of Book 9 of the *Aeneid*.

Key bibliographic and archival references have come from James Amelang, A. Katie Harris, Tatiana Seijas, David Spatz, and Daniel Wasserman-Soler. When still puzzling over the opening passage of Latino's epic, Geoffrey Parker shared his knowledge about Pedro de Deza in relation to the inner workings of the court of Philip II. Javier Castillo Fernández graciously shared a typescript of his monumental edition of Mármol Carvajal's *Historia del rebelión y castigo de los moriscos del Reino de Granada*, which is now available through the press of the Universidad de Granada. Joaneath Spicer, James A. Murnaghan Curator of Renaissance and Baroque Art at the Walters Art Gallery, kindly sent me a high quality photograph of her ingenious installation related to Juan Latino in the revelatory exhibit of 2012, *Revealing the African Presence in Renaissance Europe*.

The opportunity to debate my work-in-progress came about thanks to invitations to lecture on this project from Rolena Adorno, Laura Bass, Mercedes Blanco, Elizabeth Davis, Edward Friedman, Barbara Fuchs, Lu Ann Homza, Emiro Martínez-Osorio, Richard Rosa, Neil Safier, Phillip John Usher, Noël Valis, and Steven Wagschal. I am also grateful to the executive committee of the Asociación Internacional "Siglo de Oro" (AISO) for inviting me to give a plenary lecture on this work at the 2011 meeting in Poitiers (France), and to Santiago Fernández Mosquera for a witty and gracious introduction. At the University of Georgia, I have benefited immeasurably from conversations with Dana Bultman and Ben Ehlers, who have shared their research insights on early modern Spain. I thank Noel Fallows, Nina Hellerstein, and Stacey Casado for effective leadership and unstinting support in their respective time as heads of the Department of Romance Languages. I am also grateful to the many students enrolled in my classes who have immersed themselves in research about the people and communities of the early-modern Spanish world. Their perspectives, ideas, and creative sparks have expanded my horizons. Finally, space does not allow me to thank all my colleagues in the Department of Romance Languages, but I would note in closing how inspiring it is to walk into the cheerful, polyglot confines of Gilbert Hall each work day.

My last but most profound expression of gratitude is for Antonio Quiroga. While this book is far from his primary field of applied physics, he has been a generous supporter and perceptive interlocutor. I am sorry that I provide only passing glimpses of galley-bound soldiers who endure sword blows, storm surges, and rancid provisions. I dedicate it to him all the same, with love and thanks.

Notes on Text and Terminology

Latin texts by Juan Latino appear with the original and English translation immediately following. For his Lepanto epic, the translation is from *The Battle of Lepanto*, edited by Wright, Spence, and Lemons. His "On the Birth of Untroubled Times" is from a translation I prepared with Andrew Lemons. Most other sources are cited in English within the text, with the original in the endnotes. Unless otherwise noted, foreign-language translations are my own. Citations from Virgil's *Aeneid* will be paired with the translation by Robert Fagles, while those from Lucan's *Bellum civile* (Civil War) will appear with Susanna Morton Braund's English rendition. For Spanish-language sources from the early modern era, I modernize orthography and punctuation unless, in so doing, I would alter the meaning. For Latin citations, I follow the practice recommended by the editors of the I Tatti Renaissance Library. Thus, orthography is adapted to conform to the *Oxford Latin Dictionary*, edited by P.W. Glare, except that the *v* replaces the consonantal *u*. For terms in Arabic related to Islam and Spain's Hispano-Muslim heritage, I follow the transliteration of the *Encyclopedia of Islam and the Muslim World*, edited by Richard C. Martin (New York: Macmillan Reference, 2004), which I have accessed online via Gale Virtual Reference Library. Citations follow the author-date bibliographic citation method in order to help the reader note changes over time, whether in recent scholarship on Juan Latino or in tracing momentous changes that unfolded during his lifetime. In-text references to classic texts from antiquity or the modern era refer to the author and title. Bibliographic entries refer to the dates of the editions consulted.

Terminology

Juan Latino / John of Austria: To avoid confusion with the recurring first name, I refer to Juan Latino as such, only using the Latin Joannes Latinus when citing his published books or other documents where he is thus named. In contrast, I refer to the son of Charles V and Spanish commander at Lepanto as John of Austria, instead of Don Juan de Austria.

Isabel I of Castile / Isabella of Portugal: Queen Isabel (often called Isabella) is Isabel I of Castile. Unless otherwise noted, the Catholic Monarchs refers to Isabel I of Castile and her husband, Ferdinand II of Aragon. When I refer to the consort of Charles V and mother of Philip II, I use Empress Isabella or Isabella of Portugal.

Moriscos: I follow the historiographic convention in referring to Hispano-Muslims in Granada who were required to be baptized Christians after 1502 as Moriscos, but share the reservations that L.P. Harvey (2005, 3–9) registers. On a related note, I refer to the conflict of 1568–70 as a civil war, though it is known most widely as the Second Revolt of the Alpujarras or the Morisco Revolt.

Earlier Versions of this Research

This book draws on material from the following articles, though the ideas have been reworked and revised considerably. Once again, I am grateful to the editors and colleagues who guided these earlier works and thus helped me advance in this project:

"Modern War, Ancient Form: Lessons from Lepanto for a Latin Seminar in Post-Bellum Granada." In *Representing Imperial Rivalry in the Early Modern Mediterranean*, edited by Barbara Fuchs and Emily Weissbourd, 126–44. Toronto: University of Toronto Press, 2015.

"Scrutinizing Early Modern Warfare in Latin Hexameters: The *Austrias Carmen* of Joannes Latinus (Juan Latino)." In *Poiesis and Modernity in the Old and New Worlds*, edited by Anthony J. Cascardi and Leah Middlebrook, 139–58. Nashville: Vanderbilt University Press, 2012.

"Sombras de la *onorosa praeda*: un *exemplo* virgiliano para un aula granadina." José María Anguita and Elizabeth R. Wright. *Criticón* 115 (2012): 105–23.

"Narrating the Ineffable Lepanto: The *Austrias Carmen* of Joannes Latinus (Juan Latino)." *Hispanic Review* 77.1 (winter 2009): 71–92.

Illustrations

Abbreviations

Autoridades	Real Academia Española. *Diccionario de Autoridades.* 3 vols. Madrid: Gredos, 1976.
BAE	Biblioteca de Autores Españoles.
BH	Biblioteca Histórica Marqués de Valdecilla, Universidad Complutense de Madrid. Madrid, Spain.
BNE	Biblioteca Nacional de España. Madrid, Spain.
CODOIN	(*Colección de documentos inéditos para la historia de España*). See entry in bibliograpy.
Covarrubias	Covarrubias Orozco, Sebastián de. *Tesoro de la lengua castellana o española.* Edited by Felipe C.R. Maldonado, revised by Manuel Camarero. 2nd edition. Madrid: Castalia, 1995.
Diccionario	Real Academia: Real Academia Española. *Diccionario de la lengua española*. 21st edition. Madrid: RAE, 2001.
DLD	Brepolis. *Database of Latin Dictionaries*. Brepols Publishers Online. Accessed through GALILEO, University of Georgia Library.
LCL	Loeb Classical Library.
Lewis and Short	Charlton T. Lewis and Charles Short. *Harpers' Latin Dictionary*. New York: Harpers, 1884. Accessed through DLD above.
Nebrija	Elio Antonio de Nebrija. *Dictionarium Latinohispanicum, et vice versa Hispanicolatinum.* Antwerp: Joannes Steelsius, 1560 [1495].
OLD	*Oxford Latin Dictionary*. Edited by P.W. Glare. Rpt. Oxford: Clarendon Press. 2006 [1982].

THE EPIC OF JUAN LATINO

Introduction: A Lost Portrait and a Forgotten Name

Juan Latino (ca. 1517–ca. 1594) is Renaissance Europe's first known black poet. His landmark publication debut, the *Austrias Carmen* (hereafter *Song of John of Austria*), recounts the Battle of Lepanto of 7 October 1571. This epochal galley clash played out in a morning of fighting so intense it shocked even battle-hardened veterans, with estimates of almost 40,000 slain fighters and rowers. With John of Austria in command, a Catholic Holy League navy – comprising fleets from Spain, Venice, and the papacy – claimed victory over a formidable coalition of Muslim fleets assembled by the Ottoman sultan and his North African allies. Latino's literary commemoration of Lepanto attests to a reader and scholar steeped in Europe's classical literary heritage. It also bears the hallmarks of an innovative teacher of Latin. As would often be the case with writers from the African slave diaspora, this erudition had been hard won. Anticipating the struggle of Frederick Douglass three centuries later to gain literacy, Juan Latino followed the private lessons meant for his slightly younger master, Don Gonzalo Fernández de Córdoba, the third Duke of Sessa (1520–78). In so doing, he defied the explicit prohibitions of the grandee's adult guardians. But in time, a chronicle of the duke's family would trumpet Latino's accomplishments to draw attention to the nobleman's liberality and discernment. The Abbot of Rute (Francisco Fernández de Córdoba) thus recorded the slave's clandestine early education in his monumental history, *House of Córdoba*, but then celebrated how Latino ultimately gained renown teaching Latin in Granada in spite of bias against black Africans. This chronicle notes as well that the duke provided material support for the teaching position.[1]

Yet the ambition on display in the *Song of John of Austria* reveals a writer who aspired to more lasting glory than that on offer teaching Latin with subsidies from influential patrons. The poem's specifics on the battle suggest that as soon as news of it reached Granada, Latino gathered available bulletins and letters, while also eliciting eyewitness testimony. He then rushed to complete the poem in time for the battle's symbolically important first anniversary. To navigate the famously treacherous channels of court censorship, Latino sent the poem to King Philip II's private secretary for a kind of fast-track approval. The final publication that appeared in 1573 features a rigorously accurate and intricately allusive narration of the battle in almost two thousand Latin hexameter verses. A stunning proem in elegiac couplets, "De Natali Serenissimi" (On the Birth of Untroubled Times), prefaces this epic account, stating the case for the educator-turned-poet's lasting fame on two counts – as a noted educator of Granada and as a new kind of poet for the new, auspicious era at hand after the naval victory.[2]

How did Juan Latino attain such distinction at a time of intensifying mistreatment of blacks in Europe? Why is he so little known today? To recover this case of literacy and literary self-assertion in the first century of the Atlantic slave diaspora, I gather the scarce fragments of biographical evidence that trace a path from slavery to a distinguished teaching career. From here, my discussion will turn to the landmark epic poem with which Latino, in effect, renegotiated his hard-won freedom before the Spanish king, an international reading public, and posterity.

Throughout, I anchor my analysis in Granada, the city where Juan Latino lived almost all of his long life. By turns, I construe the Andalusian city in very specific local terms and in the broader framework of imperial Spain. For the first dimension, I hone my analysis on the noble household where Latino served, his neighbourhood, classroom, and the streets of Granada. But at the same time, the city on the Darro River is a fulcrum of Spain's imperial project, and as such, a place where the debates and violence that relate to this enterprise often originated. For this reason, it was highly appropriate if not strictly accurate when Christopher Columbus conjured the scene of Ferdinand II of Aragon and Isabel I of Castile (hereafter Ferdinand and Isabel) hoisting their standards over the Alhambra as his own point of departure for the Indies. In so doing, the Genoese mariner altered the time sequence of his negotiations to connect his expedition to Ferdinand and Isabel's triumphant entrance into the city on 2 January 1492. The pope, Alexander VI, granted them the title "Catholic Monarchs" in 1494 to honour their conquest of the last Muslim city on European soil. In like manner, Hernán Cortés's "Second Letter from Mexico" marks what we might call a "Granada pivot" at precisely the moment he transforms his expeditionary force into an unauthorized conquering army; in particular, he likens a major Tlaxcalan city to the captured Muslim metropolis, thereby certifying the wealth, sophistication, and desirability of the new land he proposes to conquer.[3] In the decades ahead, strategies and justifications for slave trading in the increasingly far-flung realms of the Spanish Monarchy would draw on the precedent of the enslavement of Granada's native Hispano-Muslims.[4]

In the case of Juan Latino's life and literary practice, we find that the extraordinary opportunities for education and social advancement he mobilized were the direct results of efforts to transform Iberia's last Muslim metropolis into a Christian city.[5] But in time, conflicts tied to this transformation undercut his accomplishments. Just before Latino published his Lepanto epic, the city was devastated by a civil war, best known today as the Second Revolt of the Alpujarras or the Morisco Revolt (1568–70). The conflict ignited when some Moriscos took up arms to resist intensifying crown repression that sought to eradicate their cultural practices and exerted intense fiscal pressure on their economic mainstays. When royal troops finally suppressed the revolt, the king ordered a mass expulsion of all Moriscos, regardless of whether or not they had rebelled. He also authorized numerous slave auctions to punish combatants and reward his soldiers. The foremost victims here were Granada's *cristianos nuevos de moros* (New Christians of [Hispano-] Muslim descent), known widely as Moriscos. These were native-born Granadinos required to undergo Catholic baptism after 1502. Though no signs indicate Juan Latino was himself a Muslim convert to Christianity or had any Muslim ancestry, the war devastated the city's economy and the fledgling educational institutions where he taught. As well, the repression targeted at Granada's Moriscos challenged his own hard-won advancement and public renown as a black educator in the city.

Against this tense backdrop, Latino's assertion of his political and cultural relevance through print publication comes into focus as a symbolic renegotiation of his stature as a free black-African Christian. The freedman, in this respect, provides another opportunity to examine issues and tensions that Laura Bass and Jorge Cañizares-Esguerra tie to self-fashioning in the Hispanic Baroque. In peninsular realms and in Spanish America, anxieties about racial difference and Christian lineage gave rise to a defining paradox of imperial Spain that both scholars illuminate: the ethnic diversity that follows from empire building coexists with a heightened emphasis on blood purity (*limpieza de sangre*). Though blood purity statutes initially targeted *conversos* and the alleged "taint" of Jewish lineage, the selective discrimination these measures institutionalized would ultimately exert pressure on individuals and communities who could not plausibly claim Christian ancestry from time immemorial. Latino, in contrast to the self-fashioners Bass and Cañizares examine, does not mobilize available narratives that would have supported a claim to be a black Old Christian. As I will discuss in detail, Latino inclines instead to representations of his Christian virtue that follow from baptism or personal will, suggesting a subtle defence of conversion.[6]

Given the pressing importance of family lineage in sixteenth-century Spain, it is poignant that reliable sources do not allow us to locate the basic touchstones of identity for Juan Latino, whether parentage, ancestral homeland, or birth date.[7] Nor do we know when or how he gained his liberty. Despite the lack of a documented manumission, I will refer to him as a freedman in the pages ahead, to emphasize the extent to which he had attained the trappings of liberty denied to the numerous enslaved blacks living nearby. Indeed, Latino bought a home with his wife Ana Carlobal, the couple raised a family, hired a couple of servants, and even invested in bonds. Intriguingly, we find no unusual remarks in period sources about the couple being interracial.[8] "Freedman" conveys as well Juan Latino's mastery of literature and poetry, pillars of the liberal arts (*artes liberales*) which correlated in classical lexicon to "the skills of freemen," in implicit contrast to the *artes iliberales* or *sordidae,* employment of slaves or the lower classes. When Latino presents himself in several instances as a black man trained in the liberal arts, he marks a distance from the majority of enslaved and free blacks in his city who specialized in demanding manual labour.[9]

"Freedman" is also pertinent, and sometimes problematic, given that Latino's reputation was so closely tied to his former master, the third Duke of Sessa. A city chronicler of the early seventeenth century reported that the duke liked to declare that "rara avis in terra, corvo simillima negro," literally my "black raven is a rare bird on earth," though explained in the Castilian rendition as "my black man is as rare on earth as the phoenix." The quip adapts a verse from Juvenal, which likens a faithful wife to a rare black swan. Sessa's celebration of Latino, revealingly, trades the misogyny of the Roman satirist for a racially charged humour gaining increasing currency in Iberia in the sixteenth century. After all, the duke gestures to a form of aristocratic ostentation, whereby elite Europeans employed and posed for portraits with black servants, trumpeting their wealth and, in some cases, making jokes about black skin colour.[10] But Latino would mobilize his own avian allusions to claim glory and royal sponsorship on his own terms. The first such instance appears in the proem in elegiac couplets already mentioned, "On the Birth of Untroubled Times," when the poetic voice hails Juan Latino's unique capacity to serve as Spain's poet of Lepanto. In support, the panegyric casts John of Austria, the hero of the battle, as a phoenix and presents the poet as an auspicious black raven. For this self-presentation to King Philip II, Latino adapts a black raven from another classical authority – the Roman historian Suetonius. I will explore this rhetorical gesture in some depth in my third chapter. My closing section will consider Latino's mobilization of yet another avian wonder in the course of assessing his contested legacy in Granada and Spanish literary history more broadly.

For now, suffice it to note the historical injustice through which the erudite and skilled poet-and-educator's fame rests in great measure today on the farcical treatment accorded him in the circa 1615 play *Juan Latino,* by Diego Ximénez de Enciso. This *comedia* is but the best known of a series of seventeenth-century fictionalizations, which explained Juan Latino's unusual social advancement and interracial marriage with racially charged, apocryphal anecdotes.[11] To draw attention to the lack of historically accurate information about the educator-and-poet's life story, art historian Joaneath Spicer hung an empty picture frame next to Latino's name in the path-breaking Walters Art Museum exhibit of 2012–13, titled *Revealing the African Presence in Renaissance Europe.*[12] Spicer's ingenious curatorial decision also drew attention to the now lost portrait of the freedman once owned by King Philip IV, a fact documented in a 1636 inventory of the Alcazar Palace. The entry notes the king owned a "portrait from the chest up of a black man, who is Juan Latino, with a label that says he was ninety years old."[13] Unfortunately, this painting is lost. It may have been destroyed in the 1734 fire that consumed countless treasures from the Alcazar Palace.

But what aspect of Juan Latino's public persona did the lost portrait recollect? Did the painter or commissioning patron honour Juan Latino's astounding upward mobility, innovative Latin poetry, and distinguished teaching career? Or was the portrait's point of inspiration the bondage in childhood, when he served a grandee? Or perhaps the likeness of the black poet-and-educator signified difference at a time where colour-based discrimination was intensifying in tandem with the expanding Atlantic slave trade? A literal reading of the inventory entry does suggest a profound degree of objectification, with the indefinite article marking the painting as a portrait of "un negro," that is, "a black man." In contrast, when the scribe moved to describe the next two canvases in the same chamber above the Hall of Orders (Sala de Órdenes), one of a nobleman in armour and the other of a woman dressed in black, he made no note of skin colour or ethnicity.[14] Nor is Philip the Fair with sceptre, hanging just before Latino's portrait in the same chamber, called a "white king"; he is, simply, Felipe I. Implied in this notarial shorthand is a normative white, European identity.

The assumption informing the scribe's grammar above brings to mind Albrecht Dürer's charcoal drawing of an unnamed black man that serves as this book's cover illustration [figure 1]. Historian Kate Lowe suggests that the bearded man was a free servant of the Portuguese merchant João Brandão who patronized the artist, noting as well that the 1508 date is questionable. She compares the confident, outward gaze of the black man with the downcast eyes of a black woman whom we know Dürer encountered in Brandão's household, though his drawing of her only records the woman as "Katharina, his Moor" [figure 2].[15] The loose terminology and its underlying legal ambiguity speak volumes about this early phase of the Atlantic slave trade. "Moor," from the Roman term for North African people (*Maurus, Mauri*), here denotes a woman of sub-Saharan ethnicity, with the added slippage of the ethnonym deployed as a synonym for "slave." Within Dürer's slippery terminology is a legal contradiction, in that a woman in Antwerp circa 1521 could not legally be enslaved, in contrast to the merchant's native Portugal. Some of the same problems posed by Dürer's portrait of Katharina will emerge repeatedly as we piece together the life and literary practice of Juan Latino in relation to the African slave diaspora. These include the European impulse to amalgamate the diverse ethnicities of sub-Saharan Africa and the Maghreb into the variable and fraught ethnonym Moor, as well as the often nebulous legality of slave-holding. Juan Latino, like Katharina before him, was the victim of a human trafficking business that was growing by way of "two thousand deceptions ... a thousand thefts, and as many raids," to use the words of jurist Tomás Mercado. On this issue, the online Trans-Atlantic Slave Trade Database offers statistical confirmation of the expansion of the morally dubious business. The database also demonstrates how, in

Figure 1 Albrecht Dürer, Portrait Study of a Black Man [name unknown], 1508? Charcoal on Paper, Albertina, Vienna, Inventory 3122. Reproduced by permission.

Art historians do not consider the 1508 date firm. As to the unnamed sitter, he may have been a free servant working in the same household where Dürer encountered Katharina, pictured in figure 2. Both portrait studies were undertaken as part of the *Four Books of Human Proportion* (1528), which ultimately involved the direct study of hundreds of men and women, whom Dürer compared to figures from classical Greek sculpture (see Spicer 2012, 46).

Figure 2 Albrecht Dürer, Study of Katharina (1521). Metalpoint on prepared light pink paper. Gabinetto Disegni e Stampe degli Uffizi, Florence (160E). Reproduced by permission.

Dürer encountered the sitter in the household of Portuguese factor João Brandão. His identification of her as "Katharina, his Moor" – understood as "his slave" – speaks to the way that *Maurus* was used as an ethnonym with little precision (Harvey 2005, 3–9). The legality here was also dubious: holding Katharina as a slave, the merchant would have been defying the law in Antwerp where he was residing, as opposed to his native Portugal (Lowe, 2012, 17). But it was precisely these legal ambiguities that fomented the growth of the Atlantic slave trade in the early sixteenth century, as jurists and theologians of the time acknowledged. See, for example, Mercado 1571, fol. 101v.

its first century, most voyages were undertaken by Spanish or Portuguese merchants.[16]

From a long-range perspective, Dürer's portrait studies, like the scribal notation to Juan Latino's now missing portrait just over a century later, anticipate a defining tension of early modernity. Viewed in isolation, the bearded man and Katharina are black, dignified, and beautiful. But examined in relation to the artistic practice from which the drawings emerged, we find a white-European impulse to deny agency and full humanity to blacks, or at least, to gauge their individual merits with a scale whose calibration mechanism is white and European. Specifically, the drawings were part of Dürer's study of human proportions, in which he compared hundreds of men and women to figures from classical Greek sculpture.[17] As visual signposts of an era of intensifying contacts between white Europeans and black Africans, Dürer's studies and Latino's lost portrait belong together conceptually. Together, they offer poignant reminders of the extent to which the emergence of Western modernity was inextricably tied to the black slave diaspora. Consequently, the history of the slave trade is not a subdiscipline for specialists in a few areas, but a fundamental part of the "ethical and intellectual heritage of the West as a whole," as Paul Gilroy underscores in *The Black Atlantic*.[18]

Mindful of the broad European and Atlantic contexts that Gilroy traces for the post-Enlightenment era, I move back in time and centre my analysis on Juan Latino's life and literary career in Granada. Again, I construe this place both in terms of the specific local context and the broader scope of Spain's imperial project. Brought by the family he served to the city some three decades after Ferdinand and Isabel accepted the surrender of the Nasrid ruler Mohammed Abi Abdilehi (Boabdil), Juan Latino spent his formative years in a city under reconstruction. During his youth, the site of a shrine to a Muslim hermit became a monastery; grammar school lessons would take place in a splendid madrasa; a succession of mosques were dismantled with their stones repurposed for Catholic churches; and the narrow streets typical of medinas of North Africa would be widened to fit Castilian notions of civic order. Most fatefully, tens of thousands of native-born Granadinos would be compelled to abandon their ancestral religion; change their surnames; and forget a regional variant of Arabic that had evolved to capture the intricacies of the silk weaving, ceramic production, and fruit cultivation that had made the region so prosperous. In the two years before the Battle of Lepanto transpired, crown officials expelled some 80,000 Moriscos to other parts of Castile, while authorizing the enslavement of another 10,000, as collective punishment for the aforementioned civil war known most often as the Second Revolt of the Alpujarras. As noted at the outset, this tragedy played out at very close range to Juan Latino's home and classroom. Granada's civil war and mass expulsion left many traces in the freedman's epic, even though the Battle of Lepanto took place across the Mediterranean.[19]

Again, with the exceedingly scarce fragments of evidence that survive, we cannot pinpoint affiliations or antipathies between Juan Latino and the Moriscos of Granada. Yet the imprint of the city's Islamic heritage was profound. The wealth and prestige of Latino's former master stemmed from the exploits of the grandfather for whom he was named, Gonzalo Fernández de Córdoba. Best known by his sobriquet as Spain's Gran Capitán (Grand Captain), this military leader attained the highest noble status of grandee through the title of the first Duke of Sessa. A relative upstart in Castile's high aristocracy, the Gran Capitán gained his military expertise and riches in the last phase of the battle for Granada, taking a pivotal role in negotiating the capitulation of Nasrid Granada in 1492.[20] Latino's own quotidian life brought many points of contact with the Hispano-Muslims and their descendants who remained in the city after 1492. Slaves and servants who were Muslim converts would have served alongside Latino in the Sessa household. Some studied with him in the grammar school and university that Charles V founded in Granada to promote evangelization of the region's Hispano-Muslims. In time, some of Latino's own grammar school students, faculty colleagues, and neighbours were acculturated Moriscos.[21] Hence my conviction that in piecing together the life story of Juan Latino in Granada, we can also cast new light on the dilemmas of race and religion that shaped Spain's imperial expansion.

A few comments are in order on race, the most mutable of my terms. In the 1611 *Tesoro de la lengua castellana o española* of Sebastián de Covarrubias (hereafter Covarrubias), we see the impact of the intensifying mania for bloody purity in the realms of the Spanish Monarchy. The lexicographer pinpoints *raza* as a term for pure-breed horses, explains its use in classifying textile fibres, and finally, registers a religious dimension that speaks to the spreading obsession about bloody purity: "race in genealogies is understood negatively as having some Moorish or Jewish race."[22] Tracing the changing meaning of "race" in Iberian vernacular languages, editors of *Rereading the Black Legend* remind us that the emerging discourses of religious and racial difference in Spanish realms would become an integral facet of western modernity.[23] Latino's own life story, literary practice, and posthumous erasure attest to this emerging discourse of colour-based discrimination construed as racial, even though the pseudoscience of racial classification by skin colour would not be codified until some two centuries after Juan Latino's life.

Yet in his literary practice, the freedman anticipates the later association of race with skin colour. Speaking to Philip II's rekindled ambitions for eastern imperial expansion in the wake of Lepanto, Latino warns the king that white bias against a black like himself in Spain is short-sighted:

> Quod si nostra tuis facies Rex nigra ministris
> displicet, Aethiopum non placet alba viris.
> Illic Auroram, sordet, qui viserit albus,
> suntque duces nigri, rex quoque fuscus adest.
> (Latino, "On the Birth of Untroubled Times," in Appendix 1, ll. 19–22; Latino 1573, 1st gathering, fol. 10r)[24]

> (For if our black face, oh king, displeases your emissaries, a white one does not please men of Aethiopia. There, a white man who visits the East is considered vile, and there are black leaders, and there is even a dark-skinned king.)

A subsequent passage of the same poem warns that illogical bias against blacks will undermine Philip II's manifest aspirations to global rule:

> Nec rerum est Dominus, qui non admiserit omnes,
> gentem ne excludat regia forte meam.
> (Latino, "On the Birth of Untroubled Times," in Appendix 1, ll. 41–2; Latino 1573, 1st gathering, fol. 10v)

> (There is no lord of states who has not admitted everyone, nor monarchy that would exclude my race capriciously).

These verses, in essence, denounce what historian James Sweet has termed "racism without race."[25] Above, "gentem ne excludat … meam" mobilizes the Latin *gens* (family, lineage) in a manner that stretches beyond the sixteenth-century notions of *raza*. So doing, the poet anticipates later usage in which the term denotes colour-based discrimination. In contrast, for other prominent poets of the day, *gens* denotes a nation or community. For instance, Pierre de Ronsard's 1572 *Franciad* adapts Virgil's *gens hectorea* in French as *race*.[26] Latino elsewhere hews to the more characteristic sixteenth-century usage in which the Latin *gens* correlates to Castilian *raza*. But in Spanish usage of the times, the term carries a negative conception of non-Christian lineage that does not signify in Ronsard. For example, early in the Lepanto epic, the poetic voice uses a form of *gens* to label the Morisco uprising as the crime of "a notorious race of evil heretics" (haereticumque malum, manifestae crimina *gentis* [emphasis added]).[27] In view of the slipperiness of *raza* or *gens* in early modern usage and in Latino's own mobilization of the term, I conceive of the "race and religion" of my title as if arrayed in non-concentric circles. At times, "race" refers to religious heritage as a sign of the growing bias against New Christians of Muslim or Jewish origins. At other times, I will construe race in terms of the colour-based discrimination Latino's verses above anticipate and refute.

As we know all too well, neither Philip II nor other European imperialists of the early modern era would heed Latino's call to an inclusive and culturally relative conception of skin colour. Events we can document in Latino's later years presage the increasing mistreatment and denigration of black Africans. We find evidence the educator became the target of racial jests by other poets of Granada. In the university, a powerful faction on the faculty sought to oust Latino from the prime classroom location he had occupied for decades. To be sure, faculty politics that I will explore in some detail cannot be ascribed with certainty to bias against a black man. Not so for the posthumous obfuscation Latino suffered in seventeenth-century Spanish letters, which unfolded soon after his death and so clearly pivoted on racist tropes.[28]

Fortunately, advances in several fields now make this a propitious moment for restoring Juan Latino to the international republic of letters in which he claimed membership. His Lepanto epic has recently appeared for the first time in an annotated edition with facing English translation, which I prepared with Sarah Spence and Andrew Lemons. Latino's epic of Lepanto is, fittingly, the first poem from Spain to appear in the I Tatti Renaissance Library, a series making great strides in recovering the neo-Latin literature from the Renaissance through accessible, bilingual editions modelled on the storied Loeb Classical Library. The I Tatti volume *The Battle of Lepanto* features Latino's poem along with works by twenty-two neo-Latin poets from Italy, thereby restoring Latino to the cosmopolitan literary realm in which he staked a claim to lasting renown.[29]

When Latino refutes colour prejudice in the elegy for Philip II, he epitomizes a facet of neo-Latin literature highlighted in a special issue of *Renæssanceforum*, whose editors explore how the Roman language became a medium for asserting and dignifying the identities of ethnic and linguistic minorities.[30] Contributors thus explore how writers from Catalonia, Wales, Ireland, and Nahua communities of Mexico embraced Latin literary expression to articulate their distinct national identities. Juan Latino's position with regards to the classical language differs from a native speaker of Nahuatl or Gaelic who chose Latin over his or her vernacular language, in that the schoolmaster belongs to the widely dispersed community of diasporic black Africans as opposed to a conquered realm or region. But what unites them is the decidedly early modern take on the ancient language. That is, the choice of Latin as the medium for expression does not simply follow from an adherence to literary tradition or from aspirations to join the ranks of the Latinate elite, though those impulses certainly operate. The language of ancient Rome is also a vehicle for asserting and dignifying a minority group or colonized people within a transnational early modern empire.

In terms of Latino's biography and his place in Hispanic studies, my search for and examination of the evidence will follow the path first charted by Antonio Marín Ocete. His landmark 1923–4 article compiled all known archival sources, leaving a paper trail that still guides scholars. At times, however, Marín Ocete filled information gaps with unverifiable or implausible anecdotes from the above-mentioned play by Ximénez de Enciso, *Juan Latino*. Reservations aside, Marín Ocete intimated a complexity of the Lepanto epic that eluded his grasp, anticipating that later generations of scholars might decipher Juan Latino's intricate epic.[31] Subsequent studies by Spratlin (1938) and Masó (1973) adhered to Marín Ocete's sources and basic narrative outline. Another step to recover the "the epic of Juan Latino" was the Spanish translation by José Sánchez Marín. Though his edition lacks annotations and sometimes suffers from overly vague translations, its transcription and facing Spanish translation gave access to Latino's work in the era before digitized copies of the *princeps* were available online.[32]

Definitive confirmation of Latino's foundational stature in African diaspora studies came in the 1990s, in Baltasar Fra Molinero's seminal *La imagen de los negros en el teatro del Siglo de Oro* and the literature review by Henry Louis Gates Jr and Maria Wolff. Gates's theory of signification also provides a theoretical model for construing Latino's self-confident poetic virtuosity. In particular, the freedman of Granada's work anticipates the feats of linguistic dexterity and wit that would anchor self-assertion by writers from the African diaspora. Though Latino uses classical Latin where the African-American writers Gates examines use vernacular expression, the idea of self-assertion through verbal acrobatics offers a useful framework for analysis, as Chantell Smith has demonstrated in a recent expansion on this line of analysis.[33]

From the perspective of Hispanic studies, documentation of Latino's unacknowledged influence on other Spanish poets came from Christopher Maurer. Through masterful philological detective work, he demonstrated that a preliminary verse from Latino's Lepanto epic was the unacknowledged source for Hernando de Acuña's famous hendecasyllable, "un Monarca, un Imperio y una Espada" (one Monarch, one Empire, and one Sword). More recently, classics scholar J. Mira Seo registered the poet's profound command of the western literary tradition, a line of inquiry further developed by Andrew Lemons, who has revealed intricacies of rhythm and versification that demonstrate the freedman's connections to classical and medieval Latin literature. John Beusterien, for his part, tied Latino's canonization in caricature to anxieties about Spain's Moorish heritage. New work on Juan Latino has also emerged from recent thesis projects.[34] Finally, special mention is due the study of slavery in sixteenth-century Granada by anthropologist Aurelia Martín Casares. Though her focus was broader, she revealed new evidence about Latino's life from her groundbreaking archival work. As important, her contextualization situates Latino's advancement in relation to the thousands of sub-Saharan Africans enslaved in sixteenth-century Andalusia.[35]

With these forerunners in mind, *The Epic of Juan Latino* retraces and contextualizes this story of Juan Latino's upward mobility and literary self-fashioning in two parts. The first emphasizes biographical analysis and the second concentrates on Latino's foremost literary accomplishment, the epic of Lepanto. Each part could stand alone. That said, the story is most meaningful when the two parts are read in sequence. Part I, "From Slave to Freedman in Granada," charts Latino's path to freedom and social advancement, supplementing the rare fragments of archival evidence with intensive contextual analysis. Here, chapter 1, "Latin Lessons amid the Remnants of Al-Andalus," pieces together the story of Latino's early life as a slave, his education, and his unusual social advancement, all of which played out against the backdrop of efforts to Christianize Granada's people and public spaces in the wake of its 1492 capture by Ferdinand of Aragon and Isabel of Castile.

Continuing, chapter 2, "Civil War, Shattered *Convivencia*," examines how the Morisco revolt of 1568–70 utterly changed the environment that had allowed Latino's upward mobility and forced a recalibration of his social stature. Crown officials used the uprising to justify what historians today consider the first modern case of a state-run ethnic cleansing campaign. The backlash against Granadinos of Hispano-Muslim origins jeopardized Latino's own hard-won social stature, even if he was not himself a Morisco. I offer a detailed narrative of this series of events out of the conviction that this conflict and its aftermath inform Latino's self-fashioning as an author of poetry in classical genres.

These first two chapters adhere to sources for which I found reasonable corroboration. Notes draw attention to problems or questions related to documents consulted. In cases where reliable period sources are not available, I draw on the broader cultural history of his home city and the wider Spanish world. A reader of Part I may, in the end, be surprised at the extent to which Juan Latino's own story of education and advancement intertwines with the history of Granada's Moriscos. I certainly was. As I delved deeper into the freedman's biography over the past half-decade, this interconnection emerged as something more profound and unsettling than I had anticipated.

Part II, "The Epic of Lepanto," concentrates on how Juan Latino reconfigured classical literary forms to speak to modern concerns. In so doing, I trace how he renegotiates the terms of his own emancipation and social advancement. As a first step, chapter 3, "A Black Poet and a Habsburg Phoenix," explores how Juan Latino deployed elegiac couplets to assert his own hard-won social position and denounce intensifying colour prejudice directed at black Africans. Chapter 4, "Christians and Muslims on the Battle Lines," interrogates the underlying tensions of the *Song of John of Austria*, the epic poem that narrates the Battle of Lepanto. Though written in Latin hexameters that emulate Virgil's *Aeneid*, the poem bears witness to the special problems that followed from empire building in the sixteenth century. I pay particular attention to how Latino airs yet ultimately undercuts the anti-Muslim propaganda that powerful sponsors in Granada and at court had used to justify the repression of the region's Moriscos. Here too, I consider evidence of the perilous waters of faction politics that the poet had to navigate to gain sponsorship in his home city. I then turn in chapter 5, "The Costs of Modern Warfare," to an exploration of literary allusions and narrative sequence. At crucial junctures, the poem draws attention to the moral implications of artillery weapons and the reliance on slave labour on Mediterranean galleys, two crucial ingredients in the victory of allied Catholic fleets at Lepanto. In addition, I consider the subtle ways the poem airs sympathy towards Muslims who fought in the battle or served as captive rowers on Spanish ships.

Ultimately, such sympathetic glimpses of Muslims at Lepanto are brief. Anti-Muslim rhetoric that jars our sensibilities today frames the opening and closing passages of the poem. Which position comes closest to that of the poet-and-educator of Granada? Is it the magnanimous Christian writer who grasps the multitude of shared experiences and beliefs that tie him to the Muslims of the Mediterranean? Or is it the avatar of the militant Catholic orthodoxy ascendant at the time of Lepanto in Philip II's inner circle of advisors? Barring the improbable re-emergence of a cache of letters or other first-person testimony, we can never pinpoint Latino's true self and sympathies. The best we can offer is a thorough and honest examination of the context in which he lived, worked, and wrote his poetry.

Hence my decision to start and end this story in the city where Latino lived for some seven decades. At first glance, this rootedness in one place seems a world away from the mobility of the most famous early writers of the black diaspora, such as Phyllis Wheatley, Olaudah Equiano, and Frederick Douglass.[36] But while it is true that Juan Latino lived most of his life in one place, his one surviving account of how he gained education and social advancement makes clear that he situated his Granada in the broader spaces of Spain's imperial expansion and the unfolding African diaspora. Chapter 1, "Latin Lessons amid the Remnants of Al-Andalus," goes to this place, at once the specific city and a symbol of Spain in the wider world.

PART ONE

From Slave to Freedman in Granada

1 Latin Lessons amid the Remnants of Al-Andalus

A Royal Ceremony and Authorial Self-Assertion

On 25 January 1574, Granada's elite convened in the city's Capilla Real (Royal Chapel) for a ceremony that King Philip II had planned with minute precision. They were arrayed by rank: first the grandee who represented the absent king; then the bishop of the neighbouring city of Jaén; and in turn, magistrates and inquisitors by seniority. As they stood solemn watch, chapel workers disinterred and then examined the remains of the monarch's departed family members. One by one, they identified and paid homage to Philip II's mother, Isabella of Portugal; his late queen-consort, María of Portugal; and two brothers who died in childhood, the Infantes Don Fernando and Don Juan. Workers then resealed the coffins for the long journey from Granada to the king's newly built Escorial Palace complex.[1] From start to finish, the transfer ceremony enacted and reaffirmed the Habsburg religious devotion that anchored Philip II's self-conception as the world's foremost Catholic king.[2]

The famously detail-oriented king did not conceive a place for Juan Latino in this dramatization of piety and power. Granada officials did, however, ask him to commemorate the ceremony with poems that highlight the city's centrality within Habsburg Spain. Ear well-tuned to the solemn occasion, Latino prefaced his book of poems on this 1576 ceremony with a brief but assertive account of his own life journey from slavery to social prominence. I quote the statement in full, given its importance as the one known autobiography and the extreme rarity of the 1576 book of occasional verse in which it appears:

> Haec, Ioannes Latinus Aethiops Christicola, ex Aethiopia usque infans advectus, excellentissimi, et invictissimi Gonsalvi Ferdinandi a Corduba, ducis Suessae Gonsalvi Magni Hispaniarum ducis nepotis servus, ab ipso infantiae lacte simul nutritus, cum ipso a rudibus animis liberalibus artibus institutus, et doctus, et tandem libertate donatus, Garnatae ab illustrissimo, pariter et Reverendissimo Petro Guerrero Garnatensi Archiepiscopo extra omnem aleam doctissimo, sanctae Ecclesiae Garnatae Cathedram Grammaticae et Latini sermonis accepit moderandam: quam per viginti annos feliciter moderatus est, sub Catholico Philippo Hispaniarum Rege translationi regalium corporum scripsit Epitaphia, ad honorem et gloriam omnipotentis Dei, et Sanctissimae virginis Mariae matris eius: Garnatae anno aetatis suae quinquagessimo octavo. (*De Translatione*, prologue, unnumbered folios)

> (Joannes Latinus, Ethiopian follower of Christ, taken out of Ethiopia in infancy, slave of the most excellent and invincible Gonzalo Fernández de Córdoba, duke of Sessa, grandson of great Gonzalo of Hispania, by him nourished with the same milk of infancy, with him from untamed mind instructed through liberal arts, and taught, and finally given liberty; from Pedro Guerrero, the most reverend archbishop of Granada, and learned beyond all doubt, he received a chair on behalf of the holy church of Granada for the teaching of Grammar and Latin language, which he has successfully taught for twenty years. During the reign of Philip II, Catholic King of Spain, he wrote these epitaphs for the translation of royal bodies, for the honor and glory of God, and the holy Virgin Mary, his mother. In Granada, in the fifty-eighth year of life.)

The count of fifty-eight years situates Latino's birth circa 1516–18, depending on whether the point from which he bases his count is 1574, when he presented the volume to crown officials for publication approval, or some two years later, when the book cleared bureaucratic hurdles and appeared in print. As positioned on the printed page (see figure 3), an ornamental initial claims the reader's attention. Much in the way sumptuous clothing might draw a viewer's focus to a painted portrait on a canvas, an oversized *H* intensifies the grammatical function of the demonstrative adjective *haec*, drawing the reader to "these epitaphs" (*haec epitaphia*).

This concise autobiography charts Latino's path from slavery to social prominence. We can trace his steps from a sub-Saharan homeland to enslavement, education, emancipation, and eventual assimilation

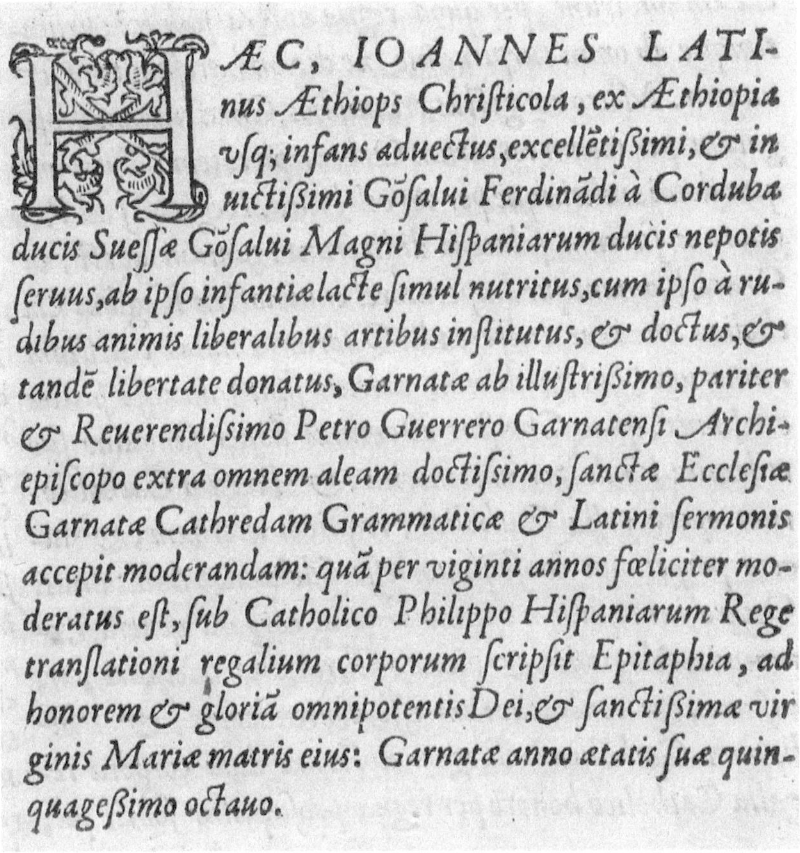

HÆC, IOANNES LATI-
nus Æthiops Chriſticola, ex Æthiopia
vſq; infans aduectus, excellẽtiſsimi, & in
uictiſsimi Gõſalui Ferdinãdi à Corduba
ducis Sueſſæ Gõſalui Magni Hiſpaniarum ducis nepotis
ſeruus, ab ipſo infantiæ lacte ſimul nutritus, cum ipſo à rudibus animis liberalibus artibus inſtitutus, & doctus, &
tandẽ libertate donatus, Garnatæ ab illuſtriſsimo, pariter
& Reuerendiſsimo Petro Guerrero Garnatenſi Archi-
epiſcopo extra omnem aleam doctiſsimo, ſanctæ Eccleſiæ
Garnatæ Cathredam Grammaticæ & Latini ſermonis
accepit moderandam: quã per viginti annos fœliciter mo-
deratus eſt, ſub Catholico Philippo Hiſpaniarum Rege
tranſlationi regalium corporum ſcripſit Epitaphia, ad
honorem & gloriã omnipotentis Dei, & ſanctiſsimæ vir
ginis Mariæ matris eius: Garnatæ anno ætatis ſuæ quin-
quageſsimo octauo.

Figure 3 Autobiography in miniature. Juan Latino, *De Translatione* (1576?). Juan Latino's only known autobiographical statement prefaces a volume of poems that commemorates the solemn transfer of Philip II's deceased family members from burial in Granada's Capilla Real to the new mausoleum at the Escorial. Asserting his own claim to lasting renown, Latino recounts his path to freedom and public recognition. No information survives to allow us to identify Latino's biological parents, nor can we ascertain how and when he gained freedom.

Source: Juan Latino, *De augusta et catholica regalium corporum translatione per Catholicum Phillipum […] Epigrammatum sive Epitaphiorum, libri duo*. Granada: Hugo Mena, circa 1576. By permission of the Biblioteca Nacional de España, R4117.

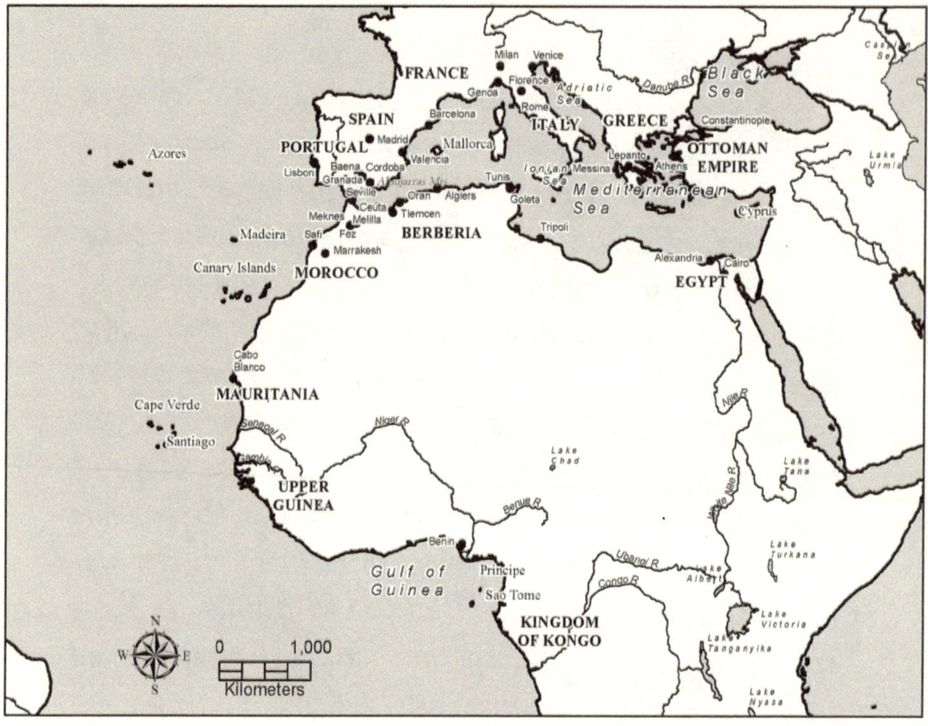

Figure 4 The World of Juan Latino, ca. 1517–ca. 1594. Surviving archival records suggest Juan Latino lived most of his life in Granada in southern Spain (Andalusia). But the city's tumultuous history and diverse social fabric would be shaped in part by events in this wider world, including Ottoman advances in the eastern Mediterranean, the resilience of corsair states in North Africa (Berberia), and the increasing numbers of people from sub-Saharan Africa kidnapped and loaded on to slave ships in West African ports.

Credit: By Thomas R. Jordan, Southern Resource Mapping

into Granada's "middling" people. What the educator-and-poet does not acknowledge in this compressed statement is a point that will emerge throughout this study: time and again, Latino's opportunities for advancement followed from efforts by church and crown officials to render Granada a Christian city. But that transformation would, in time, yield tensions that would make Latino's own gains more tenuous, even if he himself was not a Morisco and in writing would take pains to mark a distance.

Birth and Parentage?

The Ariadne's thread for Latino's autobiography in miniature is the self-assertion as a black follower of Christ, *Aethiops Christicola*. A widely used neologism from Late Latinity, *Christicola* contracts *Christus cultor*, or one who worships Christ. The term implies a piety from personal will, rather than ethnic or racial heritage. In the context of Spanish society in the mid- to late sixteenth century, the term speaks to Juan Latino's identity as a black-African New Christian, in implied contrast with Old Christians. Though *Cristiano Nuevo* referred most commonly to individuals with Jewish or Muslim ancestry, it also applied to non-European converts from sub-Saharan Africa, Asia, or the Americas. The distinction between New and Old Christians was becoming increasingly significant, with growing suspicions and pressures focused on the former. One might, in consequence, have expected the freedman to draw on available histories or myths of the ancestral Christianity of black Africans to assert his own Old Christian status. For this purpose, a black writer could have invoked the baptism of the Ethiopian eunuch by Philip recounted in the Acts of the Apostles. More suspect but still a staple of cartography and travel writing was Prester John, the fabulously rich black Christian king ruling over a mysterious kingdom near the Mountains of the Moon. With more rigour, Latino could have claimed stature as a black "Old Christian" by claiming ties to the Abyssinian Christian ruler Lebna Dengel whom Portuguese explorers met in 1520, a ruler Europeans called King David II.[3] Latino does indeed refer to the biblical account of Ethiopia's Christian heritage, as I discuss in chapter 3. But as we will see, he does not mobilize this story to buttress a claim to Christian ancestry from time immemorial, instead proposing a comparative analysis of elite biases that anticipates tools of comparative ethnography.

Turning for now to the other term in Latino's self-defining epithet, *Aethiops* signals an adherence to classical nomenclature, bypassing

Guinea, the most widely used catch-all term for sub-Saharan Africa. What signification follows from the choice of the ancient over the early modern ethnonym? Greek geographers situated the "burnt-face" nations (*Aethiops*) in a vaguely delineated land south of Libya and the Nile.[4] Pondered in relation to European book culture of the 1570s, Latino's classical geography goes against the grain of the "spacialization" of culture that Ricardo Padrón finds as a crucial impulse for changing notions of individual and collective identities. Defining himself in print so soon after the appearance of a major advance in cartography, Abraham Ortelius's magnificent *Theater of the World* (*princeps* 1570), Latino nonetheless claims a homeland that readers could not pinpoint on the land mass of the atlas's "New Map of Africa," crowded as it is with the names of regions, ports, and rivers (figure 5).[5] The sole appearance of the classical nomenclature on the Ortelius map is the "Oceanus Aethio," denoting the Atlantic Ocean south of the equator, connecting Africa to Brazil. Yet Aethiopia in this context was often used interchangeably with Guinea. For instance, a Spanish reader's annotation in a copy of Pomponius Mela's *Cosmography* glosses the Ethiopian Sea ("Mare Aethiopicum") with the vernacular equivalent rendered as "el mar de Guinea."[6] Given the extent to which sixteenth-century readers equated Aethiopia with Guinea, the implications of opting for the former rather than the latter merit some thought.

In part, the freedman's calculated archaism in naming his homeland Aethiopia rather than Guinea follows from the intellectual mission of an author who chooses classical Latin over vernacular Castilian (Spanish). But neo-Latin authors of the Renaissance had long drawn on geographic neologisms, as we see in Latino himself when he renders Granada – a city founded in the Muslim Middle Ages – as Garnata. A rigorous classicism would have dictated he refer to the realm of Granada through some version of the Roman colony Hispania Baetica, a purist's choice we do find in other contemporary books.[7] Alternately, he could have used the name of the Roman settlement of Iliberia invoked by local humanists who sought to endow the Nasrid city with a Christian history. Given that Latino was not a strict adherent to classical geographic nomenclature, the self-styling as an Aethiops was not a foregone conclusion.

One compelling benefit of using the classicizing Aethiops was its distance from a racially biased pseudo-ethnography taking shape in conjunction with the expanding Atlantic slave trade. We can see how new but fragmentary information about sub-Saharan Africa fed bias against

Figure 5 Abraham Ortelius, New Map of Africa (1570).

The Ortelius "Africae Tabula Nova" (New Map of Africa) contrasts with the "Old Africa" comprised of the three distinct regions that Greek and Roman geographers conceived as separate entities. Scholars note in this regard how the emerging Atlantic slave trade contributed to the conception of "one Africa out of many" (Lewis and Wigen 1997, 117). Here, precision about the coastal areas charted as a result of reports by European explorers, slave traders, and missionaries contrasts with the endurance of myths about still uncharted interior realms. Thus, the region just north of the Equator along the Nile River appears as the realm of Prester John. Likewise between the Equator and the Tropic of Capricorn, the cartographer locates the "Region of the Amazons." *Aethiops*, the classical ethnonym with which Juan Latino identifies himself, does not appear anywhere on the continent. The southern Atlantic linking Africa to Brazil is called the "Oceanus Aethio," which correlated in the vernacular to the Guinean Sea (Mar de Guinea).

Source: Abraham Ortelius. *Theatro d'el Orbe de la tierra*, Plate 4. Translated by Cristophe Plantin. Antwerp, Plantin, 1602. By Permission of the Biblioteca Histórica, Universidad Complutense de Madrid, FLL Res. 10.

blacks in the widely circulated and influential *Description of Africa* by Leo Africanus, born al-Hassan al-Wazzan (ca. 1486–8?). Lacking first-hand knowledge of the "Land of the Blacks," Africanus confronts regions that are "unknown and far from trade routes" by drawing on long-standing biases of Islamic geographers. In Ramusio's widely circulated Italian edition, we find a compendium of the racial stereotypes that would nourish the Atlantic slave trade: "Those of the land of blacks are most savage men, men without reason, without intelligence, and without customs: they truly have no information about what should be done. Prostitutes and thus cuckolds are numerous: some who reside elsewhere, who live in large cities have a bit more humanity."[8] By the time Africanus penned this portrait of the uncivilized savagery of blacks in sub-Saharan Africa, it was out of date. After all, greater contact with Portuguese travellers, missionaries, and traders had contradicted these commonplaces. Portuguese historian A.C. Saunders documents from many angles how more prolonged European contact with West Africans revealed customs and political systems that should have satisfied basic notions of civilization in Mediterranean cultures: "Blacks ate well, drank palm wine, lived in houses and had recognizable legal systems, states and kings." Andrew Curran, in fact, draws attention to some passages in which Africanus himself acknowledges as much in more nuanced descriptions of some ethnic groups.[9] Yet his generalizations about uncivilized savagery would gain wide resonance in European accounts of sub-Saharan Africa.

A measure of how close such fictions of sub-Saharan Africa cut to Juan Latino emerges in the *Descripción general de Africa* by Luis del Mármol Carvajal. This soldier-turned-chronicler based his account on his experience in Spanish military campaigns in the Maghreb and a seven-year captivity. Yet like Africanus before him, Mármol knew little about the lands south of the Sahara. Undeterred, he regaled readers with enticing new geographic data on the still largely uncharted lands beyond the desert, offering a tongue-twisting torrent of unfamiliar realms: "Gualata o Ganata, Guinea o Genij o Geneúa, Meli, Tombutho o Iza, Gago, Gubez, Agadez, Cano, Cacena, Perzegreg, Zanfara, Guangara, Burno, Gaoga, y Neúba [...]"[10] Acknowledging that the linguistic and religious diversity of sub-Saharan Africa defy his interpretive abilities, Mármol Carvajal reverts to the outmoded litany of stereotypes, adhering closely to Africanus's text: "They are all idolaters, and many of them are so savage that they can properly be called monsters of nature."[11] Taken together, these caricatured descriptions of the diverse people of sub-Saharan

Africa reveal the general contours of European analysis of black Africa at the time Juan Latino stepped forward as an author. Increasingly, Europeans saw evidence of a complex patchwork of ethnicities beyond the Sahara. But even as travellers, missionaries, and traders found signs of cultural sophistication, they clung to the accusations of barbarity that had first emerged to justify the capture and enslavement of men, women, and children with whom they were not at war.

Viewed in light of the era's fragmentary and often misleading information about sub-Saharan Africa, Latino's claim of a birthright in classical Aethiopia seems a pre-emptive gesture. After all, it allows the freedman to situate his birth at a remove from the racially inflected pseudo-ethnography. I delve still more into this Aethiopian self-identification in chapter 3, where I examine Latino's configuration of authorial subjectivity in print. For the moment, I continue following the autobiographical statement as a map of upward mobility, out of Africa and into Andalusia. There, he would serve as a slave for a family at the epicentre of Spain's imperial expansion.

Terms of Enslavement

The self-portrait distils the story of enslavement with the statement that Latino was "carried out of Ethiopia in infancy" (ex Aethiopia usque infans advectus). A reader attentive to the poet's profound engagement with Virgil could recall the repeated instances in the *Aeneid* where the verb *adveho,* used in a passive construction, records dangerous voyages. Most notably, the verb conveys how the storm-weary Trojans reached the shores of Dido's Carthagean realm in *Aeneid* 1.558 ("unde huc advecti"). Reconfigured in the self-portrait, *advectus* speaks to the capture and enslavement of a black African. Although the sixteenth-century expansion of African slavery is associated in popular memory with Spain's overseas colonies in the Americas, transported slaves from both the Maghreb and sub-Saharan Africa formed an integral part of Andalusia's economy throughout Latino's lifetime. They reached the region through the new routes of the Atlantic slave trade and through older, trans-Saharan channels. At least in early childhood in the first part of the 1520s, Latino would also have encountered elderly individuals who had been captured and enslaved when Malaga fell to Ferdinand and Isabel and perhaps even the last individuals from the Canary Island slave diaspora that decimated the archipelago's indigenous population.[12]

In Latino's lifetime, enslaved people would make contributions to society that extended well beyond the labour-intensive rural agriculture often associated with plantation economies of the modern era. According to the statistical documentation Aurelia Martín Casares has provided, the largest single category of Andalusian slaves were women who performed a wide range of domestic tasks. We also find slaves in the ranks of unpaid soldiery, as in the case of the unnamed bondsman who saved his master from a mountain ambush during the 1568–70 civil war in Granada. While hard manual labour was the fate of most, we also find records of enslaved men, women, and children working in the realms of literature, education, and the arts. Notably, enslaved men worked printing presses in the storied Cromberger print shop of Seville. Seeking classroom assistance and some racially charged low comedy, Flemish humanist Nicolas Cleynaerts – Clenardus in his Latin writings (1493–1542) – purchased and then taught Latin to three young black boys. They assisted his teaching in Braga, Portugal, and at least one of them accompanied Clenardus to Granada when he sojourned in the city seeking to learn Arabic. Shifting from the realm of education to the visual arts, we know it was common to find slaves in artists' workshops grinding and mixing pigments, though guilds sought to prohibit their access to the apprenticeships that would have yielded full recognition of such skills. Yet the intense contact with and implication in artists' work allowed some slaves to claim their own stature as artists. Most famously, Juan Pareja, the mulatto slave of Diego de Velázquez, defied his master's prohibitions to paint his own canvases and, among other works, left behind the only known self-portrait of a slave-artist from early modern Europe.[13] In short, Latino's concise account of enslavement bears witness to an aspect of Spain's "Golden Age" that bears more scrutiny: enslaved men and women with a diverse array of skills added to the cultural and economic vibrancy that transformed Castile from a marginal realm at the edge of Europe to the fulcrum of a world empire.

In distilling the slave trade through a passive verb construction, Latino would not necessarily be taking an oppositional stance. With few dissenters, church and crown authorities accepted the traffic in slaves and the widespread reliance on unpaid workers as routine, though some voiced concerns about the moral and ethical dangers. The changing attitudes Rolena Adorno has charted in the case of Fray Bartolomé de las Casas coincide with the arc of Juan Latino's life: in 1516 the Dominican proposed the use of black slaves in the Caribbean to spare

Amerindians from the forced labour that was decimating them. In later decades, after Las Casas studied the Atlantic slave trade in Portuguese chronicles, he denounced the enslavement of black Africans and ultimately, disavowed Spanish imperialism entirely.[14] But widespread abolitionist sentiments were two centuries away. A more typical response in the sixteenth century followed the attitudes of the young Las Casas. For instance, the seventh Duke of Medina Sidonia wrote to Philip II, urging him to use black African slaves to improve the efficiency of the crown's American mines. But this practical economic advice came with an anguished moral caveat: "speaking in conscience, I consider the trade and capture of these blacks to be iniquitous and in itself wrong, and believe God has punished Portugal for this, and pray God will not punish our Spain."[15] The Portuguese punishment alluded to here is presumably the disaster of Alcazarquivir in 1578, where King Sebastian perished without heirs. It bears mention as well that Medina Sidonia's conflicted attitude about slavery came from experience: his family had long drawn on slave labour for construction, grounds keeping, and domestic tasks.

Latino's own early years unfolded in service of yet another wealthy duke from Andalusia, as his autobiographical statement above emphasizes with a chain of superlatives. Transported from Africa, he was taken "to the most excellent and invincible Gonzalo Fernández de Córdoba, Duke of Sessa and Grand Captain, slave of his grandson the duke." The superlatives offer a rhetorical drumroll, underscoring the freedman's ties to Spain's quintessential empire builder. The Gran Capitán must have had considerable magnetism for the upwardly mobile Latin schoolmaster. Though he came from Andalusia's storied House of Córdoba, the military commander started life among the legions of unlucky "second sons" (*segundones*). Lacking both a patron and personal wealth, Don Gonzalo staked his future on the military campaigns that Ferdinand of Aragon and Isabel of Castile were waging against the last remaining Muslim kingdom of Iberia, Nasrid Granada. As I noted briefly in the introduction, the family's subsequent history presents a microcosm of Castile's rapid-fire expansion. The Gran Capitán was pivotal in negotiating the final capitulation of the last Nasrid king in 1492, which put Granada in the hands of the Catholic Monarchs. He then spearheaded the 1503 conquest of Naples, reconceiving infantry tactics in a way that brought about the *tercios,* the infantry formations based on pikes, harquebuses, and mosquetes. After the Gran Capitán died in 1515, his life story became enshrined in European letters as an example of how talent and hard work could yield great riches and lasting glory.[16] Therefore, when Latino trumpets his connection to the family, he links himself not only to an illustrious title, the Duchy of Sessa, but also to one of the era's most famous narratives of upward mobility.

The extent that Latino's account of his birth and enslavement trumpets his former master's lineage begs two basic biographical questions. Who were the freedman's parents? What did they call their son? In the context of this miniature autobiography, the unnamed father and mother loom large. Latino, after all, embeds his life story in a book honouring Philip II's own ritual of family piety, where he ordered deceased family members disinterred in a ceremony of utmost solemnity, so they could then be reburied in his own palace residence. This ceremonial affirmation of family ties in eternity mirrors the intensifying Spanish obsession with parentage and birthright. For Spaniards, lineage mattered in powerful ways, calibrating both honour and ignominy. But at the same time, the expanding international slave trade pivoted on family separation and the disruption of kinship ties. The systematic destruction of families that Frederick Douglass would denounce three centuries later in his autobiography also characterized this earliest phase of the slave trade. Douglass, retaking control of his identity, chose his own surname as freedman from Sir Walter Scott's *The Lady of the Lakes*, a gesture Paul Gilroy construes as part of a long-standing metanarrative of emancipation.[17]

What then to make of Juan Latino's vocational surname? Surviving notarial records, university documents, and the Abbot of Rute's detailed chronicle of the Dukes of Sessa, call him Juan Latino without exception. His publications list him as Joannes Latinus. Antonio Marín Ocete asserts that Latino was called Juan de Sessa until he reached the University of Granada, but provides no supporting documentation.[18] Though many slaves were indeed known by their masters' surnames, practices varied in sixteenth-century Spain. In Seville, for instance, Ruth Pike documented an enslaved man, Pedro Franco, manumitted by Genoese merchant Franco Leardo, who had presumably assigned his given name to Pedro at some earlier point. Other documents record humiliation and mockery. The aforementioned Flemish traveller Nicholas Clenardus wrote urging a friend to "hear so you might laugh" the names he assigned to the three young black men he pressed into service for Latin instructional support, listing their names as Michael Dento (toothy or even hungry Michael), Antonius Nigrinus (black Anthony), Sebastianus Carbo (Sebastian carbon).[19] Given the varied naming practices among sixteenth-century slave owners, we cannot assume the freedman was ever known as Juan Sessa before he gained literal name recognition as a skilled Latinist.

Another revealing point of comparison on the question of the freedman's name is the case of Beatriz Galindo (ca. 1465–1535), known popularly as "La Latina." Galindo gained prominence after Isabel of Castile entrusted her with teaching Latin to her children. Royal rewards for service, in turn, allowed Galindo to endow a hospital and two convents. Her education and advancement anticipate the freedman's own rise to prominence in Granada a generation later, in that in both cases Latin erudition removed barriers and refuted stereotypes. But a marked difference remains despite their shared monikers. As a woman from an elite family, Galindo signed legal documents as Beatriz Galindo and is also identified with her family name on her gravestone. La Latina was an epithet that anchored her posthumous renown.[20] Far from the elite family background of Doña Beatriz, Juan Latino may have lacked a family surname, lost in the passage into slavery.

While the unresolvable question of family name frustrates our notion of basic biography, for Spaniards of the sixteenth century, a surname could mark the difference between honour and disgrace. After all, a family name conferred a prestige or ignominy that could be passed along to descendants. Juan Latino's adulthood, moreover, coincided with a time of a spreading mania for blood purity. In its most precise juridical application, the policy reserved some of the most coveted honours and positions for those who could document Old Christian ancestry. But the idea of blood purity amplified beyond its specific application in certain institutions. Examining the earliest phase of *limpieza de sangre* statutes after the mass conversions of Sephardic Jews after 1391, David Nirenberg traces how genealogy emerged as the main form of communal memory. Noting the spread of *limpieza de sangre* statutes from the 1540s onward, John Elliott argues that this mania was more insidious even than the rise of the Inquisition.[21] As blood purity statutes proliferated, they allowed for the selective persecution and marginalization of individuals known or alleged to have non-Christian ancestors.

When pondering the impact of the mania for *limpieza de sangre* on Latino as a diasporic African, a few points of nuance are in order. Blood purity statutes were by no means universal; in fact, Granada's municipal government proved somewhat resistant to such rules. Indeed, the city's transformation after its conquest by Ferdinand and Isabel offered New Christians of both Muslim and Jewish origin comparatively more opportunities for advancement than those available in Old Castilian cities. But if *limpieza* statutes were never universal and fictions were often easy to spin for influential and ambitious Spaniards, the intensifying emphasis on Christian purity and lineage would undermine the ability of people known to be of non-European origins to gain full acceptance as part of the Spanish polity. The assessment from María Elena Martínez who traces the impact of *limpieza* statutes from late-medieval Castile to colonial Mexico apply here, when she remarks that the juridical procedures that emerged to certify blood purity "promoted an obsession with origins that laid the groundwork for the development of particularly strong links, in both Spain and Spanish America, among religion, race, and 'nation.'"[22] In Granada, conflicting notions of these touchstones of identity fomented the devastating civil war that anchors my analysis in chapter 2.

Returning to the question of Juan Latino's uncertain lineage, we find that the only hint of parentage is an oblique reference to an enslaved wet nurse. He thus speaks about his early bond to his master by noting that he grew up in Sessa's household, "ab ipso infantiae lacte simul nutritus" (by him nourished with the same milk of infancy). Through this declaration, a lost mother or maternal surrogate enters the narration as a ghostly presence, unnamed but palpable in her role as the nurse to her son and wet nurse to her master. This statement points to a central problem in early modern Spanish literature, of mothers and maternal figures whose place seems attenuated, an issue Anne Cruz has explored in some depth.[23] What then to make of Latino's indirect evocation of his mother?

Taken figuratively, the clause ("ab ipso infantiae lacte simul nutritus") could mean that the third duke's resources provided sustenance. Biographical studies in the twentieth century inclined to this kind of figurative interpretation. Unfortunately, in so doing they rendered the passage in a misleading manner that has prevented scholars without access to the rare original publication from properly interpreting this statement. In the early 1920s, Antonio Marín Ocete thus quoted the passage by eliding the *lacte:* "ab ipso [Gonzalo Fernández de Córdoba] infantiae simul nutritus" [*sic*]. No ellipses alert to the erasure of the *lacte.* Sustenance is abstract without the ablative term for milk. Six decades later, José A. Sánchez Marín transcribed the whole clause in his prologue, but elided the ablative noun in the Castilian translation, leaving "alimentado por éste ... [elipses in the original]."[24]

A full examination of the autobiographical statement requires a more direct exploration of the nursing woman given only a vague, implied presence in Latino's autobiography-in-miniature. From classical to early modern times, enslaved women were routinely required to nurse their masters' children, often to the detriment of their own children's health. An entirely plausible interpretation of the prepositional clause "by him" (ab ipso) is that Latino's mother or her surrogate nursed him and his master. A "brotherhood" of this kind between Juan Latino and the third Duke of Sessa has important implications for subjectivity. The widespread use of enslaved women as wet nurses sparked anxious reflections about the instability of racial and ethnic identities. Such fears gained currency in medieval scholasticism, when writers pondered relations between Jews and Christians. With Spain's emergence as an empire comprised of ethnically diverse realms, the fears came to encompass Moriscas who served as wet nurses in Spain, as well as Amerindian and African women who nourished Creole children in Spanish America. In Granada, these anxieties highlighted the profound unease with the region's Muslim heritage. A story thus circulated among Jesuits in which a gentleman of sixteenth-century Granada blamed his inability to eat salt pork on his father's choice of a Morisca to nurse him.[25] Latino, by implying the same woman nursed him and his master, stays far from the realm of such folklore. But, to the extent the "ab ipso lacte simul nutritus" clause portrays a brotherhood of sorts between a grandee and a black slave, it implies a positive take on the long-standing humoral interpretation of nursing: a shared wet nurse could engender fraternal bonds between a black African slave and his noble master. Such kinship, inevitably, opens the notion of nobility to a broader definition.

In fact, the history of the Sessa family mentioned at the outset corroborates Latino's account of his close relationship to his master in their formative years, though it does not speak to the potentially sensitive issue of who nursed the young grandee. The monumental *House of Córdoba* by the Abbot of Rute (Francisco Fernández de Córdoba), a second cousin of Latino's one-time master, gives the freedman a brief cameo within a lengthy chapter on this nobleman. The Abbot of Rute bases his account of the third Duke of Sessa's early years on the testimony of his younger sister and heir, Doña Francisca. From this family oral history, we get a contrasting but entirely plausible version of Latino's birth. The churchman states that Latino was born in the Sessa family seat of Baena (Córdoba) to "Guinean" parents who were slaves.[26] Where Latino embraces the classicizing "Aethiops" to convey his ethnicity, the Abbot of Rute uses the toponym through which sixteenth-century Europeans most commonly referred to the origins of black-African slaves. For the

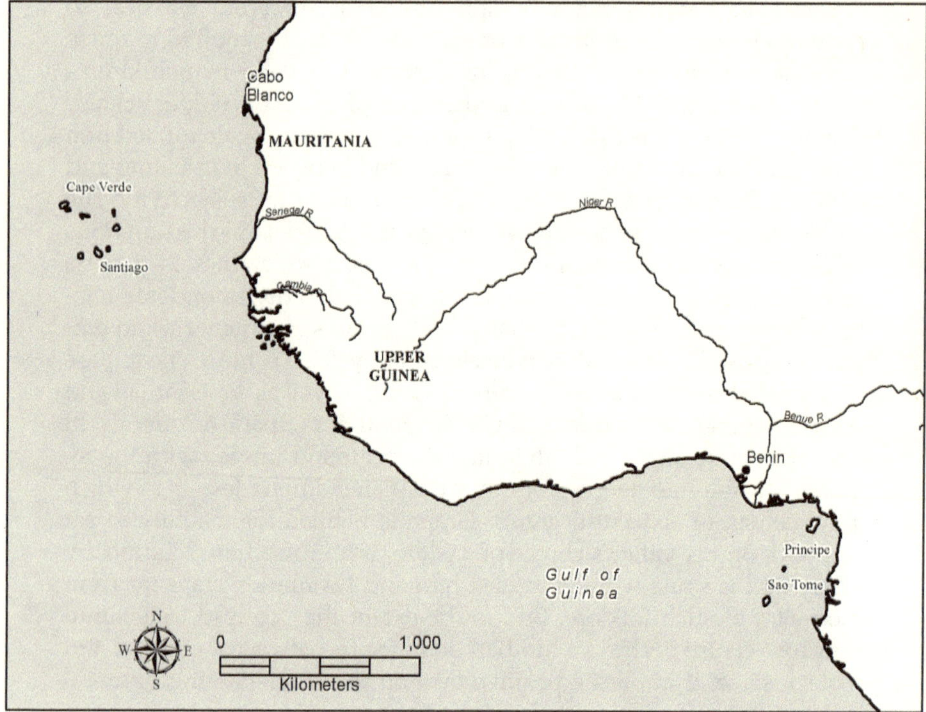

Figure 6 West Coast of Africa, circa 1517. When the family oral history of the Dukes of Sessa referred to Juan Latino and his enslaved parents as "Guinean," they gestured in vague terms to this western swath of the African continent where the Atlantic slave trade had taken root, starting with Portuguese expeditions of the 1440s. Scholars have documented individuals of Guinean, Cape Verdean, and Congolese origins in sixteenth-century Andalusia, with a significant number of Wolofs (see Martín Casares 2000, 153).

Credit: By Thomas R. Jordan, Southern Resource Mapping

specific context of slavery in Andalusia, "Guinean" conceals the diversity of black Africans in the region, who had been captured from a vast area that would coincide with present-day Senegal, Gambia, Guinea Bissau, Conackry Guinea, Mali, and Burkina Faso. The manner here that the ethnonym Guinean elides the multiple sub-Saharan ethnicities anticipates the "flexible and to some extent imaginary European geography of Africa" that Rebecca Scott and Jean Hébrard have explored in three centuries of the Atlantic slave trade.[27]

On the question of where exactly Latino was born, we do not have baptismal or notarial records through which to judge his claim of African birth against the Abbot of Rute's record of a birth in Córdoba to enslaved parents. Both versions carry a degree of authority and plausibility: Latino's that of autobiography; the churchman's, of access to family oral history. Here, Aurelia Martín Casares adds another plausible hypothesis. Unable to find records of Juan Latino's baptism or transportation to Spain in early childhood in the course of her exhaustive work in notarial archives, the anthropologist suggested he might have been fathered by the Gran Capitán. This parentage, she noted, could help account for his unusual degree of upward mobility. A nineteenth-century account of Juan Latino would, without giving attribution, label him the son of the Gran Capitán.[28] Given the nobleman's 1515 death, and Latino's claim of a circa 1516–18 birth, this hypothesis hinges on a small window of time in which the ailing military commander had either forced or consensual sex with a woman enslaved in his household. Moreover, Latino would have to have knowingly or unknowingly shed about a half-decade when he gave his age as fifty-eight in his self-portrait. The likely age gap between Latino and his one-time master (born 1520) does not readily support another possibility – that master and slave were half-brothers. The third Duke of Sessa's father – Don Luis Fernández de Córdoba, fourth Count of Cabra – married into the Sessa family in 1520 and Latino was born circa 1517. Of course, such uncertainties by no means obviate the possibility that Latino's father was another senior member of the Sessa family or a retainer.

Still, in weighing the possibility that Latino was the son of an enslaved black woman and a master or overseer, it is striking that no reliable source from Latino's lifetime alludes to a white father. This silence is noteworthy, given that the term "mulatto" had already been incorporated into Spanish usage; scribes and chroniclers applied it, albeit inconsistently, to label individuals with a mixed black and white parentage.[29] In fact, distinguished black Granadinos from the sixteenth century would be celebrated for their prominent white fathers. An early seventeenth-century history thus recalled two other famous black men of Granada, one a Dominican friar and the other a magistrate of the royal Chancillería, noting matter-of-factly that both were the sons of enslaved black women and their white masters.[30]

In the end, we are left with three different accounts of Latino's birth, each of which is conceivable: his own claims of a birth in a sub-Saharan African homeland named in classical terms as Aethiopia; the Sessa-family oral history of his birth in Baena to two black-African slaves; and the hypothesis of conception after coerced or unequal sexual relations between an enslaved black mother and white father. This unresolved question about parentage brings to mind the later case of Olaudah Equiano, known in early life as Gustavus Vassa (ca. 1745–97), who crafted a riveting account of his capture in Igboland and the dreaded Middle Passage into slavery. Yet recently discovered baptismal and naval records situate his birth in South Carolina. In the face of uncertainty about Equiano's true birthplace, Vincent Carratta proposes that his account of African birth retains its validity as "cultural memory."[31] Like Equiano two centuries later, Latino may well have asserted an African birth to fashion a heritage beyond the realm of slavery and its attendant sexual exploitation of enslaved black women. Or, he may indeed have been documenting the actual circumstances of his African birth and enslavement in early infancy. The Abbot of Rute's informant may simply have had incomplete or selective information; indeed, Martín Casares has underscored the spotty nature of the records of slave purchases, births, and baptisms in the households of Spain's high nobility. For the moment, our most reasoned course of action is to continue searching for more documents while reflecting on the deeper symbolic truth in Latino's birth narrative: black African subjectivity is ever rooted in a lost African homeland and severed kinship ties.

A Grandee's Education

Moving from Latino's birth to his education, we find that the Sessa-family chronicle fully corroborates the freedman's account of how he initiated his humanist education. In Latino's telling, he was formed by education in the liberal arts from an early age alongside his young master ("cum ipso a rudibus animis liberalibus artibus institutus"). The Abbot of Rute's family history confirms the account of a shared education, while adding tantalizing information about the personal initiative and risks involved. He notes that "against the will of those who controlled the age of minority of the duke, he [Latino] would accompany the duke to study any time he could defy the vigilance of those who blocked him."[32] Viewed in the history of the African diaspora, Latino's secretive first steps towards gaining an education anticipate later accounts of clandestine literacy in the slave diaspora, including Frederick Douglass's account of how he defied his one-time master, Hugh Auld of Baltimore, to learn to read and write. In Spain, Latino's initiative anticipates Juan Pareja's ploy to be allowed to paint, going against Diego de Velázquez's prohibition.[33]

Returning our focus to the Sessa family, we can see how Latino proved a paradoxical beneficiary of a series of untimely deaths that afflicted the noble clan. His master, born in 1520, was orphaned by age six and thus became the titular head of the family. Initially under the care of his grandmother, the duke's education was supervised by a series of adult male relatives after she died in 1527. But these guardians spent extended periods of time away at court, leaving the young nobleman behind. Complicity with his young master and turnover in the household management may well have allowed Latino to defy prohibitions and join the duke's lessons.

Another crucial detail as we compare the two accounts of education in the Sessa household is that neither version limits Juan Latino to the role of *paedagogus*, the tutor-slave who escorted a young charge or master to his lessons.[34] Latino refers to his earliest education alongside the duke as a relatively equal partnership through the prepositional phrase, "cum ipso." The Sessa-family oral history on which the Abbot of Rute relies for his chronicle likewise emphasizes companionship rather than servitude when he notes that Latino joined the duke for his lessons, initially in defiance of guardians.

By stealthily joining the young duke's lessons, Latino positioned himself to benefit from the expanding intellectual and cultural horizons of Spain's high aristocracy. Though the largest cache of Sessa papers remains in private hands – uncatalogued and inaccessible to scholars – we do know that the family epitomized the deepening engagement of noble families with intellectual currents of the Renaissance. Sessa's early education, as the Abbot of Rute describes it, blended training in arms and letters.[35] If military arts were the centuries-old mainstays of noble culture, training in letters had gained prestige in the later fifteenth century. The interest in letters intensified during the reign of Ferdinand and Isabel, when itinerant humanists such as Lucio Marineo Sículo and

Peter Martyr found new opportunities for employment in Spanish noble households.[36] For a nobleman, education typically began with private in-home tutoring around age five by a university-trained *letrado* and continued through early adolescence.

Typical of this pattern, Peter Martyr tutored the Marquis of Priego, a cousin of the Gran Capitán. Both noblemen belonged to the storied House of Córdoba, whose different clans controlled Castile's last frontier with Nasrid Granada in the fourteenth and fifteenth centuries. Historian Yuen-Gen Liang has demonstrated how the eventual integration of what had been independent castes of warriors into crown military ventures would be decisive for the emergence of the Spanish Monarchy as a global empire.[37] Estate records reveal how the Priego family changed in response to the Renaissance intellectual currents that emanated from the court of Isabel of Castile, allowing us to gauge the environment in which Latino and Sessa's early education transpired. Priego's ancestors left no records of book ownership until a 1441 inventory, which documents just eight books. A generation later, Peter Martyr's former pupil owned over 300 books upon his death in 1517. Latin authors formed the largest single category, with titles by Cicero, Ovid, Terrence, Martial, Juvenal, Seneca, Pliny, Sallust, Quintilian, Lucan, Macrobius, Livy, and Virgil.[38] Greek authors too had a prominent position in the library, with works by Aristotle, Plato, Ptolemy, Plutarch, Herodotus, and Xenophon, supplemented as well with three grammars of the Hellenic language. The notarial format of the estate inventory, transcribed and annotated in detail by María Concepción Quintanilla Raso, does not give sufficient information to establish the bibliographic specifics or document what Priego did with his books. Moreover, assiduous book collection does not signify intense reading and study of the volumes owned. But even taking these caveats to heart, the large number of titles the nobleman owned points to a growing embrace of Latin among the elite, since relatively few of the titles listed in Priego's book collection were available in Castilian translation by this date.[39] Quintanilla Raso also draws attention to the library's location in a private chamber, a detail that suggests how classical literature had come to form a key part of the cultural capital of the highest ranking Andalusian nobles.

For the Dukes of Sessa, long military service in Italy intensified the contact with intellectual and artistic projects associated with the Renaissance. In this regard, art historian Antonio Luis Callejón Peláez has documented the crucial protagonism of the Gran Capitán's wife, María de Manrique (Duchess of Terranova).[40] During her husband's prolonged military service, she resided in Genoa and Naples, with a degree of autonomy that followed from her husband's long absences during campaigns. When the Gran Capitán died in 1516, Doña Maria gained still more independence, since the couple had no male heirs. Their only surviving daughter, Doña Elvira, married a cousin, Luis Fernández de Córdoba, who was named Spain's ambassador to Rome in 1520. She died in childbirth in 1524 and Don Luis succumbed to a fever two years later, in 1526. Consequently, the third Duke of Sessa (b. 1520) and Juan Latino would have begun their education in the widowed duchess's household. Sessa, around age five, would have begun to study under a private tutor. This start of his education coincided with the moment the Duchess of Terranova took up residence in Granada in order to initiate the design and construction of the main altar of the Monastery of San Jerónimo, a lavish and innovative commission she undertook to ensure lasting glory for the family. Callejón Peláez documents how the monument emulates the Neapolitan architecture and humanism that Doña Maria had encountered two decades earlier. Drawing on an iconographic language utterly different from Granada monuments commissioned right after the city's 1492 conquest, the altar was construed to exalt the virtues and accomplishments of illustrious Sessa-family members by associating them with such heroes from antiquity as Caesar, Hannibal, Pompey, Marcellus, and Scipio, as well as Old Testament paragons and saints from the earliest Christian period.[41] When the Duchess of Terranova died in 1527, the project continued, first under the third duke's guardians, and from the mid-1530s, under the nobleman himself.

The close succession of deaths in the third duke's family would have placed the young Juan Latino in a better position to take advantage of opportunities for education. Had stronger authority figures within the family been more present or longer lived, Latino might have found some of his initiative checked; certainly, the Abbot of Rute's brief description of a clandestine education suggests as much. Again, there is much that remains in the realm of reasoned conjecture with available documents. But we can, at a minimum, infer from this Sessa family chronicle that Latino gained unique opportunities through some combination of early deaths of senior family members and the timeliness of a move from the family's rural Córdoba estate to Granada, where new and innovative educational initiatives beckoned.

But if Granada, circa 1526, proved a hotbed of new educational opportunities, the city also presented a sharp potential for dissonance related to its Islamic heritage. A question here is to what extent the embrace of humanist education agendas and scholarship required a disavowal of Andalusian points of identity. Here we can imagine how early education in the classics and quotidian life in Granada connected and contrasted. Juan Latino and the Duke of Sessa might have read Livy's *History of Rome from Its Foundation* under a *licenciado*'s tutelage in the morning and, in the afternoon, walked about twenty minutes from the Casa del Gran Capitán in the San Mateo neighbourhood to the Hieronymite convent where some of the era's most celebrated sculptors were bringing heroes known from Roman letters to life. But the route from the family palace to the funerary monument under construction brought marked contrasts. After all, the Hieronymite altar underway trumpeted family members' likenesses to heroes from ancient Rome. But the family lived amidst the splendid remnants of Al-Andalus. For one, the new monastery where the family was building its Renaissance altar was itself built atop the ruins of a Nasrid shrine to a Muslim hermit.[42] There is also convincing evidence that the Gran Capitán's Granada residence was a Nasrid palace granted to him as a prize after the 1492 capture of the city.[43]

This contrast between the endeavours associated with the European Renaissance and the region's ancestral ties to Islamic culture heightened the tension between present and past already built into humanist inquiry. Indeed, Thomas Greene movingly argues that the intellectual quests associated with the Renaissance always came charged with a profound melancholy, as Petrarch and his successors discerned and struggled with the otherness of the distant past they explored and emulated.[44] The displacement already inevitable in the humanist enterprise becomes still more pronounced as we reflect on the material conditions that marked Juan Latino's education in Granada.

Between Latinate and Arabic Cultures

The contrasts we envision in conjuring a walk from the Sessa palace to the family-sponsored altar project at the Monastery of San Jerónimo speak to a fundamental issue of the Granada where Latino claimed his education. Inevitably, the Latin apprentice in this city confronted a wide abyss between the idealized Roman past and the diverse social fabric around him. In neighbouring Córdoba, a walk to the city centre could bring classical antiquity closer at hand. This was, after all, the prestigious capital of the Roman province of Hispania Ulterior Baetica, homeland of Seneca and Lucan. Yet Granada lacked such palpable ties to Latinity. As Latino and the third Duke of Sessa studied classical antiquity, antiquarians in the city struggled to find material evidence of a Roman settlement called Iliberi, Iliberis, Eliberri, or Iliberia.[45] Such a site would, after all, provide an alternative foundation narrative for the city built by Muslim rulers.

Yet while humanist scholars and their young students searched for inscriptions or other evidence of Granada's Roman past, they walked and lived among the abundant monuments of a diverse medieval society that drew on Muslim, Christian, and Jewish cultures. The awe and anxiety fomented by this cultural crossroads emerges in one of the earliest traveller's accounts of Granada after the capture by Ferdinand and Isabel. During his stay in the city in late 1594, Hieronymous Münzer counted 200 mosques and estimated 3,000 worshippers answered the muezzin's call to pray at the main mosque. Even in the most rarefied confines of the elite, the German humanist found signs of the city's hybrid identity. When the Count of Tendilla received Münzer at his Alhambra headquarters, the nobleman conversed with his guest in Latin, but then offered him a seat on a silk cushion known as an *estrado*. This was a decidedly Andalusian luxury item that some churchmen would seek to replace with chairs, a household item deemed more Castilian.[46] Münzer, taking stock of such a different and dazzling place, found that words failed him as he tried to describe the city. He doubted that Europe had another place so magnificent and warned that a visitor might be lulled into thinking he had reached Paradise.[47] Münzer's view of Granada also records a struggle to assimilate the blend of Christian and Muslim traditions. At one point he scoffs at Mohammed as a false prophet and recoils at Islam's rejection of Catholic sacraments, yet in another place he lauds the piety and generous almsgiving of Granada's Muslims.[48]

The intermingling of Christianity and Islam yielded a fault line that would mark the city throughout Juan Latino's long life. Soon, official tolerance of Islam that the German traveller witnessed in the 1490s gave way to a policy of obligatory conversion. The resulting transformation and pressure on the native Hispano-Muslim population would yield an atmosphere similar to those of conquered Amerindian cities. Another likeness between the former Nasrid capital and its American counterparts relates to the loss of ancestral knowledge. A little less than a half-century after Granada's last Muslim sultan surrendered the city to Ferdinand and Isabel, Flemish humanist Nicholas Clenardus sought in vain to master Arabic in Granada. Initial steps seemed promising, as his host, the Marquis of Mondéjar, subsidized his purchase of a learned

Arabic speaker as a slave-tutor. This enslaved language tutor added to Clenardus's unpaid educational entourage, which already comprised at least one of the three aforementioned young black men acquired in Portugal as Latin teaching assistants, Antonius Nigrinus. But the humanist's stay in Granada was cut short by his inability to find Arabic codices, prompting him to travel to Fez.[49] What the Flemish visitor to Granada was unable to discern was the extent to which Arabic erudition had become what Vincent Barletta has memorably termed a "covert gesture." By this time the epicentre of Arabic literary production had shifted to Castile and Aragon. Back in Granada, Morisco doctors had, in effect, become the last remaining guardians of Arabic erudition. Presumably the practical implications of medicine allowed a space for cultivating Arabic letters at a time where inquisitors were increasingly associating the language with Islam. The paradoxical and tragic result was that many people judged it dangerous to own a book in Granada's ancestral language.[50]

The Granada that bewildered the visiting Clenardus is the city of Juan Latino's formative years, with Arabic etched on walls and spoken in market stalls, but its textual production was hidden from his view or exiled.[51] It was also a tense place because of a broken promise. Official religious tolerance of Islam that the Catholic Monarchs had guaranteed in the capitulation agreement of November 1491 ended in 1502 in the wake of the First Revolt of the Alpujarras (1499–1500). The forced conversions accelerated the changes already underway when Münzer visited. Hispano-Muslims who wished to stay or could not afford to emigrate underwent baptism, many in hastily organized mass ceremonies. The exodus of the most prosperous Muslims accelerated. In tandem, what had been a slow trickle of Christians relocating to Granada from other parts of Castile became a steady inflow, as crown officials removed the obstacles to legal immigration. A wide-ranging urban redesign campaign underway since 1492 intensified to allay the perception common at court and among religious leaders that the city looked too Islamic. Most notably, crown and church officials began to tear down some mosques, while transforming others into Catholic churches. Still, many mosques and a dazzling madrasa building would remain standing for decades to come.[52]

This struggle to transform Iberia's last great Muslim metropolis into a Christian city would inform Latino's enslavement, education, and upward mobility in manifold ways, conditioning bondage in early life, yielding opportunities for education and advancement in adulthood, and then ultimately setting limits. A crucial series of events and programs transpired before he was born, but left many unresolved tensions that lingered throughout Latino's long life in Granada. The city's first Catholic prelate, Hernando de Talavera (archbishop of Granada 1492–1507), designed an evangelization program in Granada based on the promise that baptism removed racial and ethnic divisions.[53] But the trauma of the 1499 revolt, bitterness among Moriscos because the crown reneged on the terms of the 1491 *Capitulaciones*, plus the attachment of many Granadinos to their ancestral religious traditions sowed tensions that would haunt the city during the early sixteenth century. Hispano-Muslim communities of Granada showed a diversity of reactions. A *fatwa* (advisory opinion on law and tradition) issued in 1504 authorized Muslims to use the dissimulation known as *taqiyya* to remain in Spain.[54] Just how many of the thousands of Muslims who converted to Catholicism in the early sixteenth century clung secretly to Islam and how many embraced Christianity is impossible to know. Documents provide examples of both extremes and still more numerous examples of hybrid religious practices. In this respect, Julio Caro Baroja underscored Granada's array of ambiguous identities (*personalidades equívocas*) that resulted from the conquest, forced conversions, and uneven assimilation.[55]

It is in the context of this tense coexistence of Christian- and Islamic identities that Juan Latino's enslavement and early education in Granada played out. Until all surviving Sessa family papers are available for study, the grandee's household will remain the subject of conjecture. But some contextual clues help us understand how unusual chances for education and advancement resulted from Granada's hybrid society. Service to this high-ranking family would have brought contact with the churchmen and officials who promoted the Hispanization of the Muslim city and its native population. These would have included priests and friars serving as confessors to family members. In fact, the Franciscan monastery that stood across the street from the Casa del Gran Capitán was connected by a walkway. Yet at the same time, a wealthy noble household would have relied on the labour of New Christians of diverse origins, whether as paid servants or slaves. Surviving estate inventories for Andalusian nobility record servants and slaves from North Africa, sub-Saharan Africa, and even Morisco communities of Andalusia.[56] Since the Sessa home was probably a former Nasrid noble palace that the Gran Capitán claimed as war spoil, Juan Latino as a boy would have lived and worked in the shadow of intricate Arabic script and ceramic tiles of the kind that survive today in the Alhambra.

In the spaces beyond the Casa del Gran Capitán, this interconnection of Christian and Muslim heritages remained palpable. We could suppose, for instance, an errand in which Juan Latino was dispatched from the palace to take a message to the city centre. Such a walk would have situated the young Latin apprentice at a cultural crossroads quite different from the encounters between past and present that nourished Italian humanist inquiry. Though muezzins's calls to prayers that made Hieronymous Münzer feel he was in a "Saracen" city no longer echoed from minarets in Latino's childhood, he would have walked among repurposed, idled, or newly demolished mosques. Also, a walk from the Casa del Gran Capitán to the centre would have required he pass the abandoned homes of recently expelled Muslims and Jews.

This hypothetical errand to the city centre from the Sessa family's home in the San Mateo neighbourhood would have included the city's most emblematic street for trade, the Calle Zacatín. The name derives from the Hispano-Arabic term *saqqattín* (rag merchant), an occupation heavily represented in the street's lower section which ran parallel to the Darro river and connected to the Plaza Nueva. The natural associations of the Zacatín – in Granada as elsewhere – with the market culture of Islamic cities appears in the cornerstone of Spanish lexicography, the Sebastián de Covarrubias *Tesoro*, which draws on the examples of Fez and other Berber cities to illustrate this kind of commercial hub. In Granada, alleyways running from the lower Zacatín to the Darro housed the workshops and stalls of tanners, dyers, and other water-intensive trades as they had in the Muslim period. Continuing towards the centre, the less gritty upper Zacatín housed cobblers, silversmiths, and tailors.[57]

Upon reaching the Bibarrambla plaza where he would one day teach in the grammar school, Latino would have encountered particularly splendid remnants of Islamic Granada. The minaret of the main mosque, retooled for the cathedral complex, remained intact when Latino came of age in the city, as did the fourteenth-century madrasa.[58] Exiting the Bibarrambla, Latino would likely have entered the Alcaicería or central silk market. This warren of some two hundred shops or stalls had struck Italian humanist Lucio Marineo Sículo as a miniature city within Granada. Throughout the first half of the sixteenth century, the Alcaicería's lingua franca remained Arabic, a resilience that followed from its nuanced silk-trading vocabulary. Transactions negotiated here, in turn, sustained thousands of Moriscos in a cottage industry focused on raising silk worms, weaving, sewing, and embroidering.[59] But alongside its practical economic relevance for the silk trade, the Arabic language retained a profound association with Islamic religious practices, becoming – according to Mercedes García-Arenal and Fernando Rodríguez-Mediano – a cultural battlefield.[60]

Did the young Juan Latino, while studying the Roman language, pause to consider how Arabic had an equal claim to reverence as, arguably, Granada's true classical language? Again, the place names suggest as much. The silk market's Castilianized name derived from the Hispano-Arabic term *alqaysaríyya,* which, in turn, came from the Latin *Caesarea.* Revealingly, this case of Latin-to-Arabic cultural cross-fertilization prompted Sebastián de Covarrubias to marshal the Alcaicería's etymology as proof of Granada's Roman heritage. The lexicographer thus notes that the name derives from *cayzar,* an Arabic corruption of *Caesar,* which reflects how the earliest trade came about through Roman licence to Arab traders. Covarrubias's *Tesoro* (dictionary), according to Georgina Dopico and Jacques Lezra, hinges time and again on this kind of negotiation between the ideal of political unity under the Spanish Monarchy and the awareness of the ineluctable cultural diversity of Castilian lexicon. In effect, the "treasures" of this would-be language of a world empire were as much Arabic as Latinate.[61] Juan Latino's classical education in Granada offers an analogous duality. Inevitably, the classical culture inculcated in his lessons would have emerged in juxtaposition with the Hispano-Muslim people and places encountered in servants' quarters or on the city streets. Since we lack a direct account from Juan Latino on this problem, recollections from Emperor Charles V's sojourn in the city open a window onto the city in which a young slave gained such unusual access to opportunities for higher education. During the royal residency, the discrepancy between a desired cultural unity under the Spanish Monarchy and Granada's palpable Islamic heritage comes into sharp focus.

When Emperor Charles V and Empress Isabella entered Granada in June of 1526, a group of women from the Morisco community dazzled them with *leilas* (traditional dances) performed in their honour. Though charmed by the intrepid dancers, members of the emperor's large retinue suffered a kind of cultural vertigo as they contended with Granada's duality. The same city that stood as a symbolic and practical starting point for Castile's international empire – as Christopher Columbus and Hernán Cortés cannily expressed in writing about their respective American expeditions – was the most visible testament to Iberia's Hispano-Muslim heritage. The five-month visit would have profound implications for city life for years to come. Royal chroniclers and city boosters would allege that newlyweds Charles V and Empress Isabella conceived the future Philip II in the city. Poets would celebrate that the quintessential metrical innovation of the Spanish Renaissance – the Hispanized Italian hendecasyllable – resulted from the Granada encounter between Catalan poet Joan Boscán and the Venetian polymath Andrea Navagero.[62]

But Navagero also left behind an account of the unease that followed from Granada's duality. The Venetian marvelled at ingeniously designed fountains and canals that remained from the Muslim period. He also waxed poetic about fruit orchards bursting with cherries, figs, apricots, and other Mediterranean delicacies still meticulously tended by Moriscos. Echoing Peter Martyr and other humanist visitors before him, Navagero called Granada the perfect setting for a life of tranquil, contented contemplation. But as he admired the handiwork of the engineers and artisans of the bygone Nasrid era, the Venetian visitor looked askance at their descendants. Voicing the prejudices that linked elites across Western Europe, he lamented that the all the noble Moors (*cavalieri et persone nobili*) had moved to North Africa, leaving plebeians and low-born people (*popolo et gente vile*). He also contended that the Moriscos clung to Arabic, spurned the Spanish language, converted to Christianity only by force, and received scant instruction in its doctrine.[63] To be sure, recent scholarship adds nuance to Navagero's broad-brush characterization: the region's diverse Morisco communities still included some families descended from the Nasrid ruling elite, though the massive emigration waves after the 1492 capitulation did leave the communities largely bereft of their religious and political leaders. Likewise, there would be numerous converts who fully assimilated into the majority population.[64] But what mattered at the time is that the Venetian's simplification would be widely shared within the ranks of crown and church authorities.

Fatefully for the regions's Moriscos, a crown *visita* (audit) registered the same generalizations in a report prepared for Charles V.[65] In response, the king enacted a series of new decrees and educational initiatives that would have far-reaching implications. He outlawed a wide range of cultural, religious, and economic practices associated with the region's people of Hispano-Muslim origin, ranging from the use of Arabic to halal butchering to circumcision. As Antonio Domínguez Ortiz and Bernard Vincent noted in their landmark study, the measures codified Moriscos as aliens in their own land who could not be considered loyal subjects of the king unless they abandoned a wide array of time-tested traditions that structured their social, religious, and economic lives.[66] Acutely aware of the financial ruin these measures would bring, Morisco leaders paid a massive donation to the strained royal coffers in exchange for a forty-year suspension of enforcement. Of course, no amount of *escudos* and *reales* could dispel the shadow cast by a series of marginalizing and punitive measures that put Granada's Moriscos in a colonial relationship with crown authorities and immigrants from Castile. However harmful such crown pressures would be for the region's Moriscos in the long run, the array of educational initiatives Charles V authorized to bring about this minority's Hispanization created extraordinary opportunities for Juan Latino.

These openings relate to higher education. Spurred to action during his Granada sojourn, the king founded three closely related institutions with the goal of energizing a lethargic evangelization enterprise. An Estudio General (hereafter, university) would train the priests and theologians needed for the evangelization. At the same time, a cathedral school, the Colegio Real de Santa Cruz de la Fe (hereafter Colegio Real), would prepare students for higher education with Latin grammar. Finally, a boarding school would take in at least one hundred sons of New Christians to inculcate them in Christianity and Spanish-Christian culture from earliest childhood. The residential school resembled missions in Spain's American colonies, where evangelization programs often sought to separate talented children from their families and cultural traditions. Nonetheless, the decree is striking in the context of the times, given that it conceives of a path for New Christians of Hispano-Muslim to become full stakeholders in Granada's Christian polity. That is, the royal grant envisions that the educational initiatives would prepare "good people to preach and instruct in religious doctrine and so they could inform faithful Christians, particularly the newly converted, of what they should do and carry out."[67] This promise of inclusion for converts would not last for Latino's entire lifetime, but it was operative at a critical juncture.

Juan Latino's path to higher education benefited from propitious timing on still another level. The educational initiatives designed to promote the acculturation and evangelization of Hispano-Muslims coincided with a broader wave of curricular reforms in Spain. Serendipitously, he intensified his education just as the humanist educational methods that Erasmus and Nebrija championed were taking root across Iberia. Among other changes, grammar school instruction moved away from the medieval emphasis on listening and memorization.[68] Chapters 3 to 5, which focus on Latino's literary practice, will explore the poetic gestures that reflect humanist teaching methodologies, since his Lepanto volume brings the Renaissance classroom to life on the printed page with interplay between the Latin verse in the text and didactic notes in the margins.

Evidence suggests that these new educational opportunities arose just when his opportunity for private, in-house education in the Sessa household had ended. In 1533, when he was thirteen, his master presided at the nascent university's first degree-granting ceremony in his capacity as one of the city's most powerful noblemen.[69] The following year, the grandee took full control of his estates, previously under the tutelage of an uncle serving as his guardian. At sixteen, Sessa relocated to Valladolid where Empress Isabella was in residence. The duke's formal training in Latin and the liberal arts would have ended here. Now his studies focused on the practical, high-stakes scrutiny of self and peers that powered courtly ambition. A telling irony emerges as the Abbot of Rute's chronicle recounts Sessa's legal emancipation in the same sentence in which he records Juan Latino's education.[70] The chronicler details the precise juridical means through which the duke took control of his estates, going so far as to note exactly where that document could be found. We have, in essence, a narrative of emancipation, though one focused on the nobleman's passage from tutelage under an uncle to full control of his family wealth. Left unanswered in the Abbot of Rute's history is the question of Juan Latino's own emancipation. What became of Juan Latino after his master moved to court?

Sessa's departure for court around 1536 left Latino – then probably in his early twenties – to continue his education alone. Unless Sessa manumitted his former companion prior to his departure, Latino would have been left to contend with the overseers or surrogates the duke left in charge of his affairs in Andalusia. Unfortunately, the family chronicle, so meticulous about Sessa's own emancipation, is silent on whether and how the duke manumitted Latino. In fact, the freedman's own autobiographical statement, that he was "finally given liberty" by Sessa (et tandem libertate donatus) is the only plausible reference to a manumission, oblique as it may be.[71] The ambiguity within the adverbial qualification "tandem" insinuates that freedom was a long struggle.

Once he left Granada in 1536, the duke's activities, artistic patronage, and aspirations would be focused outside Andalusia, though he retained an important presence in Granada through retainers, relatives, and such ongoing building projects as the funeral monument to the Gran Capitán still under construction. The grandee also provided crucial material support to Juan Latino. Thus, the Abbot of Rute's *House of Córdoba* celebrates that the grandee provided his former childhood companion with "asiento y mesa." This formulation indicates in-kind support akin to "room and board," suggesting that sponsorship allowed Latino to establish work or residence (*asiento*) and draw on basic sustenance (*mesa*). Such dependency would not necessarily be demeaning or associated with bondage, since it formed a mainstay of aristocratic patronage. In fact, support from a grandee would remain a point of pride and ostentation into the seventeenth century; thus, two generations later, Lope de Vega would trumpet his dependence on the sixth Duke of Sessa – grand-nephew of Latino's one-time master – even after he gained unprecedented popular acclaim and a steady income writing plays.[72]

In the evidence of the relationship between Latino and the third Duke of Sessa, the first archival record of the one-time slave's activities after the nobleman's departure from the city dates from 1546, when the university granted the freedman the degree of *bachiller* (baccalaureate).[73] The fact that Latino received this credential around the age of thirty suggests that he advanced his studies outside the Sessa household after an interruption, or that he combined continuing education with work obligations. A precise account of the freedman's advanced study beyond the baccalaureate degree of 1546 remains elusive, due in part to the destruction of a large number of university records in an 1877 fire. Surviving records do not corroborate two often repeated assertions about Latino's university studies. Notably, Marín Ocete reported he continued his higher education while still a slave, following the fictionalized account of Latino's life from seventeenth-century playwright Ximénez de Enciso. Likewise, no university records survive to support the account of a public oration Latino delivered to secure his licentiate degree.[74] That said, both notions of Latino's higher education – the lack of a formal manumission and the public oration to secure an advanced degree – stand as reasonable inferences based on what we can glean about the early years of Granada's fledgling university.

One more intriguing yet uncorroborated account of Juan Latino's path to higher education appears in a city history by Francisco Bermúdez de Pedraza, published a decade after the freedman's likely death. His discussion of the former slave's specific academic vocation is revealing in the context of Granada's scholarly traditions, past and present: "he had wanted to study medicine, and on the advice of his friends he desisted, whereupon he immersed himself in Grammar study."[75] True or apocryphal, the chronicler's allegation that the freedman had wanted to study medicine speaks to the continuing importance in Granada of Hispano-Muslim medical science and to the prestige of the medical faculty at the fledgling University of Granada. The advice against studying medicine might well follow from the perceptions throughout the sixteenth century that Arabic erudition was risky, since it could invite Inquisitorial scrutiny.[76] This anecdote may, however, be apocryphal, but bears mention for what it suggests about the environment for advanced learning in the former Nasrid city.

One point that seems clear amid uncertainties about Latino's path to higher education in Granada is that it came at a relatively advanced age. The older age at which he received his baccalaureate degree suggests he balanced advanced study with other work, whether as a slave or freedman. Such an advanced age for study would have set him apart from the elite segment of the university population preparing for university studies in early adolescence. Nonetheless, there are indications that some other slaves and servants did find at least a limited access to advanced instruction. For instance, among the estimated 200 Latin apprentices who attended Nicolas Clenardus's Latin class in Braga, Portugal, there were black slaves, in addition to his own three slaves pressed into service as teaching auxiliaries, the already mentioned Antonius, Sebastian, and Michael. Latino's older age for study also meshes with a general tendency in Spanish universities of the sixteenth century, whose relatively large informal student population followed in some measure from the burden of fees that delayed progress towards degrees.[77]

Whether slave or free at the time of his foray into higher education, Latino would have been contending with changed prospects given that his childhood companion had departed from Andalusia for court. The inner politics of a sprawling aristocratic family might not have been so favourable; after all, a decade earlier, senior family members had sought to block the young slave's access to early education. What seems to have been decisive for Latino upon the Duke of Sessa's departure from Granada was his ability to cultivate new patronage alliances. The same year Latino took his baccalaureate degree, 1546, Granada welcomed an energetic new archbishop, Pedro de Guerrero. This churchman embodied the reforming zeal that church and crown officials would deploy in their efforts to reshape Granada into an orthodox Christian polity.[78] Along the way, the prelate made a lasting mark on the city, serving a three-decade tenure as prelate, though this term included two long absences when he represented Spain in the Second and Third Councils of

Trent (1551–2, 1562–3, respectively). Latino's autobiographical statement records the influence this churchman had on his career as an educator, when it notes that he gained his position teaching Grammar and Latin from Pedro Guerrero, archbishop of Granada. The Guerrero connection gave him crucial support for his position in the Colegio Real and university, the educational institutions Charles V founded in the aftermath of his 1526 visit. An intriguingly ambiguous turn of phrase underscores the freedman's praise of this sponsoring prelate. He lauds Guerrero as "extra omnem aleam," which in the context hails him as "learned beyond all doubt," following from a passage in Pliny's *Natural History* that thus praises Cicero.[79] At the same time, "extra omnem aleam" could more generally convey "all obstacles or risks"; consequently, a reader might also read the passage as a chronicle of the poet's own advancement and mobility against many difficulties.

Whether taken as a homage to the learned churchman or a subtle reference to his own courage, Latino here marks an important alliance at a delicate juncture. After the departure of the Duke of Sessa from Granada, the prelate's support and sponsorship would be critical. Because the new University of Granada and its partner institution of the Colegio Real grew without sizeable endowments of their own and were situated within the sprawling cathedral complex, the city's archbishop was the most powerful single official in their day-to-day operations. The university's first permanent building, now called the Curia Episcopal, towered over the northeast corner of Granada's Bibarrambla plaza.[80]

A commercial nerve centre since the Nasrid era, the Bibarrambla plaza neighbourhood where Latino studied and taught housed the ecclesiastical and educational institutions charged with Christianizing the city. The university's mission is recorded in an inscription that is still visible on the Curia Palace today, despite several façade alterations since the sixteenth century: "This house of learning was founded to dispel the darkness of infidels."[81] Latino, who taught for four decades inside the building, was part of a teaching faculty whose ultimate justification pivoted on this goal of converting Muslims, a project variously defined as the instruction of Morisco grammar school students or, more commonly, as the training in Latin of the future priests who would give instruction to Granadinos of Muslim descent. Graduation records identify a small number of Moriscos who took degrees at the new university. We can reasonably assume quite a few more of the graduates listed in university graduation records came from families who had attained sufficient assimilation to pass as members of the city's Christian immigrant population.

The main thrust of Juan Latino's vocation as an educator would be the guidance of young Granadinos preparing for university studies. Indeed, the freedman would make this a point of pride in his 1573 volume of commemorative poetry on the Battle of Lepanto. The frontispiece thus heralds him as a "guide for studies of the youth of Granada" ([per] Magistrum Ioannem Latinum, Garnatae studiosae adolescentiae moderatorem). As such, Latino would have been a gatekeeper to university studies and the prestigious positions in the growing crown bureaucracy such study could yield. What records survive from an archive fire in the nineteenth century indicate that, like Latino himself, some in his Latin class were older. Some were servants. Also significant was the somewhat precarious nature of the university and Colegio Real, due to chronic underfunding. These institutional problems may, in fact, have opened a door for Juan Latino to gain a quasi-permanent position on the faculty. To the extent this is the case, Latino's skills as an educator, the special problems of a new university, and well-calibrated alliances with patrons trumped the era's mistreatment of black Africans. But when we dig deeper into his life in Granada, we always find signs of the vulnerability of an educator who came from an oppressed minority.

Assimilation and Its Discontents

At first glance, Latino's work teaching in the grammar school and university would seem to shield him from the bias against black Africans. University archives portray Latino as a regular member of the faculty, marking no distinction as to race. The freedman typically appears as "Maestro Juan Latino," as in the minutes of the faculty senate (*claustro*) from November of 1558, where members discussed the absenteeism of a canon law specialist. Latino similarly appears in minutes for sessions in the following two years. As on the occasion two decades earlier when the *claustro* awarded him the baccalaureate degree, the recording secretary did not make any indication of his skin colour or slave status.[82] Instead of race or ethnicity, the significant distinction here emerges from long-standing university hierarchies stemming from degree and discipline. That is, each time Latino is named in faculty senate minutes, his name, along with one or two other *maestros*, appears after the *doctores* in theology, civil law, canon law, and medicine. This scribal format suggests that, despite its fledgling nature, the University of Granada's early operations still showed the hallmarks of the traditional academic hierarchy. Here, humanist teachers remained relative newcomers, compared to the traditional higher faculties of theology, law, and medicine.[83]

Notwithstanding this secondary rank in the university faculty, Juan Latino's title of *maestro* carried, at a minimum, the public recognition that he had the credentials to teach an academic subject.[84] Though at the University of Salamanca, *maestro* was also an honorific for someone who had studied theology, there is no evidence this usage applied at the University of Granada, nor is there any indication Latino undertook advanced study in this most traditional of university disciplines. With so many gaps in Granada's university archives, we can only affirm the title of *maestro* (*magister*) conferred a stature as an educator. This recognition likely required that Latino undergo some kind of public examination, though again, no records survive.

Another indication of the notable respectability Latino's teaching position conferred comes to light in documents where outside observers upgraded Latino's position to that of a *catedrático*, understood as the holder of a permanent teaching chair. The royal secretary who approved the freedman's first book for publication thus labelled the author a "catedrático de Gramática en la Universidad de Granada" (a chair of Grammar at the University of Granada). Likewise, the scribes from crown-taxing authorities with whom Latino maintained a dispute over debts owed on his property (*censo*) identify him as a *catedrático de gramática* affiliated with the university. The Abbot of Rute's detailed chronicle of the third Duke of Sessa's life upgrades Latino's rank still more, stating that the freedman gained the surname of Latino in recognition of his language skills, then attained the chair in Latinity and rhetoric at the university, and thereafter, enjoyed a leadership role as a dean in the university. After retracing the steps of the freedman's teaching career in the early twentieth century, Antonio Marín Ocete protested that Latino could not have been a *catedrático* since the fledgling University of Granada failed to endow a chair in Grammar until much later.[85] Granada scholars José Antonio Sánchez Marín and María Nieves Muñoz Martín propose the university chair was nonetheless official, granted by the city's archbishop.[86] My own reading of the remaining documents from the university's early years suggests that the intertwining of the Colegio Real and the university made Latino appear as a fully vested faculty member, much in the way adjunct instructors in American universities perform critical duties and thus often appear indistinguishable from tenured professors to outside observers.

Whatever the precise terms and title of his teaching post, the freedman's success there brought assimilation into Granada's upwardly mobile population of *letrados* and other members of liberal professions. At some point in the 1540s, he married Ana de Carlobal (or Carleval), sister of one of the University of Granada's first graduates. One historian reported that the Carlobals were also dependents of the Duke of Sessa, with the father serving as a governor of ducal estates, but did not provide specific documentation.[87] Certainly, a union with another Sessa-family retainer would help explain Latino's marriage to a white woman in a context where scholars have found interracial marriages relatively rare. But again, available sources do not confirm this supposition.[88]

What is beyond a doubt is the Latino-Carlobal family's assimilation into Granada's growing professional class. The couple purchased a house in the city's Santa Ana parish three years after Latino had earned his baccalaureate degree.[89] The Santa Ana neighbourhood where the couple started their family remained a contact zone well into the sixteenth century, blending Christian and Muslim cultures. When the couple bought their house, the parish church was being built over the ruins of the Almanzora mosque that had remained largely intact until the 1530s. The church's strategic location, perched under the Alhambra between the older Muslim quarter of the Albaicín and the newer quarter below, remains a testament to the city's transformation. Its elegant Mudejar belltower likewise speaks to the cultural hybridity of the place where Juan Latino and Ana Carlobal started a family. Facing it is the spacious Plaza Nueva, carved out in an effort to widen the narrow streets and alleyways typical of Muslim cities. When the family settled in Santa Ana, a stately Renaissance palace was being constructed as the headquarters of the royal Audiencia and Chancillería (Provincial High Court and Chancery).[90] The expanding crown bureaucracy to be housed in the new building, in turn, attracted upwardly mobile *letrados* and their families to the neighbourhood. In fact, later records from a dispute over the crown's levy on *censos* suggest the extent to which Latino embodied this aspect of the quarter, as documents show he expanded his property investments from one house to a cluster of them. So doing, he partook of an emerging credit economy that was itself a sign of a society undergoing momentous changes.[91]

Thus settled in the dynamic Santa Ana neighbourhood, the Latino-Carlobal household belonged to the growing segment of the city population that nobleman Diego Hurtado de Mendoza called the "middling people between the great [high-born] and small." Affiliations to this *letrado* class in Granada brought opportunities to Latino and others that may have been more difficult to find elsewhere in Castile or even a nearby town like Córdoba. Looking at the city overall, David Coleman documents striking feats of mobility for New Christians who successfully assimilated to what were perceived as Old Christian ways. These included a converso merchant who relocated there from Toledo and a prosperous Morisco family who eventually passed themselves off as the descendants of Milanese émigrés.[92] If recent interest in Latino follows from his foundational importance within the global African diaspora, from another angle his family life is a story about Granada after 1492. But at the same time as this city offered new avenues for social mobility, it also suffered racial and ethnic tensions.

Signs of both the city's social dynamism and its underlying tensions inform the *Vecindario* of 1561, a parish-by-parish registry of households that survives in the Simancas state archive. The book took shape when church officials ordered a house-by-house, parish-by-parish tally of individuals "old enough to confess."[93] The pages for the Santa Ana parish confirm the freedman's integration into the realm of "middling people"; thus, as head of household, he is listed first, as "el maestro Juan Latino," with no indication of his minority status as a black African or his one-time enslavement. Living with him are his wife, Ana de Carlobal; a daughter, Juana; a housekeeper, María Gracia; his son-in-law, Francisco de Cordova; and a servant, Pedro. A seventeenth-century history recalled Latino's son-in-law was a lawyer with the neighbouring royal chancery, a plausible claim that requires further archival research to corroborate.[94] Notable here is how the scribe identified Latino through his honorific, as *maestro*. Most male heads of household are identified by their first and last names, plus a trade or occupation, if applicable. We can thus see how a large number of Latino's neighbours earned their living in the silk trade. This business was still dominated by Moriscos, despite inroads in the business by Christian immigrants. Records that survive for the many neighbours involved in the silk trade do not allow for a determination of ethnic identity. Most of those neighbours had Hispanized surnames – among others Carrera, Bautista, Roma, Aguilar, Sánchez, Díaz, Contreras – and were not specifically labelled as New Christians. As such, they could be either acculturated Moriscos or Christian immigrants who entered the business. Indeed, scholars have documented Santa Ana's integration of Moriscos and Christian immigrants, in contrast to the segregation of the almost entirely Morisco Albaicín on higher ground, or the Christian-majority parishes in the lower part of the city.[95]

Taking stock of Latino's degree of integration, the census record of his household might, at a glance, seem to indicate a more benign attitude towards black Africans in Spain. Some twentieth-century scholars would present Latino's social advancement in Granada as evidence of greater racial tolerance in the Hispanic world, in contrast to the racism of the English-speaking Atlantic world.[96] But a closer look at the census registry complicates the picture.

Paging through the census, we find many signs of the expanding Atlantic slave trade. Slavery, in turn, informs perceptions of blackness. Time and again, the scribes who recorded information about residents conceive blackness as a metonym for slave status. For instance, an enslaved woman in the household headed by one Antón Pérez appears as "Beatriz su negra" (Beatriz his black). A Morisco head-of-household has a slave identified as "Felipe su negro" (Felipe his black).[97] Scribes record other households with black "criadas" or "criados" (servants), which likely indicate paid domestics. Records for the San Matías parish label enslaved black Africans "esclavos bozales," a term widely used to describe recently kidnapped and enslaved sub-Saharan Africans, often with the implication they were not yet proficient in a European language.[98] Most census takers do not use this classification term, so it is difficult to ascertain whether this term literally refers to recently transported slaves or simply presents a denigrating term for black Africans.

Free blacks do appear, though in marginal social positions and occupations. One household in the Albaicín was led by a free black washerwoman, Catalina Hernández, and either her daughter or sister, Cecilia Hernández, who worked in the wool trade. Elsewhere, a scribe registered a household comprised of a freedwoman, Francisca, and a man listed as "Pedro, negro tullido" (Pedro, a maimed/disabled black).[99] Symptomatic of colour prejudice, the scribe did not note a surname for Pedro, in contrast to the practice with which other households are registered.

On first inspection, the "Maestro Juan Latino" might seem a world apart from other blacks in Granada. His prosperous household would appear to insulate him from the hundreds of enslaved black Africans reduced in the register to "his black" (su negro / negra), or from the harsh lives of other free blacks, whether Catalina Hernández the washerwoman, or the disabled Pedro. Yet the *Vecindario* features one unsettling reminder of Latino's own past. In the Santiago parish household of a cathedral canon identified only as "el canónigo Carvajal," we find two slaves, "Juan de Valencia, esclavo / Juan Latino otro" (Juan de

Valencia, a slave, Juan Latino, another).[100] What to make of this namesake? It could be a form of mockery, a tribute with comic overtones, or even a godson given Latino's name in baptism. Without more context, there is no way to interpret this homonym, who might have been a slave of North African or sub-Saharan African origin. Whether the intentions behind this name were friendly, comic, or derisive, the enslaved Juan Latino and the Maestro Juan Latino moved in overlapping professional circles, given the educator's close ties to Granada's cathedral chapter. Consequently, when the freedman walked the centre-city streets near his classroom, he would likely have encountered an enslaved namesake who, intentionally or not, reminded him and others of the shackles he had cast off with great effort.

From another vantage point, the 1561 *Vecindario* demonstrates that "Juan" had become a quintessential slave name, reflecting a typecasting akin to twentieth-century popular culture, where "James" was the stock name for a chauffeur. Thus, records from the Albaicín parish of San Miguel list "Juan negro" in a series of households in close proximity to one another.[101] By no means the only frequently recurring slave name, "Juan" does nevertheless stand out in the census rolls as a very typical one.

More problematic still, the numerous enslaved black men and women of Granada identified as "su negro" or "negra" bear witness to a trope that would become a hallmark of early modernity: blackness becomes conceived in figurative terms as enslavement. Latino was thus a minority twice over. As either the son of two black slaves or of a black mother and white father, or himself a captured native of the Senegal river region, Latino was a visible Cristiano Nuevo at a time where the spreading *limpieza de sangre* mania was fomenting discrimination against individuals who could not document Old Christian ancestry from time immemorial. A converso merchant who had relocated to Granada might redesign his family tree, commission a new genealogy, or alter family oral history to claim Old-Christian lineage. Latino, as a prominent black African, could not so easily have taken this route to assimilation. Rather, his profile in the city, as the census report suggests, would hinge on a duality. In the context of Granada's dynamic population of *gente media* tied to the growing crown bureaucracy and to educational establishments, Latino would be one more member of the *letrado* class, as "Maestro Juan Latino." But at critical junctures where deepening distinctions of race and ethnicity come into play, his affiliation would be with the city's other black residents, including the slave of the cathedral canon named Juan Latino.

The freedman-and-educator's contradictory identity, known widely as both a member of a vibrant professional class and a high-profile representative of an oppressed minority, connects his story to the broader narrative of Spain's emergence as the first global empire of the modern era. That is, the nascent modern bureaucracy that nurtured the educational institutions where Latino secured social advancement also normalized racial and ethnic discrimination under the guise of defending and spreading the Catholic faith. At some points, the growing bureaucracy of the Spanish Monarchy could empower individuals to rise outside the inherited strictures of family and community. But at other points, the same constellation of royal councils and ecclesiastical institutions could inhibit or aggressively block that freedom. Earlier, I noted how the growing if uneven application of blood-purity statutes would become one such check on individual advancement throughout Spanish realms. Now, from the specific vantage point of the Granada portrayed in the 1561 census book, we can glimpse another case where the embryonic modern state limits individual agency. The census book's very existence speaks to this dimension. Priests and scribes prepared a house-by-house tally of Granadinos of an age where they are obliged to hear confession. This book stands, in effect, as a prototype of a modern government registry. On its face, the survey undertaken to insure Catholic piety does not discriminate based on race or ethnicity. In theory, any Granadino who regularly follows the requirement to confess his or her own sins would be equal in the eyes of religious authorities. But any time a Granadino is labelled *negro* or *su negro,* the state is certifying or fixing a racial identity. We also see new statecraft hewing ethnic difference into the permanent record each time a census taker notes Morisco identity. For instance, on the title page for the San Cristóbal parish of the Albaicín, a hand other than the census taker wrote "es todo de moriscos" (it is all Moriscos). Is this disdain or a matter-of-fact classification? This taxonomy was not systematic. Other hands in the census made no special issue of the Morisco-majority parishes they surveyed, as, for instance, in the registry of the Albaicín's San Nicolás parish. But this ability of the growing state to certify and enforce ethnic difference would, however uneven, soon yield dire results for Granada.

A half-decade after the census, Philip II sent an inquisitor affiliated with the most orthodox faction at the royal court to serve in Granada. Pedro de Deza arrived in the city as president of the royal Audiencia and Chancillería (hereafter Audiencia). The highest branch of the crown judiciary with jurisdiction over all of Andalusia, the Janus-like appeals court-and-chancery typified the labyrinthine nature of the professional royal judiciary as it had evolved in the sixteenth century. Intersecting channels of authority, privilege, and patronage gave an ambitious, well-connected official like Deza wide berth.[102] His impact on Juan Latino's life would be decisive in both good and bad ways. The ambitious new president of the Audiencia became yet another influential sponsor for the freedman; in time, Deza would open the doors at court that allowed Latino to assert himself as the author of epic poetry at a time where gaining access to print was difficult. Yet from another angle, Deza would sow great destruction and suffering in Granada. With ruthless efficiency, he spearheaded a series of measures that ignited the devastating civil war, also known as the Morisco Rebellion or the Second Revolt of the Alpujarras. The crown official's bitter legacy would be the mass oppression of Granada's autochthonous population of Hispano-Muslim descent. More broadly, the inquisitor's arrival in the city precipitated a series of events that would upend the idea of what it meant to be a Christian in Granada.

Chapter 2 retells the story of the events that transformed Granada in the wake of Deza's arrival. In particular, I recount the traumatic turn of events that would devastate the city and also more sharply mark ethnic and racial distinctions. The newly acute problem of group identity in Granada, I argue, would inform Juan Latino's literary practice and self-fashioning as an author deserving lasting renown. Where this first chapter has cast a wide net in order to glean fragments of scarce evidence about Juan Latino's path to social advancement, the chapter ahead details Granada's civil war.

2 Civil War, Shattered *Convivencia*

Usque adeo miserum est, civili vincere bello?
(Is victory in civil war so very terrible?)

Lucan, *De bellum civile* (1.370)

Publicizing Edicts of Intolerance (New Year's Day, 1567)

A parade of constables and magistrates rang in the new year of 1567. While Granada's royal and municipal officials had long greeted each new year with celebrations marking the Nasrid king's capitulation to Ferdinand and Isabel on 2 January 1492, this time was different. The traditional commemoration of the *Toma* (capture) of 1492, as A. Katie Harris shows, had emerged in the sixteenth century as a forum for elite self-expression and competition.[1] Yet, rather than look back to the deeds of Ferdinand and Isabel, the parade of constables that opened 1567 admonished Granadinos of Muslim ancestry about new perils ahead. To the accompaniment of horns and kettle drums, judicial officials from the royal Audiencia and others from the municipal government marched to each of the city's public gathering places. In every plaza or churchyard where they paused, a crier read aloud five edicts (*pragmáticas*) issued in Philip II's name. Each of the five proclamations prohibited a distinctive custom or business practice associated with Granada's Morisco communities. Though crown officials had previously issued decrees on the same range of topics, they had not devoted great energy or resources to their enforcement. In essence, the constables' parade heralded a new leader's implacable resolve.[2]

This chapter tells the story that began with the New Year's Day proclamations and culminated with the civil war, known to scholars as the Second Revolt of the Alpujarras or simply, the Morisco Revolt. But I follow the traumatized soldier-chronicler Ginés Pérez de Hita who insisted that "civil war" is the proper term "since they were Christians fighting Christians, and all within one city and one realm."[3] Whatever one calls Granada's horrific war of attrition that played out from late 1568 to 1570, there is little doubt it challenged Philip II within his Iberian realms as never before. As in the civil war Lucan narrated in his devastating epic, the stronger side ultimately prevailed in Granada. But as in ancient Rome, the cost of such a victory would be so high as to test the power of language itself.

Events that played out from 1567 to 1570 are relevant on several counts for the *Epic of Juan Latino.* First, the violent end to the tense *convivencia* between Moriscos and Christians would inform the freedman's self-fashioning as the author of an epic poem about the Battle of Lepanto. That poem, as subsequent chapters will discuss in detail, would seem to displace questions of Christian-Muslim relations to the distant eastern Mediterranean, where the Battle of Lepanto transpired not long after Granada's civil war. But even in a work that commemorates a naval battle abroad, the conflict that unfolded at home would be palpable. A second reason for pausing to reflect on the rebellion in Granada before delving into his Lepanto epic is more diffuse, but as pressing. The expulsion and enslavement en masse of Granada's Moriscos after the rebellion of 1568–70 would pivot on the official effort to deracinate and then forget this autochthonous population. The goal of erasing the Moriscos of Granada from a conception of Spanish polity, while never complete, would have a profound impact on what it meant to be a *vecino* (resident) of the city.

On this note, a caveat about the freedman bears repetition before beginning. With no reliable evidence of Muslim ancestry or Morisco kin, Juan Latino and his family were not the explicit targets of the five edicts read on New Year's Day 1567. But the *pragmáticas* articulated both licit and illicit identities in a way that undermined the idea of Christianity's universal reach. Key measures and assumptions within the text of the new laws cast a shadow on any individual of non-European ancestry. In this respect, the edicts did affect Juan Latino, regardless of his affiliations with or antipathies towards Moriscos of Granada. Moreover, the uprising these new policies incited in very short order would devastate the city where Latino had secured freedom, social advancement, and public admiration as an educator. However tense and uneven the *convivencia* between Christians and Moriscos had been before the rebellion, the city that emerged from it would be less open to individuals readily identified as New Christians with ancestors from outside Europe.

The edicts, individually and together, pivot on a desire to calibrate the measure of Christian spirituality to outward physical appearance and in reference to cultural practices associated with populations of Old Castile. The first decree gave Morisca women three years to phase out their distinctive dress and adopt the women's clothing favoured in Old Castile. The second announced the prohibition of *zambras* and *leilas*, the same festive dances with which Moriscas had greeted Charles V and Empress Isabella on the occasion of the royal visit that had been so decisive for Latino's education and social advancement. The third decree outlawed the public baths that had survived from the Nasrid era and had so captivated the imaginations of visitors. Less connected to Hispano-Muslim traditions but increasingly important to the most prosperous Moriscos who had remained in the city after 1492, the fourth edict prohibited Morisco ownership of black slaves. The fifth law prohibited contracts in Arabic. Each edict came with a range of punishments for violation, ranging from steep fines to exile, imprisonment, and even five years in the galleys. The enforcement mechanisms outlined also carried a moral hazard common in ancien régime justice, in that individuals who denounced offenders and the judges who presided over criminal processes stood to gain a share of property confiscated as punishment.

As noted above, a particularly crucial dimension of the edicts is the insistence on external appearance as a reliable marker of inner Christian virtue. For instance, the first edict, on dress, codifies the hallmarks of true Christian religiosity with reference to the regional costume of the women of Valladolid, Burgos, and Medina del Campo, with cloaks (*mantos*), smocks (*sayas*), head coverings (*tocas*), and exposed faces (*rostros descubiertos*). The garments in question were the distinctive tunics (*marlotas*) and outward veils (*almalafas*) favoured by Granadinas of Hispano-Muslim ancestry. Here, the timing is particularly ironic given that such Morisca garments, long a point of fascination for visitors, were literally being etched in the visual memory of book consumers across Europe in the first edition of Georgius Braun's atlas of city views, the *Civitates Orbis Terrarum*. Just as crown officials were publishing the large fines for wearing *marlotas* and *almalafas*, they figured in Braun's city view as a defining feature of Granada's allure to outsiders. Figure 7

Figure 7 Georg Braun, Granada, 1565. This view of Granada (from the east) is based on the drawings of Flemish engraver Franz Hogenberg. Braun embellished his collaborator's city view with scenes from daily life that capture its allure as Iberia's last Muslim metropolis. In the right foreground, there is an allegorical depiction of the evangelization of Hispano-Muslims (Moriscos). Above the evangelization scene, a woman depicted atop a mule and another walking to her left wear the *marlotas* (tunics) and outward veils (*almalafas*) favoured by Moriscas. Garden plots shown in the centre right were the specialty of Morisco gardeners, renowned for their ability to coax an agricultural bounty from even the tiniest plots. Ironically, by the time this city view appeared in print for the first time (1581), it was an anachronism. The distinctive Morisca garments had been prohibited in the Pragmatic of 1567 and more dramatically, the mass expulsion and – enslavement of Moriscos that took place between 1570 and 1571 had negated the earlier goal of mass evangelization. Nonetheless, the city view stands as a record of the city in which Juan Latino studied, started a family, and negotiated his social mobility.

Source: Georg Braun, *Urbium praecipuarum totius mundi. Liber Tertius*, 1581, plate 15. Reprinted, Cologne: Bertram Bucholtz, 1593. By permission of the Biblioteca Histórica, Universidad Complutense de Madrid, BH FLL Res 15.

shows one such city view from the third instalment of the Braun atlas of city views.

At first glance, the prohibitions would not seem to alter the daily life of thoroughly Hispanized Moriscos, Christian immigrants from Castile, or even black men and women. But in examining the letter of the new laws, we can see how the decrees cast a shadow on any Granadino who could not plausibly conform in outward appearance to features associated with the people of Old Castile. Note, for instance, how the text of the first edict equates physical appearance with interior qualities: "so that in all that concerns the interior as well as the exterior, they would conform with the true Christians."[4] The language of illicit deviance likewise offers logic applicable beyond the realm of women's clothing: "the difference and distinction in outward habit has been and is a major cause for inward difference, which has very much offended our Lord God."[5] To the extent the logic of the edict is associable to other realms, the definition of physical non-conformity threatens other individuals from minority groups, or even those with a highly visible physical disability.

Even so, one can imagine a well-assimilated black Granadino like Juan Latino could have shrugged off a decree so explicitly aimed at Moriscas. But the fourth of the five edicts and reactions to it would have been impossible to dismiss for any black resident of the city. That is, Granada's New Christians of Muslim descent were forbidden from owning black slaves. This law hinged on the allegation that Moriscos were inculcating black African slaves into Islam. In purely economic terms, the prohibition amplified the negative impact of other measures that Moriscos interpreted as extortionist, most notably the increasing taxes on the silk industry.[6]

In ethical terms, the decree affirmed and amplified demeaning conceptions of blacks that were gaining traction in tandem with the growing Atlantic slave trade. In particular, the prohibition hinges on the notion that black Africans are uniformly receptive or susceptible to Islamic proselytizing. Going back centuries in medieval Iberia, there was an iconographic tradition that portrayed black Africans in support positions for invading Muslim armies, an idea codified in the term "blackamoor."[7] Closer at hand, Inquisition records from the mid-sixteenth century showed that officials erroneously conceived the newly captured blacks from sub-Saharan Africa as religious blank slates. This misconception stemmed from the fact that Europeans lacked the ethnographic analytical tools needed to identify animist religions of West Africa.[8]

Soldier-chronicler Luis del Mármol Carvajal airs both generalizations about blacks – as natural subalterns to hostile Muslim armies and religious tabulae rasae – in his discussion of the edicts of 1567. He thus ties prohibition to the fear of "the harm from the fact that Moriscos of the realm of Granada should have blacks from Guinea in their service, because they would purchase them freshly transported to draw on their service, and having them in their homes, they inculcated them in Muhammad's sect, and they assimilated them to their customs, and besides those souls being lost, that *the Morisco nation was growing by the hour* with less assurance of their loyalty [to the crown]" (emphasis added).[9] The idea that the Morisco population "grows hourly" through the inculcation of black slaves into crypto-Islamic practices builds on a series of distortions that anthropologist Julio Caro Baroja identifies in his classic study of Granada's people of Hispano-Muslim descent: fecund and industrious families, conceived as hallmarks of normative Spanishness in other contexts, are viewed negatively in regards to Moriscos. Caro Baroja notes how often officials and anti-Morisco polemicists accused these Granadinos of threatening Spanish realms with unfettered reproduction and the hoarding of scarce resources. Note as well the negative conception of "Morisco nation" (*nación morisca*), typifying a logic that had been used to label Spaniards descended from converted Sephardic Jews as an alien group as well. This negative charge renders one of the nations ruled by the composite Spanish Monarchy – along with Castilians, Basques, Galicians, Catalans, Navarrese, and others – into an alien group within, sapping the strength of Spain's body politic.[10]

Taking stock of this discourse of a black-Morisco menace, the position of a relatively privileged free black like Juan Latino bears some reflection. Accepted as an esteemed educator and property owner, he might not immediately seem vulnerable to the edict and its underlying logic that black Africans were natural subalterns for Muslim enemies. He was not, after all, part of the Morisco population as best we can tell. As an erudite schoolmaster, he would not have been plausibly mistaken for a recently captured black African who did not yet speak Spanish. But what of the "other" Juan Latino? As I discussed in chapter 1, the registry from the 1561 census of Granada listed another slave in the city named for the freedman. This second Juan Latino, in symbolic terms, stands as an enslaved doppelganger. Or for that matter, one might also consider the significant number of other black slaves named Juan. In theory, these other black or enslaved Juans were more vulnerable to accusations of susceptibility to Islamic proselytizing. In a sense, once there is an official statement on how blacks in the city can augment a Muslim threat, Juan Latino the educator becomes subject to at least some measure of guilt by association and generalization. His vulnerability is the same as that facing a prosperous and well-connected member of the Morisco community who finds himself accused of being a member of a secretive Muslim fifth-column.

A final existential peril for Juan Latino that follows from all the edicts of 1567 bears consideration. The turn away from the earlier goal of gradual assimilation towards a policy of implacable enforcement negated the defining mission of the educational establishments where Latino studied and worked. As noted in chapter 1, the foundation and ongoing operations of both the Colegio Real and University of Granada followed from the idea that a full Christianization of Granada's Moriscos depended on sending well-educated priests and friars to pastoral missions in Morisco communities. Despite the contentious faculty politics and chronic underfunding that plagued these twin institutions in the years Latino had studied and worked there, the evangelization mission remained a point of pride. Minutes of the faculty senate from the years just before the edicts celebrate that the university had trained a generation of qualified clergymen, thus improving the quality of pastoral attention in the entire region.[11] The well-educated priests mentioned in the faculty senate minutes were, moreover, Juan Latino's former classmates and students. This assimilationist agenda had remained alive, if not without criticism, until the constables' parade of 1 January 1567. Now the crown signalled its commitment to coercion instead of persuasion. The actions and negotiations that followed the publication of the edicts would have drastic and ultimately dire consequences in relatively short order.

Intolerance Enforced and Contested

After reading the five proclamations in Granada's plazas, the phalanx of officials set out immediately to destroy the public baths (*hammams*), known in Spanish parlance as *baños artificiales*. To set an example, the constables first destroyed those in the Alhambra, which had been incorporated into the vast royal patrimony after 1492. Hammer blows shattered the splendid marble baths that had inspired the German traveller Hieronymous Münzer to imagine naked concubines bathing under the watchful eye of a Nasrid king.[12] But where Münzer's host seven decades earlier in the Alhambra had been the Islamophilic Count of Tendilla, the hammer-wielding officials of 1567 were led by the new Audiencia president, Pedro de Deza. This inquisitor's elevation to high rank followed from his ties to the newly ascendant faction at court led by Cardinal Diego de Espinosa; this official, in turn, was doubly powerful, as the president of the Council of Castile and Inquisitor General.[13]

Morisco communities grasped the dangers at hand right away. One crowd gathered in an Albaicín plaza to hear the edicts read aloud on 1 January 1567 panicked and almost rioted.[14] Community leaders, lamenting that Philip II had succumbed to bad advisors, drafted their own letters to the king and his inner circle. Most famously, a descendant of Nasrid rulers, Francisco Núñez Muley, wrote to Pedro de Deza in his capacity as the region's highest ranking crown official. With methodical point-by-point arguments, Núñez Muley reminds the Audiencia president that Moriscos were *naturales* (natives) of Granada and thus one nation among the many within Hispania. The offending Morisca veils and cloaks were not signs of secret adherence to Islam, but the regional costume of a Spanish province. Such points of distinction, notes editor and translator Vincent Barletta, bring to light the inner conflict of even an elite Morisco, who sought to show his affiliation with the Catholic Monarchy's imperial project as a loyal subject, while resisting measures that threatened his community's very survival. No indications suggest Núñez Muley had ties to Juan Latino, but the conflicted identity Barletta finds in this memorandum anticipates the kinds of inner conflicts that would inform the freedman's Lepanto epic composed just a half-decade later.[15]

Núñez Muley's defence of Morisco Spanishness hinges on his endorsement of the intensifying mistreatment of enslaved black Africans. For instance, he defends the Morisco dances prohibited in the second edict by noting the tolerance for the traditional dances of sub-Saharan Africans. On the subject, he asks: "Can we say that there is a lower race than the black slaves of Guinea?" On the question of black slave ownership, he proffers another rhetorical question: "Don't these black slaves deserve their wretched state? Must everyone be seen as equals? Let them bring the water pitcher on their backs, or carry burdens, or handle the plow."[16] Within a half decade, Juan Latino would refute this formulation that equates black Africans with unpaid, backbreaking labour with his own feat of erudite, pedagogically engaged Latin poetry – the subject of the next chapter. But for now, let us follow the story of the edicts and the conflict they incited.

When Philip II failed to heed Núñez Muley and others who opposed the edicts, tensions reached a breaking point. Among Morisco communities, apocalyptic prophecies (*jofores*) gained adherents. Across the wider city population, fears of violence were palpable. On Easter Sunday of 1568, neighbourhood sentries in a part of the city with a majority of Christian immigrants mistook the flashing torches of crown soldiers for a Morisco call to arms. Panicked Franciscan friars from one monastery took up arms, joining angry mobs who were threatening to sack Morisco homes. Only a timely rain storm and the posting of armed guards in key neighbourhoods staved off a massacre.[17] Ultimately, however, premonitions of violence proved accurate.

A Christmas Eve Call to Arms

Two days before Christmas in 1568, Hernando de Córdoba y Válor, a member of the city council who descended from Nasrid royalty, escaped from a house arrest, the result of the unlawful carrying of a dagger into the city council chambers (*cabildo*). His alleged accomplices in the escape, in Mármol Carvajal's telling, were a Morisca and a black slave.[18] The escapees made for Válor's family seat in the eponymous mountain village. There, he took back his ancestral surname, aben Humeya. Rebels declared him king, based in great measure on the prestige of his family, regarded as direct descendants of the prophet Mohammad.[19] Spurred to action, a silk dyer from the Albaicín, Farax aben Farax, slipped into the city's outskirts in the sleety darkness of Christmas Day with a motley band of followers.

Aben Farax and his men stole pikes and tools from an unguarded mill, and donned colourful Turkish bonnets. As daybreak neared, they attacked a small group of sentries huddled around a camp fire in the plaza of the Albaicín's largest church, San Salvador. They then approached the home of a prominent Jesuit of Morisco origin, Juan Albotodo, mocking him as a *perro renegado* (renegade dog) as they sought, in vain, to break down his door. Unable to reach the churchman, the rebels sought a pharmacist known to be a familiar of the Inquisition, shattering his jars and flasks when he was nowhere to be found.

From here, the raiding party stood atop a hill with a view over the Albaicín, just beyond the church of San Nicolás. Aben Farax called his neighbours to arms with the Muslim *shahada* or profession of faith, "There are none but God and Muhammad." The rebel then invited oppressed Moriscos to take revenge, promising the support of the king of

Algiers and the Ottoman sultan. But the call to arms was met with silence. A couple of witnesses reported hearing a voice from one rooftop urging the rebels to disband, reminding them they were too few in number and had no time. Indeed, the canon of San Salvador was already ringing the bells in alarm. An angry Farax aben Farax then climbed a tower, from which he insulted the same neighbours he had just beckoned with the call to prayers, as "dogs, cuckolds, and cowards." Their call to arms unanswered, rebels retreated to rejoin their waiting allies.[20] From here, they removed to their mountain strongholds.

This vivid, even melodramatic account of the events that night comes from Mármol Carvajal's history of the rebellion, based on information he gleaned from other witnesses and in the course of his work as a provisioning official for the crown forces charged with subduing the revolt.[21] When he pieced together the different accounts of the start of what would be a prolonged war of attrition, Mármol Carvajal sees a Granada of "equivocal identities," to apply Caro Baroja's term. The soldier-chronicler thus distils action to the Christian renegade who reverts to Islam, his black and Morisca confederates, an artisan and obstinate Muslim, and a Morisco Jesuit. To take adequate measure of the historical memory of the civil war, one must compare Mármol Carvajal's account to the two other classic accounts that were also composed by writers who witnessed at least some of the events from within the city. We find a more Olympian perspective from nobleman-diplomat Diego Hurtado de Mendoza, who analyses the war's outbreak from a tactical vantage point. A second soldier-chronicler, shoemaker Ginés Pérez de Hita, drew on his own experience fighting the rebels within a contingent from Murcia led by the Marquis de los Vélez. But he adds even more manifestly literary flourishes than Mármol Carvajal, a pattern Mary Quinn considers in relation to early-modern subject formation.[22] Notwithstanding their contrasting styles of narration, the three classic chronicles of Granada's war that began on Christmas in 1568 converge in that they tell of a conflict that dragged on longer than anticipated and engendered violence so fierce it shocked even hardened veterans of Spanish wars in Flanders, Italy, and the Mediterranean. The three chroniclers also echo one another in recording fateful consequences for the city and its people.[23]

Indeed, the rebellion that hardly seemed to be able to get going on Christmas Eve would upend life in Granada and undermine the already fragile local patterns of coexistence that had brought Moriscos, Christian immigrants, and black Africans together, if always with degrees of tension. As regards the specific case of Juan Latino and his family, though we lack testimony of their affiliations and actions during the two-year conflict, Granada's civil war and its harsh crown response would, in short order, leave profound and unsettling traces in his Lepanto epic. Since his commemoration of the naval battle of 1571 is hardly legible without a nuanced understanding of the rebellion that broke out in Granada a half a decade before, a careful reading of the chronicles is necessary, even if the freedman himself momentarily stands in the background.

Granada at War

As the unanswered call to arms might suggest, crown and city officials assumed the scattered rebels with scant followers would be easily stopped. But a series of inept yet exceedingly violent counterstrikes by crown units under two noblemen of the region allowed the rebels to endure and their cause to gain adherents. Indeed, L.P. Harvey argues convincingly that such misdeeds caused an uprising that could have been resolved with a negotiated rebel surrender after three months to drag on for two years.[24] Time and again, the indiscriminate brutality and frenetic plunder of the anti-insurgent forces gave oxygen to rebel bands. Within the first season, the string of lush valleys at the entrance to the Alpujarras Mountains, long associated with bountiful harvests of fruits and nuts, became newly famous among Spaniards as fields of martyrdom. Chroniclers would recount in gruesome detail how Morisco rebels tortured and killed priests and Christian immigrants. Yet even reading through these new "martyrologies" of the Alpujarras, with their over-determined rhetoric of Christian-Muslim incompatibility, one still finds evidence of the region's longer patterns of coexistence. For instance, chroniclers celebrated the Morisca widow of a Christian immigrant who reportedly proclaimed her Catholic faith even as knife-wielding rebels killed her.[25]

Officials, in turn, cited such rebel excesses as justification for a new slave trade. For soldiers and their commanders, the sale of captured Moriscos became a central goal of the military expeditions charged with quelling the revolt. Theologians warned it was sinful and illegal to enslave baptized Christians. To counter this obstacle, jurists based in the royal Audiencia marshalled a legal precedent from a rebellion of Jews in medieval Toledo: Moriscos deemed to have called out to Muhammad or declared themselves Moors could be sold as slaves.[26] The ruling opened an easy loophole for seizing and selling captives. It is at this point in the rebellion's trajectory that the chronicle of Granada's Moriscos reverses the "epic of Juan Latino," understood in figurative terms. That is, in contrast to the educator's well-known journey from slavery to freedom, the region was now engendering thousands of emancipation stories in reverse, where once free people were enslaved.

A frenzied, improvised slave trade soon overwhelmed tactical calculations on the ground. In a particularly notorious but highly representative sortie in the first spring after the outbreak of fighting, two captains led a search party of 800 men to hunt for Aben Humeya, the rebel leader, near his ancestral village of Válor. Frustrated in their search for their nemesis, soldiers captured and killed rebel emissaries, after which they slaughtered unarmed villagers and sacked their homes. When the initial target of their raid – Aben Humeya – arrived with his fighters at daybreak, the crown soldiers were too laden with their plunder to escape. Hundreds from the crown's raiding party died still clinging to war spoils, with some 40 of the original 800 returning alive to Granada. This search party doomed by plunder was but an exaggerated case of a general pattern.[27]

To capture the extent and impact of the obsession with looting, soldier-chronicler Pérez de Hita adapted the time-honoured epic catalogue to take measure of the greed he saw in his comrades-in-arms and even himself. A particularly devastating passage recounts the obsession with plunder, so "there were men who would even carry away cats, cauldrons, sieves, troughs, reels, winding frames, cowbells, hoes, and other trivial things, all not to lose the habit of theft. I will not single out here the people who did this, for all together were thieves and I foremost."[28] On closer inspection, the household goods in this looters' catalogue are far from trivial things, or *vagezas*. Rather, the chronicler bears witness to how he and his comrades-in-arms dismantled the delicately intertwined pieces of Granada's economy. The agricultural implements fighters seize when they cannot find captives to be sold as slaves were, after all, the tools with which Hispano-Muslims had long coaxed an agricultural bounty from the craggy mountain terrain of the Alpujarras. Likewise, the reels and winding frames belonged to the household weaving operations that supplied raw materials for Granada's famed silk trade.[29]

Such narratives of frenzied looting merit close attention in relation to the story of Juan Latino for two reasons. For one, his own Lepanto epic stands out within the vast corpus of narrative poems on the battle for the frankness with which it recounts how ostensibly heroic fighters become rapacious looters and slave traders, an issue chapter 5 explores at length. A second point of interest relates to the more nebulous but no less critical question of his own witness to Granada's civil war. Here, many indices show that the turmoil of Granada's civil war struck close to Latino at home. Pérez de Hita's devastating self-recrimination – "I foremost" – invites the vexing question about Latino and his family. What ties did they have to the traffic in war spoils or the newly rekindled slave trade? Might the Latino-Carlobal family have purchased or been given a slave? We saw in the 1561 census that the household had two servants. What happens when traders and soldiers bring captured Moriscos into the city? Baptismal records of their parish neighbourhood show families in the area begin to receive slaves captured in the Alpujarras during military campaigns. No indices survive that would allow definitive answers to the kinds of questions about complicity that Pérez de Hita acknowledges in his devastating self-examination.

What can we determine about the wartime life of the freedman and his family? Naturally, the kinds of raiding in Granada's mountain hinterlands described above disrupted city supply chains. Scarcity, in turn, exposed long-simmering conflicts. Hurtado de Mendoza's portrait of Granada as wartime home front recalls the devastating early scenes from Lucan (*De bellum civile* 1.257–65), where Romans sense the civil war is about to destroy their city. Conveying a dread of Lucanian dimensions in his eloquent prose, Hurtado de Mendoza blames the undue confusion to the city's recent embrace of so many new settlers:

> Moved to believe and affirm true and false rumors alike; to spread news, whether harmful or beneficial, and stubbornly follow them. *New city*, a body comprised of settlers from many regions, who were poor and helpless in their lands, and moved by profit to resettle here. [emphasis added][30]

The "new city" the nobleman disdains is, from another perspective, the Granada that allowed Juan Latino and others to attain remarkable upward mobility. The Santa Ana neighbourhood where he and Ana Carlobal settled was, as chapter 1 notes, home to a number of Christian immigrants drawn to opportunities in the sprawling judicial bureaucracy of the Audiencia. Latino's own family may have belonged to what Hurtado calls the new city. According to a seventeenth-century chronicle of the city, Latino's son-in-law worked in the Audiencia, an entirely plausible connection that nonetheless requires further documentary corroboration.

Pondering the question of where Latino stood in the city at war, it is also important to recall his alliances with the elite. His former master and life-long sponsor, the Duke of Sessa, owned family lands in Órgiva, a rebel stronghold. By coincidence, Sessa had returned to Andalusia from a posting in Milan shortly before the rebellion. He led battalions of crown forces sent out to attack rebel hideouts and deliberated about policies towards Moriscos, though by the time the war ended his reputation was sullied, as yet another casualty of the chronic infighting among the lead commanders of crown troops.[31]

Notwithstanding a lifelong tie to this grandee, Latino would nonetheless have been vulnerable to the disruptions of a city at war. The influx of soldiers and fortune seekers who flooded into Granada destabilized prices for food and other necessities. Refugees displaced by fighting in the mountains flooded into the city. The city's crucial silk trade – already under the stress of increasing taxes – was devastated, with the intricate seasonal rhythms of silk worm breeding upended. Harmful aftershocks would have extended beyond the families directly dependent on the silk industry, given that historians estimate that commerce connected to the central silk exchange (Alcaicería) sustained an estimated 10 per cent of city residents. Again, many in Latino's Santa Ana neighbourhood worked in some aspect of the silk trade or other cottage industries that were closely related, including tailors, velvet weavers, and embroiderers.[32]

Charting the war's course as it drags on from 1569 to 1570, the encroachment on city life becomes palpable. Of course, the most direct harm befell the city's people known to be of Hispano-Muslim origins. Crown officials billeted crown troops in Morisco homes, relishing the idea that they would shoulder the heavy burden of room and board.[33] Following the civil war in the three classic chronicles of the revolt, one can see a delicate social fabric fraying beyond repair. Along the way, slavery became even more entrenched in city life as an influx of men, women, and children captured in the mountain communities altered the population balance. The parish registry of the Santa Ana church at the heart of Latino's neighbourhood shows a series of infants born to enslaved women from the Alpujarras Mountains within three months from the initial outbreak of violence. As the revolt and repression ran their course, almost 5,000 Morisco men, women, and children were sold into slavery in the region. By the end of the rebellion, an estimated

14 per cent of city residents would be slaves.[34] Did Latino and his family see these newly enslaved Granadinos as fellow travellers in a struggle he and his kin had endured? Or, as I asked above, might they have benefited directly or indirectly from the new slave traffic? Again, these queries have no reasonable answer with good sources, but do provide points of context and contrast when slave trading comes into view in the Lepanto epic.

In light of such pressing questions about Latino's life during wartime, the archives of the university and grammar school are a natural point of curiosity. Given that the educational institutions where he studied and taught had been endowed to support the training of clergy charged with pastoral missions among Moriscos, one must ask what happens when the mission of assimilation is negated. Unfortunately, faculty senate records are missing from 1570 to 1574, ostensibly a casualty of a fire in 1877. Histories of the university's first century of operations were written by faculty members and, despite varying perspectives, avoid direct discussions of the rebellion.[35] It is impossible, for the moment, to determine whether teaching continued as usual, or whether the war caused a hiatus. Where one does find a more direct acknowledgment of the magnitude of disruption is in the Morisco historiography. Here scholars record how the revolt and ensuing mass punishment devastated the university. In existential terms, the king's decision to treat all Granadinos known to be of Hispano-Muslim origins as culprits of the uprising negated the institutions' long-standing support for the goal of Christian conversion and assimilation. In practical terms, the university suffered a brain drain as persecution of this native population intensified, particularly in the faculty of medicine, which had long benefited from the deeply rooted Hispano-Muslim traditions in the medical sciences.[36]

With the limitations on precise documentation in mind, there is, nonetheless, a moment in the chronicles where the violence initially isolated in the mountains outside the city contaminates life in the city. Two months after the rebellion began, a constable distributed arms to non-Morisco prisoners housed in the palace of the royal Audiencia, a place visible from the higher ground of Latino's neighbourhood. Guards and armed inmates massacred over one hundred prominent Moriscos who had been targeted for preventive detention based on their stature as community leaders or property owners from the Albaicín. What followed was another stark case of justice in an old regime monarchy. Widows and children of the victims flocked to the headquarters of the

Audiencia, hoping for compensation and a return of embargoed property. Instead, crown officials confiscated their assets.[37]

Like the disastrous expedition to Válor, the prison massacre spread news of disorder, embarrassed many crown officials, and brought new adherents to the initially unpopular rebel side. In response to such turns of events, Philip II sent his half-brother, John of Austria, to take control of the campaign against rebels and restore order. The young Habsburg military commander's arrival and actions in the region would be decisive in the story this book tells, propelling Juan Latino's self-fashioning as an epic poet. An examination of his arrival in war-torn Granada gives a sense of how John of Austria inspired the poet.

Enter John of Austria

The traumatized city displayed its war wounds for John of Austria in a highly choreographed ceremonial entry. Its highest-ranking nobleman and military commander, the Marquis of Mondéjar, bedecked his troops in Moorish dress and ceremonial livery. Weeping Christian-immigrant women, displaced from villages in the rebel strongholds of the Alpujarras, filed in procession before the young Habsburg to beg for his protection. An entourage of legal officials from the Audiencia also paid homage.[38] Its president, Pedro de Deza, hosted John of Austria in the palace of the Audiencia, from which the Habsburg commander would reorganize the crown's efforts to quell the revolt.

For residents of the Santa Ana parish – including the family of Juan Latino and Ana Carlobal – John of Austria's activities played out in view, given that the Audiencia palace sits below the neighbourhood streets, like the stage in an out-sized theatre. At least once, the young Habsburg crossed the Plaza Nueva from the chancery palace to the parish church. Its registry notes a baptism, in early June of 1569, in which John of Austria served as godfather to the newborn daughter of Don Diego de Mexía and Doña Ana de Córdoba.[39] This baptism coincided with deliberations about the fate of Granada's Morisco communities. The main interlocutors were all well known to Latino; a few were important sponsors. Latino's former master, the Duke of Sessa, sided with Deza in advocating a mass expulsion. The city's archbishop – another of Latino's sponsors – aired practical concerns about the feasibility of taking people out of their homes. Only the Marquis of Mondéjar unequivocally defended the right of Moriscos to remain in their ancestral homeland, noting their central role in sustaining the region's food supply.[40] Morisco community leaders, for their part, recounted abuses and petitioned John of Austria for justice. These advocates of mercy or moderation did not prevail.

Just two weeks after John of Austria entered the Santa Ana parish to vow to support the Christian upbringing of a newborn infant, he supervised the expulsion of hundreds of baptized New Christians from the city. This would be the first wave of two mass expulsions. Viewed from a distance of centuries, John of Austria's emptying out of the Albaicín marks a sad modern milestone, where a nascent professional bureaucracy organized and executed a large-scale ethnic cleansing campaign.[41] But even within the context of the times, the expulsion was theologically problematic, given that it denied the efficacy of baptism. The mass reprisals also negated the earlier model of assimilation through evangelization, an ideal associated most closely in Granada with Hernando de Talavera's programs outlined briefly in chapter 1.

The officials who charted the logistics of the expulsion again took advantage of the festive calendar, as was the case with their publication of the Edicts of 1567 on New Year's Day. This time the dissonance between festive traditions and official violence would be even greater. Throughout Spain, Saint John's Eve (*la Noche de San Juan*) marked the pinnacle of what Julio Caro Baroja has called the "season of love," when men, women, and children gathered in city streets and country meadows for reverie that heralded new, optimistic beginnings.[42] But on Midsummer Night of 1569, John of Austria dispatched troops to round up Moriscos over ten- and under sixty years old from the Albaicín and other quarters.[43] Squadrons of soldiers – one led by Latino's former master, the Duke of Sessa – fanned out across city neighbourhoods, moving house-to-house to find Morisco men, then marching them in groups to parish churches. Women were allowed several days to sell family possessions.

After a night in the parish churches, the Moriscos – hands tied and bound together – were marched through the Puerta Elvira to the Hospital Real, which the Reyes Católicos had endowed as a charitable hospital for the indigent and the mentally disabled. Violence flared at several points. One squadron leader marched his prisoners behind a cross draped in black, inciting panic as the bound men and their trailing families assumed they were about to be executed. A frightened boy who reportedly lunged at John of Austria was slain on the spot by sword-wielding crown soldiers.[44]

Aside from the hard-line stance of Pedro de Deza and his allies at court, much evidence suggests widespread unease about the mass retribution. Notably, John of Austria's letters to allies at court air guarded sympathy for the Moriscos and considerable discomfort with the implacable Deza. He notes as well how some priests in Granada and Guadix spoke against the persecution in their sermons. Exasperated with Deza's intransigence towards even moderate Moriscos or potentially repentant rebels, John of Austria even recommended that Philip II name Deza bishop somewhere beyond Granada, with the ecclesiastical sinecure offering a face-saving way out for the crown official and a path to peace for the region.[45]

Such qualms invite still more questions about how Juan Latino and his family observed these events. From the Santa Ana neighbourhood alongside the Darro and above the Plaza Nueva, residents would have watched the hundreds of Moriscos marched out of the lower Albaicín parish of San Juan de los Reyes as they filed down alongside the river. Soldiers also rounded up about a third of the Santa Ana residents in the same first wave of expulsions. Yet the only direct statements from Latino about the expulsion of Moriscos from Granada are the words of praise that open and close the Lepanto epic, points I explore in due course. The endorsement of the expulsion may have followed from a sincere conviction, the cautious calculations of a black Granadino with some potential vulnerability of his own, the ambitions of an aspiring author who needed to gain publication licence, or most plausibly, a complicated mixture of motives. As I will discuss in chapters 4 and 5, more subtle allusions and descriptions within the poem suggest that the rhetoric of holy war envelops more anguished and nuanced reflections. As a black African, Latino may have felt the sting of Morisco scorn for black Africans, as recorded in Francisco Núñez Muley's defence of embattled Morisco communities. Or, perhaps, like Núñez Muley heaping scorn on black Africans, Latino hailing the expulsion was contending with what Vincent Barletta calls the "paradoxical intersections between collaboration/emulation and resistance."[46] Indeed, much about the freedman's life in Granada suggests Moriscos were frequently fellow travellers in the quest for social validation and advancement. After all, Latino studied, and then worked with students and colleagues of Morisco heritage at the city's grammar school and university. In more profound existential terms, he too was a New Christian easily identified with a misunderstood region beyond the heart of

Western Europe. Even setting aside the private opinions or unpublished thoughts we can never hope to recover, it is also clear that after the expulsion, all but the most elite Granadinos paid a high price for the mass retribution. Suddenly, billeted royal troops had no one to feed and lodge them. Already notoriously undisciplined, hungry soldiers looted abandoned homes. Inevitably, the expulsion defended as a way to calm the region gave new impetus to the revolt playing out in the mountains, with rebel ranks growing with the addition of Moriscos who escaped the Night of Saint John roundup that emptied the Albaicín and other quarters.[47]

The rebellion and repression played out for a year after John of Austria supervised the expulsion of Moriscos from the city. Ultimately, the rebel side was doomed by the fratricidal treachery among leaders and an inability to attract significant assistance from the Ottoman sultan and Muslim rulers in North Africa.[48] In the end, the side with the most firepower won. The numerically superior crown forces under John of Austria brought out heavy artillery and avenged setbacks with scorched-earth tactics.

On this point, narratives of John of Austria's deeds show a duality that anticipates a tension within the later chronicles and poems of Lepanto. Repeatedly, visions of John of Austria as a hero bound for glory in single combat clash with the details of military victories secured with heavy artillery weapons. Accounts of one major siege he initiated in January 1570, ten months after his arrival in Granada, show this dissonance. Frustrated at forced idleness in Granada and impatient to claim his birthright as the "son and brother of such great princes," John of Austria set out to crush a rebel stronghold in the castle of La Galera. Chronicler Diego Hurtado de Mendoza provides both epic colourings and the contrary evidence of an impersonal modern warfare. The historian sounds an epic note when describing how word spreads around Spain that the young Habsburg commander is poised for a heroic undertaking in Granada. But then the impersonal siege tactics come into view. Moving into the area, Don John removed old artillery that remained from Ferdinand of Aragon's campaigns, bringing in new, larger bronze cannons. A first assault failed disastrously, with rebels slaughtering an entire company of Catalan fighters. Vowing revenge, Don John mined the walls and unleashed the full force of cannon fire. With rebel resistance thus overcome, his troops massacred an estimated 400 non-combatants on his orders. Before leaving the area, Don John also allowed soldiers to fill their packs with silk, jewels, and other spoils. As a parting gesture, he ordered La Galera's fields and gardens sown with salt.[49]

When it was clear that crown forces would prevail, John of Austria left Granada, never to return again. A final phase of fighting continued through early spring 1571, bringing the drawn-out military conflict to a gruesome and tragic end with some unsettling ethical questions related to freedom and vassalage, and others about how victors should treat the vanquished. A band of one-time allies cornered and killed the last rebel leader, Aben Abóo, carrying his body back to Granada in an effort to win favourable surrender terms for themselves. There, officials cut off his head. Young boys dragged his headless torso around the city before it was finally burned. The severed head remained displayed in a cage at the city's Puerta del Rastro, as part trophy, part admonition. While he was collecting his notes and eyewitness reminiscences of the revolt for his monumental history in progress, soldier-turned-chronicler Mármol Carvajal regularly walked by this ghoulish relic.[50] A final wave of expulsions of Moriscos focused on mountain hamlets. Scholars estimate a total of 80,000 men, women, and children were expelled in three phases. Many died of typhus and other maladies as they were herded to resettlement in Castile and Extremadura.[51]

Within Granada itself, the end of the revolt brought a wave of public slave auctions. In legal parlance, those enslaved were *moriscos de guerra* (bellicose Moriscos), called thus based on allegations they took up arms against the crown. Since the auctions and direct sales compensated division commanders and soldiers, there were clear incentives to grab any vulnerable resident of the mountain communities associated with the rebel cause. In fact, Moriscos captured in Granada were so abundant in Spanish cities that slave traders transported many to Italy to avoid the depressed prices.[52] Again, one must ask how a freedman like Juan Latino responded to the intensification of the slave trade that played out, sometimes within earshot.

A New Slave Trade

In the first months of 1571, some one hundred men, women, and children were auctioned as slaves in the Bibarrambla Plaza. If Latino's classes at the grammar school and university were in session – a determination that requires further archival research beyond the university's fire-diminished records – the auctions would have echoed within earshot of Juan Latino's classroom in the plaza's northeast corner. Another battalion captain turned slave trader offered another thirty Moriscos for sale in the Plaza Nueva, a space visible below Latino's Santa Ana neighbourhood. In total, almost six hundred individuals were sold into slavery in ad hoc markets improvised in prominent gathering places around the city between February and May of 1571.[53]

The last slave auctions coincided with the start of a repopulation campaign that also had notable implications for notions of identity. Starting in February of 1571, Pedro de Deza spearheaded a repopulation campaign designed to attract new settlers to Granada from northern Castile. Officials envisioned an influx of hearty Old Christian farmers who would become the stewards of the fields and orchards once tended by Moriscos, following the pattern of colonization that Castilian kings had long used to settle reconquered lands. It would not take long for the officials to learn that the program attracted mostly desperately poor, dispossessed northern peasants with little knowledge to replace the time-tested agricultural practices of Hispano-Muslims of Granada. Underlying the fledgling homesteading program we find the same artificial vision for Granada that anchored the edicts of 1567: a top-down reconfiguration of a population could remake the last realm of Al-Andalus to fit a vision of Christian purity hewn in the image of the people and customs of Old Castile.[54]

Where would a black-African educator fit in this new Granada? Would a realm that crown officials reconceived as paradise for Old Christian settlers be as welcoming a place for a black New Christian? The city that emerged from the revolt and expulsion was, in key respects, unlike the frontier city where Juan Latino and others had gained a degree of upward mobility that was unusual for the era. A royal *visita* (crown audit or supervisory visit), compiled in the aftermath of the rebellion, records the lingering conflicts in the war-torn city. Pedro de Deza, on whom Juan Latino depended to at least some degree, comes in for stinging criticism as cruel, corrupt, and lascivious. Along with accusations of Deza's lavish lifestyle, sexual escapades, and unruly servants, the audit accuses him of selling free Moriscas to slave traders from Portugal and Ceuta.[55] To be sure, such accusations may follow in some measure from Deza's implication in high-stakes faction politics which yielded many enemies eager to air incendiary accusations. Nonetheless, the dossier's overall picture – of a ruined city in the thrall of venal officials – meshes to a great extent with the accounts from Hurtado de Mendoza, Mármol Carvajal, and Pérez de Hita, as well with John of Austria's dispatches during his time in the city. Granada after the civil war was also a place of ruin and rubble. Historian Manuel Barrios Aguilera estimates as many as 6,000 empty homes would begin collapsing into ruins or be taken apart by scavengers.[56]

The city on the Darro River was, in short, a place in which all but the most exalted elite residents might need new strategies for survival or advancement. It was also a place where anyone with obvious New Christian lineage was in a potentially more precarious position. And not least, Juan Latino's home city in 1571 was a place hungry for good news. Appropriately enough, John of Austria would provide it.

Victory Overseas

News that the former leader of crown forces in Granada had attained a stunning victory at sea on 7 October 1571 had a special resonance. The Holy League coalition fleet that John of Austria commanded brought together Spanish fleets, a Venetian contingent, and a small but symbolically powerful papal navy. Together, these Catholic fleets had defied expectations and defeated an armada assembled by the Ottoman sultan. In short order, the Battle of Lepanto would be enshrined in the realms of the Spanish Monarchy as the foremost victory at sea, or *gran batalla naval*. Juan Latino responded to this international news event right away, in tandem with dozens of poets across Europe. To fully grasp the naval battle's importance to the freedman, I set aside the longer-range debates of the battle's geopolitical legacy that have long dominated Lepanto historiography. Shifting perspective to the naval victory's first life as a news story, chapter 3 asks how word about Lepanto reached the war-weary Andalusian city.

PART TWO

The Epic of Lepanto

3 A Black Poet and a Habsburg Phoenix

Breaking News

On a Thursday morning in late October 1571, the *Angelo Gabrieli* rowed in to the port of Venice. True to their messenger-angel patron, the crew members brought joyful news to a wary city, still anxious about Ottoman invaders in the wake of the violent siege and takeover of its prized eastern colony of Cyprus.[1] The Holy League coalition fleet, which united the Serenissima's navy with forces from Spain and the papacy, had crushed Sultan Selim II's formidable armada in a half-day of combat so intense and bloody it stunned even the most battle-tested veterans.

The news from the *Angelo Gabrieli* was healing balm for many wounds. Venetians, still mourning the macabre ordeal of the noblemen and soldiers who died defending Cyprus, judged the naval victory divinely sanctioned revenge. When the bulletin reached Spain, citizens and leaders alike sensed a new day dawning. Though there were thousands of dead to mourn and wounded to treat, the reports from Lepanto at least offered a decisive victory claimed quickly, in marked contrast to the prolonged war of attrition that had recently played out in Granada's mountains.

Perspectives today are markedly different from these first impressions, shaped as they are by such brilliant narrators as the Venetian chronicler Pablo Paruta and Spanish literary titan Miguel de Cervantes, both of whom reflected on the events from the distance of two decades. Studies today also embed Lepanto chronicles within considerations of longer term geopolitical questions as well as Christian-Muslim relations in our times.[2] But to take full measure of Juan Latino's self-assertion as a poet of Lepanto, it is necessary to momentarily set aside

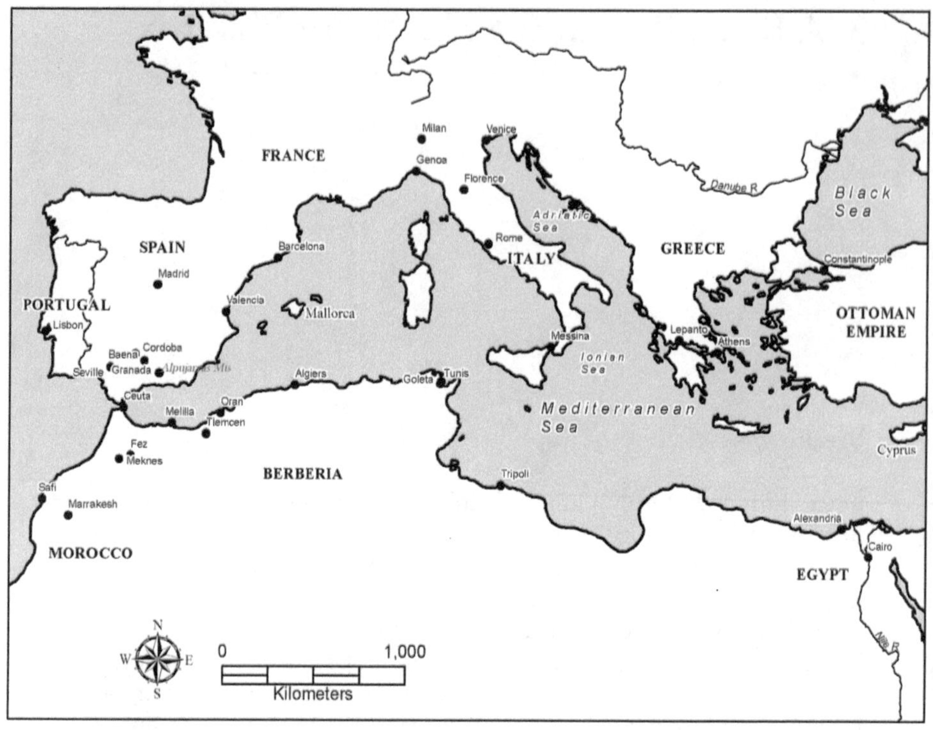

Figure 8 The Mediterranean, circa 1571. Latino's *Song of John of Austria* draws profound inspiration from the increasingly efficient channels of communication that connected individuals and communities across the Mediterranean. Indeed, couriers aboard a galley brought news of the victory at Lepanto on 7 October 1571 to Venice (18 October). From there, word spread to Naples (24 October) and Madrid (31 October) (Braudel 1966 [1949], 1:330). Latino's epic commemoration adapts and tames Virgil's personification allegory of Fama to convey this fast dissemination of the first reports.

Credit: By Thomas R. Jordan, Southern Resource Mapping

the more distant views of the battle's implications. This allows a reader to take stock of the battle described in the news bulletins disseminated from port to port in the fall of 1571. It is this first glimpse of events that would inspire Juan Latino's publication debut and shape his self-fashioning as an epic poet for a new era.

The dispatch delivered aboard the *Angelo Gabrieli* described how, at daybreak on the feast of Saint Giustina (7 October 1571), Holy League forces caught sight of the Ottoman navy at the Curzolaris Islands near the Gulf of Corinth in western Greece. With no time to waste, the fleets of Venice, Spain, and the papacy arrayed in the line-abreast formation their commander, John of Austria, had devised. Ottoman forces, for their part, fanned out in their signature half-moon formation, which followed from their tactical reliance on their expert archers but also drew on the symbolic power of the Islamic crescent. Combat began with lethal volleys of artillery fire spewed by a vanguard of Venetian merchant ships retrofitted with heavy cannons. As the opposing fleets lumbered closer to one another amid the deadly rain of bullets and arrows, fighting began to resemble hand-to-hand combat on land. Survivors told of a living hell, where they shot, stabbed, and clawed at one another through dark, sulfurous smoke. Seizing the initiative after a couple of hours, Spaniards under John of Austria rammed and then stormed the Ottoman flagship. Inevitably, the fog of war blurs many details, though a general sequence emerges as we draw on other eyewitnesses where the Venetian bulletin abbreviates.[3] Spaniards surged forward towards the Ottoman mainmast. Crack Janissary forces repelled them. Dead and maimed bodies crowded the narrow deck. Soldiers still standing slashed and fired on enemy fighters at point-blank range. Many fell or were pushed overboard. Thrashing in the waves, men resumed desperate fighting. By turns they clawed or clutched at one another, clinging with free hands to any bits of prow or plank they could grasp. The Ionian sea waters turned blood-red.

Most first-line bulletins describe how Spaniards trapped the Ottoman admiral, Ali Pasha, after three charges to the Turkish flagship's mainmast.[4] Spanish nobleman Nicolás Augusto de Benavides, recovering from battle wounds and a fever in the days after the battle, gave a dramatic account of a confrontation that transpired after John of Austria and his lieutenants cornered Ali Pasha. A Spanish guard demanded this brother-in-law of the Ottoman sultan surrender. Ali haughtily refused and brandished his scimitar. But a Spanish rapier struck first. After slaying the Turkish admiral, Spanish guards found the slain commander's teen-aged sons. With royal disdain, the two Ottoman princes refused to surrender to mere foot soldiers. John of Austria himself promised they would be safe in his hands and pulled out their servants from a line-up of captives. Initially relieved, they nonetheless wept bitterly when they saw their father's captive flagship: instead of flying the Sultan's sumptuous silk banner woven with Qur'anic verses, it displayed the pasha's severed head. "No doubt, a strange trophy," the gentleman-soldier Benavides added.[5] With the severed head as ghoulish victory herald, Holy League soldiers and commanders exalted.

Holy League forces had no sooner declared themselves vanquishers than they transformed the naval battle field into a maritime trading post. Fighters clamoured for valuable prizes that could be seized, counted, classified, and sold in the markets and bazaars of Spain and Italy. Hungry and ill-clad Spanish soldiers, who had arrived at Lepanto being owed months of wages, lunged for any item, large or small: swords, guns, battle standards, dinner services, and goblets. Even the elegant burnished parchment paper on which Benavides penned his letter while recovering from his wounds at the battle site was sold to him on the spot by a raiding soldier.[6] But the prizes soldiers most coveted were Ottoman fighters who could be sold as galley slaves or ransomed to relatives. Examining the first-line battlefield reports, we find a grim triage that played out as victors judged which captives could command a ransom or row in galleys. They slaughtered the rest. Thus, the first detailed account sent from John of Austria's command element includes the matter-of-fact report that Spaniards slit the throats of some five hundred Turks along with Ali Pasha.[7]

These vivid reports of a decisive and unexpected Holy League victory struck a nerve with statesmen, map makers, and poets based in the Holy League realms. Within three weeks of the battle, copies of the Venetian report had travelled with what seemed to be lightning speed to Rome, Naples, and Spain. In the months ahead, Western Europe witnessed an unprecedented outpouring of celebrations and responses. Lepanto's deep resonance came, in great measure, from the sense of an event whose scale and intensity surpassed any in recent memory. A concise note from John of Austria to Philip II registers the profound impact felt by even seasoned veterans as they looked out on two armadas, each of unprecedented size, each under respected commanders and well stocked with experienced fighters. The bulletin suggests that the mutual respect of military veterans on both sides survived their danse macabre of brutality and revenge. In this sense, commanders' first impressions of the battle's epochal nature hold up to the analysis of military historian J.F. Guilmartin: "Lepanto is a rarity in military history: a battle in which both sides fought skillfully and well, where the random strokes of chance that infest the battlefield were largely neutralized by the skill of the commanders against whom they fell, and where the stronger side won – though by a narrow margin and not in the expected way."[8]

For the Western Europeans who digested the earliest reports of Lepanto, its historical parallels magnified the initial assessments of a victory for the ages. Scouring maps and charts of western Greece to pinpoint the naval battle's exact location, they noted that it played out just south of the site of antiquity's largest and most famous naval clash, the Battle of Actium (31 BC). Lettered Europeans shared an image of Actium based on the *Aeneid* 8.675–728, in which Virgil's vivid ekphrasis transformed the culmination of a Roman civil war into an epochal clash between East and West. Renaissance poets and scholars had long memorized and emulated the Mantuan's tour-de-force narration, which etches the clash on the shield that Aeneas carried into battle. Wasting no time, chroniclers, cartographers, and poets documented and glossed the Lepanto-to-Actium connection, an issue illuminated by a notable cluster of critics, including David Quint, James Nicolopulos, Elizabeth Davis, and Mercedes Blanco.[9]

At the same time, individuals and communities also examined reports of the naval victory through the filter of local concerns. Venetians credited Saint Giustina – a Christian martyr already revered in the Veneto region – with guiding the fleet to victory on her feast day. In the years ahead, devotion to her spread. In France, a Venetian diplomat urged the French king to launch a campaign against Protestants on Lepanto's first anniversary, attesting to how early modern numerology informed strategic deliberations at the highest levels.[10] In Spain, the joy Lepanto unleashed soon redoubled as Queen Anna of Austria gave birth to a new royal heir, the Infante Don Fernando.

Philip II credited the royal birth and naval victory to God's favour. In a flurry of thanksgiving gestures, he commissioned his favourite painter, Titian, to prepare an *ex voto*. The thanksgiving offering depicts the king presenting his newborn heir to a descending angel whose banner promises greater glory to come (see figure 9, *Allegory of Lepanto*). A canvas in the background reveals the naval combat of 7 October. Though the version that now hangs in the Prado Museum was expanded in the seventeenth century, the view of the battle on the canvas is particularly relevant for Juan Latino's take on Lepanto. In the left foreground, a bound Turkish captive casts his eyes downward. His turban, crescent-embossed shield, and quiver recall past military exploits. Sinewy back muscles suggest the strength and experience needed to wield the composite recurved bow that elite Turkish units favoured. Now that same muscle power advertises his potential value as a captive oarsman. Our interpretation depends on whether we focus on the enactment of divine favour bestowed on the Spanish king or hone instead on the human drama distilled in the Turkish captive. In the smaller original that Titian sent to Philip II, the central focus would have rested on the celebratory nativity scene, connected to Lepanto by the winged allegory of Victory heralding more empire building ahead.[11]

This providential interpretation of Lepanto as proof that God had smiled on Habsburg Spain shaped crown policies and deliberations. Most notably, historian Geoffrey Parker records the proposal that Philip revive the title "Emperor of the East." What this meant in practice and in negotiations with the papacy was that advisors envisioned Lepanto as a point of departure for a new eastward expansion, first to retake Constantinople and from there, to reconquer Jerusalem. This longing for eastward expansion would, in time, leave profound literary traces, as Frederick de Armas notes with reference to Don Quixote's conjuring of rule in Trebizond.[12] Looking westward as well, a busy Philip II drafted a memorandum to his viceroys, prelates, and Audiencia presidents in the Americas, notifying them of "an occurrence of momentous importance for the peace and calm of all Christendom."[13]

Pausing to reflect on how this news reached Granada, we can imagine that the predictions of peace and tranquillity would have been particularly welcome in a city still suffering the trauma of the civil war and mass expulsion of Moriscos. As we saw at the close of chapter 2, the precipitous loss of so many industrious food producers and skilled artisans had devastated the economy, with bitter recriminations adding new perils to civic life. When news of Lepanto reached the city, a crown auditor (*visitador*) was still at work there, compiling damning evidence of corrupt actions during and after the revolt. It was also becoming clear that the violent and theologically dubious expulsion defended by proponents as necessary to protect Granada did not so much eliminate fears of Muslim attack as fan more fanciful invasion scenarios.[14] Viewed in the light of Granada's postwar turmoil, Philip II's Lepanto-inspired predictions of peace and calm must have tapped into a deep yearning for normalcy in the Andalusian city.

Figure 9 Titian, *Allegory of Lepanto*, 1575.

Philip II commissioned this scene as an offering of thanks, or *ex voto*, for the victory at sea and the birth less than two months later of his son. As he lifts up his heir Don Fernando in joyful gratitude for the twin blessings, a winged allegory of Victory promises the crown prince more conquests ahead (*maiora tibi*). The naval clash of 7 October 1571 is depicted in the background. Scholars believe that Alonso Sánchez Coello added the bound Turkish captive – left foreground – when the canvas arrived in Spain, with a second augmentation by Vicente Carducho in 1625. The latter emendation added the prisoner's quiver (see Panofsky 1969, 72–4; Checa 1994, 52–4; and Falomir Faus 2003, 288–9).

[Titian, *Felipe II, después de la victoria de Lepanto, ofrece al cielo al príncipe.* © Madrid, Museo Nacional del Prado, Cat. P00431.]

At the same time, news of the naval battle carried other echoes particular to Granada. The same unit commanders who toiled long and frustrating months to suppress the rebellion in the Alpujarras had now won a decisive victory in half a day. The *tercios* (infantry units) who had devastated many mountain villages in Granada with ignominious looting were now the heroes of a foreign war. The treasures they hauled away came out of the trunks of Turkish captains with unfamiliar, exotic names, instead of the homes and gardens of native Granadinos.

Juan Latino took note of Lepanto's local significance immediately. Available evidence suggests he set to work commemorating the victory overseas as soon as the news reached him. In time for the battle's symbolically important first anniversary, he presented his volume of commemorative poetry to court censors. Crown bureaucracy and the technical requirements of manual printing took another half year, but his book of Lepanto poetry appeared in print in what was still very short order, in the spring of 1573. The poet's ambition is on immediate display on the title page presenting the book to none other than the king himself: "Ad catholicum, pariter et invictissimum Philippum Dei gratia Hispaniarum regem" (to the Catholic and also equally invincible Philip, king of Hispania's realms by God's grace).[15] By publishing a literary response to the battle in such short order, the schoolmaster of Granada joined an international literary conversation that was playing out on a scale never before seen in the print era. Poets from across Italy, Spain, and even in Spanish America reacted quickly to the news story. Taking stock of the rapid-fire outpouring of poetic responses to the battle in *Los poetas de Lepanto*, José López de Toro spoke of a "volcanic eruption" that brought forth scores of poems. For his part, Carlo Dionisotti found a "poetic plebiscite" that united poets across Italy, transcending regional and linguistic barriers, as well as the elite humanist confines of literary academies.[16]

Against this backdrop, Juan Latino's choice to commemorate the battle in Latin rather than Castilian (Spanish) draws attention to the internationalist responses to Lepanto sometimes underplayed in literary studies. Scholars have, for the most part, concentrated their analysis on ways that poetry on Lepanto in Castilian (Spanish) and Italian (Tuscan) nourished emerging national identities of Spain and Italy.[17] This point of emphasis, in turn, followed from the context of literary histories hewn to the boundaries of modern nation-states, as well as from the division of literary and linguistic study in universities, where modern and classic languages usually reside in separate departments.

But as we take full stock of the literary responses to Lepanto, language and identity remain points of negotiation, yielding a rich cacophony not unlike the mix of languages and dialects that would have echoed on both sides of the battle lines at Lepanto. Appropriately, some poets found in the clash of two multinational armadas a fitting occasion to exalt their own language. Thus, Joan Pujol published a three-canto epic in Catalan, *La singular y admirable victoria*, offering an apt poetic homage to the Catalan commanders and troops who played a central role in Spain's victory. The anthology Sebastiano Ventura published in Venice shortly after the battle, titled *Raccolta di varii poemi Latini, Greci, e Volgari,* includes poems in Bolognese, Pavese, and other Italian dialects.

Latino, for his part, stood with the dozens of poets who chose Europe's one cosmopolitan literary language for their Lepanto reflections. His embrace of classical Latin offers yet another reminder of its continued vibrancy and relevance. The Roman language, after all, gave the poet a voice in international communications and politics. As well, the ability to craft suitable Latin verse conferred membership in the international "republic of letters" (*respublica litterarum*).[18]

The Roman language may also have provided Juan Latino some measure of safety from local tensions. After all, he made his claim to surpassing cultural relevance as an author at a time when he was also a member of a stigmatized minority writing in a city so recently devastated by an ethnic cleansing campaign directed at another discriminated-against group. On a related note, the more limited reach of Latin texts – accessible to advanced grammar school students, highly educated members of the clergy and religious orders, plus others with advanced education – may also have allowed the freedman to narrate politically sensitive actions in the naval battle, a point to which I return in chapter 5 when I discuss how his epic of Lepanto airs the victors' misdeeds at Lepanto. In short, Juan Latino may have had some powerful reasons to speak in a less immediately accessible, but still widely known and revered language.

The pull of Latin as a publication medium was not merely defensive. Strong positive attractions remained. Not least among Latin's enticements was how the cosmopolitan literary language harmonized with the Spanish Monarchy's intensifying ambitions to world dominance. Philip II, aiming to expand his empire eastward towards Constantinople and Jerusalem, needed poets and chroniclers who could tell his story for subjects based in faraway lands. While sailors and merchants across the Mediterranean traded and gossiped in the region's many vernacular languages or in the mariner's lingua franca, Latin remained the one international language for print publications.

Taking measure of Juan Latino's 1573 Lepanto volume, the reader finds a literary statement on Lepanto akin to Titian's *Allegory of Lepanto*. In common with the Venetian's two-tiered view of events, which connects the naval battle to the birth of a new royal heir, Latino's book merges the two auspicious occurrences. We can see from the precise and accurate battle account that Juan Latino took care to adhere to reliable news bulletins and eyewitness testimony on the battle. At the same time, he synthesized classical and medieval literary traditions through dense webs of allusion characteristic of Latin poetry in the Renaissance.

To this already demanding artistic agenda, Latino added an educational program that follows from his career as an educator in Granada. Thus, margin glosses speak for the Latin teacher, identifying some citations, figures of speech, rhetorical devices, and metrical peculiarities.[19] In this dimension, the poet took on an extra task that sets the book apart from other contemporary literary publications. Though editions of classic texts with commentary remained common for schoolbooks, the dominant publication format for original works of poetry was, by this point, the italic book free of marginalia, a style that the storied Manutius publishing dynasty of Venice had popularized in the early 1500s. Compare, in this regard, Latino's folios, which feature concise pedagogical explanations in the margins, to the clean margins of the roughly contemporary editions of Alonso de Ercilla's *Araucana*.[20] Yet Latino's didactic use of margin glosses follows, not from an anachronistic impulse, but from the goals of the author whose title page proclaims him an educator of Granada, "Garnatae studiosae adolescentiae moderatorem" (guide for studies of the youth of Granada).

A prefatory elegy addressed to Philip II sets the agenda for Juan Latino's self-assigned role as Spain's poet of Lepanto. Like a road map to new, higher ambitions, the poem lays out the goals that have propelled the respected educator to move from work concentrated in a local grammar school and university setting to situate himself in the international arena delineated by the Spanish empire. By itself, this connection of Latin poetry and energized imperial ambitions was not unusual in the wake of Lepanto. Latino's preparation of his Lepanto volume coincided with the Tuscan bibliophile Pietro Gherardi's preparation of an anthology of poems on Lepanto by Italy's one hundred best neo-Latin poets.[21] What is striking and unprecedented in the case of Juan Latino, nevertheless, is the freedman's specific assertion that the new, auspicious era for empire signalled by the naval victory demands a recalibration of attitudes and hierarchies related to skin colour and ethnicity.

Between Elegy and Admonition

The proem to Philip II, titled "On the Birth of Untroubled Times," comprises thirty-six elegiac couplets (see Appendix 1). Ear carefully tuned to the historical occasion at hand, the poet speaks to Philip II's intensifying aspirations for global empire. Yet intertwined in the prophecy of good times ahead we find a pointed warning against the era's intensifying racism. A painstakingly crafted argument that unfolds within the couplets admonishes the king that ill-informed bias against blacks will stand in the way of his ambitions to add eastern realms to his empire.

By speaking in classical elegy, Latino implies a kinship to illustrious Roman predecessors who cultivated the metre to air personal sentiments, with Ovid and Martial most prominent among them. Thanks in large part to Baltasar Fra Molinero's seminal study of blacks in Golden Age Spanish letters, critics have long known of this elegy's impassioned defence of blackness; yet Fra Molinero's consideration of the poem itself was necessarily brief, given that his study concentrated on how seventeenth-century Spanish writers rendered Juan Latino a fictional caricature.[22] Since then, the specific contours of Latino's self-fashioning as an author through the elegiac couplets have not been widely examined. This obscurity stems from the lack of a printed translation in English or Spanish, as well as from the emphasis within Hispanic studies on early modern lyric poetry in Castilian (Spanish). Recently, classics scholar Holt Parker has made available a concise introduction and annotated translation in the blog *Renaissance Latin Poem of the Week.*[23] The time is thus propitious for delving into this early and eloquent statement of pride from a diasporic African based in Europe.

In a manner quite fitting for the educator who taught Latin to generations of future lawyers, Latino's poetic voice subjects Philip II's new imperial horizons to a caveat: eastward imperial expansion hinges on a more inclusive attitude towards blacks. The notion that the embrace of black vassals is a pre-condition for eastern empire building comes forth in a lawyerly refutation of the era's growing bias and oppression that marginalized sub-Saharan Africans. Since his is an early voice raised against early modernity's institutionalization of colour prejudice, Juan Latino's refutation merits examination, point by point.

To begin, the title, "On the Birth of Untroubled Times," distils the king's own assessment of divine favour after Lepanto. Latino's choice of words follows from Philip II's celebrations. *Natalis* – the day of one's birth or the fact of being born – pairs with *serenus*, understood both as calm weather and in terms of Habsburg iconography. This formulation of an uncloudy day marks the birth of the Infante Don Fernando to Queen Anna of Austria with an ear tuned to Philip II's own image making. The most common Spanish terms contemporaries used to describe Philip's assiduously cultivated regal gravity were *sosiego* (tranquillity, calm) and *moderación*, both of which fall within the lexical range of the Latin adjective *serenus*.[24]

While the formulation of a *natalis serenus* speaks to the Habsburg image making that Philip II honed into a personal trademark, it resounds powerfully with recent events. Not least was the civil war in Granada detailed in the previous chapter. The conflict had ignited the same year in which the king's volatile heir Don Carlos died in murky circumstances. Philip II's queen, Isabel of Valois, succumbed to complications from childbirth in the same year. After a turbulent and tragic half-decade, the fall of 1571 did seem to bring a change of weather.

Building on the title, the three opening couplets assert Juan Latino's surpassing cultural relevance in this auspicious new era at hand. Note here the claim that alterity or being from another world beyond Europe confers a unique power to recount the momentous naval victory:

Unicus est victor, scriptorem quaeritat unum,
  res nova vult vatem regibus esse novum.
Auribus alme tuis non haec victoria ponto est
  audita, hic scriptor nec fuit orbe satus,
Aethiopum terris venit, qui gesta Latinus
  Austriadae mira carminis arte canat.

(The victor is unique, he demands a unique writer; a new event requires a new bard for kings. Such a naval triumph, benevolent one, has never reached your ears; this writer was not engendered in this world: he came from lands of Aethiopia, Latinus, who sings the Austriad's wondrous deeds with his skill in song.)[25]

The assertion is bold. Spain has secured an unprecedented naval victory. How could the king entrust its commemoration to an ordinary poet? This self-fashioning as a dazzling outsider, though so natural to us today, contrasts with the dominant literary practice of Renaissance Spain. After all, the poetic revolution of the previous generation arose when a brilliant group of writers strove, as Leah Middlebrook notes, "to rehearse and elaborate the image of the courtier as the new masculine ideal."[26] Given this pattern, we might have expected Juan Latino to follow such illustrious predecessors as Garcilaso de la Vega and Joan Boscán, rooting his claim to international prominence in his own elite credentials. The freedman could have drawn on the prestige that followed from his lifelong ties to Spain's consummate empire builder, the Gran Capitán, whose family he had served as a slave in childhood and from which he continued to receive material support for his teaching position in Granada. At other key moments, Latino did in fact herald this relationship, as I discuss in chapter 1. He might also have trumpeted his ties to Granada's archbishop, Pedro de Guerrero, whose prestige had increased when he represented Philip II in the second and third sessions of the Council of Trent. But with this new literary calling card as a poet from another world to king and court, the freedman swerves momentarily from his alliances with Spain's elite.

To proffer his own claim to outsider credentials, Latino draws on an emerging cartographic discourse. The poet is not from this world or realm ("nec fuit orbe satus"), but from Ethiopia ("Aethiopum terris venit"). Because he is from another world, he can serve the king as a new bard ("vatem novum") at a time of new-found glory. Through the notion of "res nova" (new things), the poet signals an alternate conception of modernity. We have, in effect, a spirit of literary renovation in step with the agenda Middlebrook outlines in *Imperial Lyric*. But in the passages above, the measure of cultural currency inverts, elevating the outsider poet over the nobleman.

Framing the self-portrait as a new poet ("vatem novum") in geographic terms with the "nec fuit orbe satus," Latino turns the era's enduring cartographic mysteries about sub-Saharan Africa into an advantage. Though today most analysis of an early modern "mundus novus" (new world) emphasizes European conceptions of the Americas, sixteenth-century map makers also contended with the uncharted African lands south of the Senegal River as another new world. Francesc Relaño notes, in this respect, how cartographers distinguished the *Africa vecchia* (Old Africa) known to ancient geographers and medieval travellers from the *Africa nuova* (New Africa) that Portuguese expeditions and the slave trade had partially revealed. Over the course of the sixteenth century, chroniclers and map makers continued to piece together what

Relaño calls "the African puzzle." A striking illustration of the intellectual demands that followed as Europeans selectively and incompletely pieced together this puzzle emerges in the mid-sixteenth-century updates to Ptolemy's *Geographia*; here, map makers like Giacomo Gastaldi advertised that their charts offered "infinite modern names for the cities, provinces, and fortresses" never before listed, while retaining the ancient geographer's organizational scheme and hierarchy. They also repeated many of Ptolemy's fantastical names for the still-unknown people and places of sub-Saharan Africa. Gastaldi's annotations to the chart for sub-Saharan Africa illustrate the European puzzling in action, where some long-standing myths about the region are codified while others are replaced with new facts gleaned from navigators. The Italian cartographer thus annotates the Latin translation of Ptolemy with bracketed comments that sometimes confirm myths and sometimes bring in new facts from exploration. On the same page we read Ptolemy's "near this Gulf live the Ethiopian Anthropophagi" with Gastaldi's comments added in parenthesis, "(that is, those who eat men)," but then just below, Ptolemy's "those Ethiopians that are commonly called Hesperii" is glossed by Gastaldi with factual information from Portuguese voyages, as "(Realm of Senegal, of Gambia, and of Guinea)."[27]

This blend of fact and fantasy would have been impossible for someone in Juan Latino's position to bypass. In fact, an important expression of the mixing of old myths and new geographic facts emerged close at hand. Luis del Mármol Carvajal's monumental study of Africa was completed and submitted for publication approval just three months before Latino finished his Lepanto volume. Latino also contracted his services as a legal representative in litigation at court, suggesting the two men knew one another to at least some extent. Mármol Carvajal's portrayal of black Africa, mentioned in chapter 1, thus bears consideration once more, given that it records prevailing Spanish attitudes towards the region and its people at the moment the freedman drafted this elegy. Though Mármol's travels as a soldier and captive gave him extensive knowledge of the people, languages, and lands of North Africa, he conceded that sub-Saharan Africa remained a mystery: "There are countless provinces [...] most uncharted." But he filled the information gaps with a litany of racist stereotypes discussed in chapter 1, labelling black Africans uncivilized idolaters.[28] Juan Latino, as we have seen above, charts the same course through a still-unknown land to present himself to the public and the king as a poet. Yet he transforms the "other worldly" status that informed Mármol's racist dismissal of blacks into a hallmark of unique insight.

With Latino's poetic credentials thus grounded in racial and geographic difference, the poem moves to the subject of Lepanto and its place in Spanish historical memory. To ensure the naval battle lives on in hearts and minds, the freedman asks Philip II to entrust him with the task of commemorating the deeds of John of Austria:

Is genibus flexis orat te, invicte Philippe,
cantator fratris possit ut esse tui.
Nam si nobilitant Austriadae bella poetam,
Phoenicem Austriadam, quod niger, ille facit.

("On the Birth of Untroubled Times," Appendix 1, ll. 9–12; Latino 1573, 1st gathering, fol. 9v.)

(He beseeches you on bended knee, invincible Philip, so he can be singer for your brother. Now if the wars of the Austriad ennoble the poet, he, as a black, renders the Austrian a Phoenix.)

In other words, Juan Latino will celebrate John of Austria in Latin verse. His poems will transform the flesh-and-blood military commander to an immortal phoenix. In exchange, he seeks the same reward sought by so many Renaissance poets: court patronage and social validation.

Beyond this simple trade of praise for patronage, however, the role as "cantator fratris" (singer for your brother) hinges on a special bond between the poet and John of Austria. Though at first glance Philip II's younger half-brother might seem far removed from the black-African educator in terms of Spain's social and political hierarchy, their life stories offered compelling parallels. Latino, as noted in the first chapter, parlayed his position as a slave to a young grandee to gain a clandestine education. The questions about his birthright that we cannot fully answer due to a lack of reliable evidence most likely echo questions that haunted Latino himself in a society increasingly fixated on Old-Christian lineage and birthright. Who were the freedman's parents? Was he the son born out of wedlock of a black slave and a white master or overseer? Given such mysteries about parentage, John of Austria may have had a special magnetism. The illegitimate son of Charles V and the volatile commoner, Barbara Blumberg or Plumberger, he lived his early childhood under the tutelage of a court musician in a village south of Madrid, completely unaware of his royal birthright. His father sent for him when he was seven, thus beginning the apprenticeship that led to the highest military command. But as Don John fought to quell the Morisco revolt in Granada and then led the victorious coalition navy in Lepanto, he sought, in vain, to gain full royal status. His dispatches record many slights and humiliations, where haughty advisors refused to dine with him and seemingly elemental tactical decisions required the approval of those same scornful aristocrats.[29]

Within the passage of the elegy quoted above, John of Austria stands as the focal point of artistic inspiration. A poetic sleight of hand redraws the Habsburg "bastard" as a dazzling phoenix and heralds Latino's special insights as a black poet ("Nam si nobilitant Austriadae bella poetam, / Phoenicem Austriadam, quod niger, ille facit"). The black poet here claims the power to render the hero of Lepanto a phoenix. The natural concision of classical Latin showcases Juan Latino's literary magic. Here too, blackness has shed negative associations and instead, confers special vatic powers. The bard's capacity to make John of Austria a phoenix, stated in the accusative "Phoenicem Austriadam," comes because he is a black ("quod niger"); *quod* in grammatical terms justifies the assertion of creative faculties, "ille facit." Along the way, Latino negates the allegations of black inferiority aired in Mármol Carvajal, Leo Africanus, and other sixteenth-century sources that forged European conceptions of sub-Saharan Africans. Now blackness confers unique linguistic dexterity and keen poetic insight.

One sign of this conceptual shift is the poet's mobilization of the phoenix imagery. Presented as an emblem for John of Austria, its symbolism draws on both classical philology and medieval theories of kingship. Crucially, Pliny's *Natural History* regaled readers with the description of the most dazzling of the east's "indescribable birds" (*inenarrabiles aves*). A beguiling gloss detailed a bird as large as an eagle, with a gold flourish marking a purple neck, rose-coloured feathers adorning the tail, and tufts of feathers crowning the head. Most tantalizing, this avian wonder lived for centuries. Before dying, the phoenix made a nest from sprigs of cinnamon and frankincense, from which a maggot-like new hatchling would spring. Pliny's paradoxical bird inspired European poets from antiquity to the Spanish Golden Age. Perhaps best known, the phoenix would become both emblem and epithet for the playwright-and-poet, Lope de Vega, whose popularity and output astounded his contemporaries.[30]

In the realm of political theory, medieval jurists drew on Pliny's wondrous, regenerating bird to explain the paradoxical concept of the king's two bodies. Dynastic power, like the phoenix, regenerated to continue for eternity, even after a single king died. The Habsburgs, like other European dynasties, invoked the avian marvel to legitimize their succession, from their foundation in the thirteenth century to the rise of the Spanish Habsburgs in the early sixteenth century. The freedman's patronage formulation, in which his song as a new Habsburg poet will transform the king's half-brother into a phoenix, draws on three centuries of royal precedent.[31]

The terms of the patronage exchange proposed here include a pointed self-aggrandizement. Typically, ancien regime patronage required unsupported or incompletely supported writers to contort with ostentatious self-effacement as they spoke to the mighty. The case of Lope de Vega, the *fénix* of the next generation, would be paradigmatic, as Alison Weber has shown with reference to his religious poetry.[32] Yet in this case, Juan Latino, at least momentarily, casts aside the seemingly obligatory language of servility. In its place, the patronage formulation above hinges on the unique ability of a black poet ("quod niger, ille facit"). That is, the poet will render Juan de Austria a splendid phoenix, because he is a black man (*quod*), not in spite of this minority status. The claim here of transformative powers ignores the racist rhetoric and discriminatory legal structures taking shape to justify the enslavement and oppression of blacks, both at home in Granada and abroad.

Instead, the poetic voice beckons to tropes of black piety, wisdom, and power that pre-dated the Atlantic slave trade. A limited but powerful range of motifs conceived blacks as agents of positive cross-cultural contact and as confirmation of Christianity's ecumenical nature, thereby contrasting to negative conceptions, such as the representation of blacks as subalterns within invading Muslim armies. Most famously, the black magus depicted in many nativity scenes from the twelfth century onward dramatized the universal reach of Christianity (see figure 10).[33]

Gesturing to such positive notions of blackness, Latino roots his claim to prestige and power in a pointed application of a well-known biblical conversion narrative. The angriest passage I have found in Latino's surviving texts invokes the only black (Ethiopian) mentioned in the Bible, the Ethiopian emissary of Queen Candace in Acts of the Apostles 8.27–39. Recalling his conversion, the poet warns the king against racist exclusion:

Figure 10 *Adoration of the Magi* right panel from *Retable Depicting Madonna and Child, Nativity, and Adoration of the Magi*, ca. 1468. The scene with a black magus is from the right-side panel of a travelling altar (165.2 × 200.8 cm) made for Pedro de Montoya, Bishop of Osma (1454–75). It features intricate needlework in silk floss and creped yarns, with padding added to approximate a sculpted Gothic altar. The black magus emerged from the twelfth century onward, gaining resonance across Europe as a testament to the ecumenical reach of Christianity (Snowden 1983, 107; Kaplan 1985, 79–80; and Koerner 2010, 16).

Quod si nostra tuis facies Rex nigra ministris
displicet, Aethiopum non placet alba viris.
Illic Auroram, sordet, qui viserit albus,
suntque duces nigri, rex quoque fuscus adest.
Candace Regina genus, nigrumque ministrum
vel curru Christo miserat illa suum.
Legerat ille genus non enarrabile Christi,
Austriadae pugnas non canet iste tui?
Obvius Aethiopem Christum docet ore Philippus,
discipulum Christus mittit ad Aethiopem:
non temere Aethiopi caelo datus ergo Philippus,
ne Aethiopi haec forte Philippe neges.

("On the Birth of Untroubled Times," Appendix 1, ll. 19–30; Latino 1573, 1st gathering, fol. 10r; emphasis added)

(For if our black-face, oh king, displeases your emissaries, a white one does not please men of Aethiopia. There, a white man who visits the East is considered vile, and *there are black leaders, and there is even a dark-skinned king*. Queen Candace sent her people and black emissary to Christ in a chariot. He had read of the ineffable people of Christ; will this man not sing the battles of your Austriad? En route Philip teaches the Aethiopian face-to-face about Christ, Christ sends a disciple to the Aethiopian, not by chance, therefore, Philip was brought under Aethiopian sky, nor, o Philip, should you, by accident, deny these just reasons.)

Embedded in these verses are arguments for the embrace and inclusion of blacks on both political and religious grounds. The political or imperial point of argument – highlighted in italics – draws Philip II's attention to the fact that eastern imperial expansion will bring his emissaries into lands where blacks rule, that is, sub-Saharan Africa or Ethiopia. Latino's geography here draws on long-standing conceptions of Ethiopia as part of the East or India, a facet of medieval cartography quite different from the modern organization of the world by continents.[34] Intriguingly, the specific political dimensions of this Ethiopian east evoke a scene from one of the treasures of the library of Isabel of Castile. Several illuminations from the late thirteenth-century *Books of Chess, Dice, and Board Games* prepared for Alfonso X of Castile depicted blacks in eastern lands as kings and courtiers (see figure 11). Though now in the Escorial Palace, the codex was housed in Granada's Capilla Real during most of Juan Latino's lifetime. Just around the corner from his

Figure 11 Books of Chess, Dice, and Board Games.

This scene of the court of a black ruler is from the illuminated manuscript completed in Seville in 1283 for Alonso X (the Wise) of Castile (1252–84). A notable aspect of the manuscript is the religious and ethnic inclusiveness of its scenes, which depict Christians, Muslims, and Jews, with phenotypes suggesting blacks, whites, and Asians (see Constable 2007, 314). Prior to its transfer to the Escorial Palace in 1591, the manuscript was housed in Granada's Capilla Real, as part of Isabel I of Castile's library.

Alfonso X, *Libros de ajedrez, dados, y tablas*, fol. 22r. [Reproduced from Codex T.I.6. of the Biblioteca de El Escorial, Spain. © Patrimonio Nacional.]

seminar room and under the custodianship of the same church officials who supervised the activities of the grammar school where he taught, this volume would have been accessible to the freedman. Game 25 shows a black ruler playing chess with a courtier, attended by servants and a musician, substantiating Latino's claim in the elegy that in eastern realms there are black kings and courtiers. Reconfiguring such a distant realm in his poem, Latino warns that these black courtiers could scorn white Europeans visiting them just as whites disdain blacks among them.[35]

Turning to the religious argument for inclusion, we see how the poet draws on the biblical narrative of cross-cultural contact and conversion ("Candace Regina ... Philippe neges"). The episode alluded to is from Acts of the Apostles 8, where Philip the evangelizer meets the Ethiopian eunuch, an emissary of Queen Candace. On seeing that the black man strives to read the Book of Isaiah, Philip strikes up a conversation. The Ethiopian, in turn, asks for instruction and baptism. This black convert is the first non-Jew baptized in the New Testament and the only "Aethiops" mentioned in the Bible. Early biblical exegetes commented on and illustrated the scene, attracted to its testimony of Christianity's embrace of converts and its illustration of a diligent student of scripture.[36]

One might ask whether the poet or his readers grasped the unflattering contrast implied through the insertion of this particular biblical allusion into a poem addressed to the Spanish king. That story's emphasis on conversion and ecumenism contrasts with the justification for the recent mass expulsion of Granada's population of Moriscos. This action, explored in depth in chapter 2, essentially denied the efficacy of Christian conversion for all Granadinos of Hispano-Muslim origins. On this point, a caution is in order. Any subversive intent or interpretation that arose from the poet's choice of biblical stories remains cloaked in silence or rests on the subtlest of allusions or contrasts. This was no time for a poet and educator who depended on high-ranking crown and church officials for his livelihood to speak out directly against the hard-line religious orthodoxy that had recently prevailed over alternative traditions of engagement and inclusion. Allusions and narrative choices in the freedman's epic of Lepanto – the focus of chapters 4 and 5 – bear witness to a poet negotiating among differing attitudes towards the Mediterranean region's Muslim heritage, ranging from viciously negative to deeply sympathetic positions. Still, the focus on a non-European Christian neophyte in the elegy suggests the lingering appeal of conversion narratives, even after church and state officials had rejected the efficacy of Hispano-Muslim conversions in the poet's home city.

Delving still more into the choice here of conversion stories, I am also struck by one seemingly obvious message that the freedman sidesteps here. A reader might reasonably have expected Latino to embrace the biblical story of the Ethiopian convert as proof of his own Christian lineage from time immemorial. He could, after all, have cited this passage to claim a special Old Christian status, as a descendant of one of the first converts in the Bible. What might seem a far-fetched fictionalization to us would, nonetheless, have been plausible and expedient in Spain, particularly given the spread of *limpieza de sangre* statutes and the genealogical fabrications they engendered. A claim to biblical lineage by Latino would have been no more or less fanciful than the genealogical fictions that elite Spaniards mobilized to hide their Jewish or Muslim ancestors. In fact, the Ethiopian emissary from Acts might have been quite reasonable by comparison to such family histories as the one commissioned by the Avila-based marquises of Velada, who claimed descent from Hercules. A particularly prominent family in Latino's home city, the Granada Venegas, claimed descent from Visigothic royalty of Zaragoza, while retaining respected Taifa kings of Muslim Spain in their family tree. An idea of the proliferation of implausible lineages comes from a spirited Lope de Vega heroine in the 1615 urban marriage comedy *Los ramilletes de Madrid*: she assures her wary brother that the gentleman she hopes to marry descends from Adam himself. Even as urban audiences laughed at jokes about patently absurd genealogical claims, writers-for-hire did a brisk business fabricating such lineages.[37]

Given the common practice of certifying Christian lineage from time immemorial, Juan Latino would have had much to gain from concocting his own. Yet as the passage above shows, he bypasses the genealogical argument available to craft his own narrative of Old Christian ancestry. Instead, he marshals the story of the Ethiopian convert to denounce European colour prejudice and deliver a stern warning to Philip II. This logic anticipates modes of ethnographic and anthropological analysis that would gain traction much later in the early modern era. The freedman's comparative framework calls attention to faraway lands where a black elite will disdain and recoil from white visitors ("there, a white man who visits the East is considered vile, and there are black leaders, and there is even a dark-skinned king"). Reading these lines in the context of the poem's own times, one gets the sense of a black scholar trying to turn back a tide of racist rhetoric with reminders of alternative hierarchies of value.

While intensifying colour prejudice was a broad European phenomenon closely tied to the growing Atlantic slave trade, the status of black Africans had been a specific point of contention in the poet's home city in recent times. The most prominent defender of Morisco rights, Francisco Núñez Muley, had defended Hispano-Muslim cultural practices by reaffirming biases against black Africans and defending the rights of his community to own black slaves, an issue considered in chapter 2.[38] Against this backdrop, the poetic voice's reminder above that there are black leaders and black kings in the distant lands where Philip II would extend his imperial power ("suntque duces nigri, rex quoque fuscus adest") carries a message with pressing implications for readers closest at hand.

Continuing from here, the poetic voice warns that racist exclusion impedes the new empire building that Philip II and his advisors envisioned after Lepanto:

> Nec rerum est Dominus, qui non admiserit omnes,
> gentem ne excludat regia forte meam.
> ("On the Birth of Untroubled Times," Appendix 1, ll. 41–2; Latino 1573, 1st gathering, fol. 10v)

> (There is no lord of states who has not admitted everyone, nor monarchy that would exclude my race capriciously.)

In other words, universal monarchs are universally inclusive. Such logic echoes the *Brevíssima relación de la destrucción de las Indias* (*Brief Treatise on the Destruction of the Indies*) by Fray Bartolomé de las Casas, which was first published two decades earlier (1552).[39] If Juan Latino's poetic voice takes a rhetorical position that steers well clear of the Dominican's vehemence, the warning nonetheless presents the same line of reasoning: the king undercuts his own imperial ambitions when he permits the oppression of loyal non-European subjects.

But where Las Casas warns of hell fires that await tyrannical conquistadors, Latino seeks to entice his royal dedicatee with wondrous new imperial horizons. With the poetic voice acting as a chess grandmaster, the final passage marches Philip II's armies eastward. A triumphant John of Austria becomes a new Julius Caesar as he carries the Habsburg standard into new battles:

Et miles pugnat, ceptis fit Caesar in armis,
prudens consilio crescit, et ingenio.
Dum natus princeps paulatim surgit in hostes,
conficiet frater grandia bella tibi.

("On the Birth of Untroubled Times," Appendix 1, ll. 67–70; Latino 1573, 1st gathering, fol. 11r)

(And as soldier he fights, becomes a Caesar in battles waged, prudent, matures through council and intelligence. As born leader he rises against enemies, the brother will carry out great battles for you.)

On another front, the king's newborn heir Don Fernando undergoes his royal apprenticeship, embracing the military command that comes as his birthright:

Fernandusque tuus, spes nostri, et gloria saecli
res gerere, et Martem discet amare suum.

("On the Birth of Untroubled Times," Appendix 1, ll. 71–2; Latino 1573, 1st gathering, fol. 11r)

(And your Ferdinand, our hope, and glory of ages, will learn to govern affairs and love Mars himself.)

With brother and heir both extending Spanish rule, Philip II would regain control of Christ's tomb in Jerusalem for Western Christendom and place the Ottoman Turks under his yoke:

Virtute et patrem referens nil linquet inausum,
sub iuga Turcarum mittet et imperium:
sub te iam Christi reddet pietate sepulchrum,
regibus et fato debita regna tuis.

("On the Birth of Untroubled Times," Appendix 1, ll. 73–6; Latino 1573, 1st gathering, fol. 11r)

(Recalling the father in virtue, he will leave nothing undared, he will submit the empire of the Turks under the yoke: he will piously restore the sepulcher of Christ to you, and the realms destined by fate to your rulers.)

The Ottoman advance over the last century is safely checked and Habsburg power extends to the place that had long eluded European monarchs – Christ's tomb in Jerusalem.[40]

An Auspicious Black Raven

To sign off, the poet reprises his assertion of auspicious blackness. Like the court painter who signs the king's portrait in a discrete but easily visible corner, the closing couplet fixes a place for Juan Latino in this world empire:

> Haec tibi certa suo promittit carmine cornix,
> felix cuncta bene et prospera, dixit, erunt.
> ("On the Birth of Untroubled Times," Appendix 1, ll. 77–8; Latino 1573, 1st gathering, fol. 11r)

> (A raven promises you in his song these things are certain, auspicious, he announced all will be well and prosperous.)

Latino heralds himself a *cornix* or black raven. This avian imagery stakes a terrain that would later become fertile ground for baroque artistic innovation. Dana Bultman in particular has illuminated how the controversial Luis de Góngora and women writers embraced such symbols as the "pájaro ladino" (foreign-speaking bird) and the turtledove to signify their flight out of the bounds of traditional literary practice.[41]

The allusive power of Latino's own avian image amplifies with a pedagogical gesture. A margin note, speaking in the voice of a classroom teacher, identifies the *cornix* as an "allusio ad cornicem Tarpeiam" (allusion to the Tarpeian raven). Following the clue leads the Latin learner to Suetonius's *Life of Domitian* 23.2. The chronicler thus records the interpretation of a black bird's appearance just before the death of the tyrannical emperor: "Nuper Tarpeio, quae sedit culmine cornix./ 'Est bene' non potuit dicere; dixit, 'Erit'" (Recently a crow which was sitting on a Tarpeian rooftop/Could not say "It is well," only declared "It will be").[42] Imagine for a moment a Latin apprentice in Granada who, prompted by the margin note, found the passage in Suetonius. On an elementary level, the allusion supports basic grammar study. The Roman text offers a practical illustration of how to use the verb *sum* (to be), contrasting the present indicative active *est* with the future *erit*. But for the apprentice who had already mastered verb conjugation, the lesson deepens, imparting worldly wisdom. The witty line in Suetonius could be added to a list of handy citations or commonplaces; one day, he might gloss advice to a powerful minister with a particularly urbane allusion.[43] What aspiring minister or diplomat couldn't use a handy reference to Suetonius's *Lives of the Caesars*?

Latino's own adaptation of Suetonius typifies the era's poetic ideal of *imitatio*, where writers and theorists sought artful emulation, not mere repetition. Going well beyond simple imitation, the practice demanded an artful and ingenious adaptation that theorists from Seneca to Petrarch had explained with the metaphor of a busy bee digesting pollen from a field of flowers to spread new life.[44] Latino's offer of celebratory poetry for royal patronage "digests" Suetonius's *culmine cornix* with a marked didactic purpose. The freedman's *carmine cornix* retains the ablative-nominative grammatical construction of the source text, while changing ablative *culmine* to *carmine*. "All will be well," says the raven perched on Rome's Capitoline Hill (*culmine cornix*). That auspicious declaration still rings out with Latino offering his own song (*carmine*). The lexicon has changed the hilltop place into the poet's song. But the accent remains on auspicious.

In this recalibration of the black bird, the poet does not deign to consider the range of negative associations often associated with the colour black in European letters and folklore. On the contrary, this raven sings of a dawning age of prosperous, blessed events. Blackness here has shed its baggage as a marker of slave status or disdain. Now it signifies God's grace. Having refuted racial bias with the earlier story of the Ethiopian convert, the poetic voice has soared to a place beyond.

From here, the poet as black bard stands ready to present his auspicious *Song of John of Austria*. Chapters 4 and 5 explore how Latino as epic poet brings forth an innovative proposal for chronicling a world-shattering event. Artistic and technical difficulties that result from the composition of an epic narration in such short order intensify with the pedagogical duties the freedman assumed. But as we will see, at key moments the vocation as educator – already given a virtuoso display with the black raven – sometimes elicits critical assessments of Spanish imperial policy. In particular, echoes of the repression of Granada's Moriscos and intimations of the moral pitfalls of modern warfare complicate the poet's stated mission of enshrining the Habsburg phoenix, John of Austria, in the modern epic canon.

4 Christians and Muslims on the Battle Lines

From News Bulletin to Latin Verse

The Song of John of Austria is an epic poem divided into two books of just over 1,800 Latin hexameter verses. Throughout, explanatory margin glosses approximate the voice of a schoolmaster, drawing attention to rhetorical devices; translating classical toponyms; and revealing some literary allusions, while leaving others to the readers' own devices. The temporal proximity between the poem's composition and the events recounted – Latino submitted it to a royal secretary two months before the battle's first anniversary – informs the narrative structure from the outset. Using the metaliterary framework of the news of the battle, the poem replays the moment that word of the victory at Lepanto reached the poet and his fellow Granadinos. This striking immediacy offers a resounding statement of relevance, but also adds complications of the kind Torquato Tasso had in mind when he advised poets to avoid recent history as the explicit topic of an epic poem.[1]

From the beginning, the shadow of recent events at home hovers over the depiction of the battle overseas. An encomiastic opening sequence hails Pedro de Deza, the controversial Audiencia president. Chapter 2 details how, in the half-decade leading up to Lepanto, the official had spearheaded the enforcement of the pragmatics of 1567; promoted a hard-line response to the uprising the new laws incited; and finally, supervised the mass punishment directed at all the Moriscos of Granada, even those who had not taken up arms or supported rebels. Opening verses to the *Song of John of Austria* hail Deza as Granada's guardian and saviour. Continuing, the poem juxtaposes the rebellion and the naval battle through the conceit of a news bulletin.

That is, the poem dramatizes at the beginning how, while city leaders and residents are offering prayers of thanksgiving for deliverance from the civil war, news of the triumph at Lepanto arrives. Here, the poet recasts Virgil's allegory of Fama in a benevolent guise. Gone is the dreaded flying monster – with an eye, ear, and mouth under each wing – whose rumour-mongering dooms Dido in *Aeneid* 4.137–88. Taming the personification allegory, Latino conjures a figure to concretize the seeming explosion of information that has resulted from the advances in print technology and greater efficiency within Mediterranean courier networks.[2]

As if breaking the seal on a letter or news bulletin, the poetic voice recounts how the two massive armadas encountered one another in the waters of western Greece. In the details of forming battle lines and fighting, the verse narration adheres to the basic outline of events found in the first-line letters and bulletins. Tools of the epic poet – harangues, similes, and figures of speech – add texture and drama. Taking a bird's-eye view, the poet details how both the Ottoman coalition fleet and its Holy League counterpart moved into formation. Direct discourse records the harangues with which Christian and Muslim commanders rally their fighters; at other moments, speeches conjure more private moments of tactical deliberations, prayers, and even premonitions. Once firing begins, *The Song of John of Austria* offers a vivid direct narration of combat. At this point, Latino diverges in key respects from other poets who crafted verse narrations of Lepanto and also veers from his praise for Pedro de Deza's hard-line policies in Granada. In particular, he pays more anguished attention to the death in combat of the Ottoman admiral Ali Pasha than do his best known contemporaries. Also striking in comparison to other epics is how *The Song of John of Austria* pays close attention to what happens when Spain and its allies claim victory after a morning of fighting. Along with the prayers of thanksgiving and shouts of victory we find in contemporary poems on the battle, the freedman recounts the frenzied looting of Spanish soldiers in unusual detail, going so far as to expose a near-mutiny against commanders. Here too, Latino's epic also stands out for how it acknowledges the one major setback that Holy League commanders conceded right away, showing how Algerian corsair governor and galley warfare mastermind Uluç Ali outwitted his Holy League adversaries, destroyed the fleet of the Knights of Malta, and fled the carnage relatively unscathed. In his telling, the poet imagines the dread of Christian captives in Algiers who, having heard the news of the Holy League victory, cower in anticipation of Uluç Ali's wrath upon return. In reality, the Calabrian remained in the eastern Mediterranean in the months after the battle.

Recovering the celebratory mood to conclude, the poet draws still more on the framing device of the news bulletin. Verses recount how word of the victory travelled from the eastern Mediterranean, to Pope Pius V in Rome, then to Philip II's Escorial Palace, and finally to Granada. Closing verses add one more joyous piece of news: as the city celebrates the naval victory, word arrives that Queen Anna of Austria has given birth to the Infante Don Fernando. The closing sequence thus offers a configuration analogous to Titian's *Allegory of Lepanto* (see figure 9): the naval victory and royal birth, together, affirm divine favour. Going one step further, Latino's closing verses extend the blessing to post-rebellion Granada, heralding a new era of peace and prosperity for the city. This ending, in effect, reprises the key premise of the elegy to Philip II explored in chapter 3: Juan Latino is a new kind of bard offering a song of good tidings and predictions of more empire building ahead. This Habsburg song, in turn, merits royal approbation and sponsorship. But if we look more carefully at the social context in which the poem took shape and its allusive environment, some dissonant notes become detectable. The pages ahead ponder this counterpoint, first in terms of the Granada-to-Lepanto sequencing of events in the panegyric opening passage. From here, some distinctive narrative choices come into focus.

Viewing Lepanto from Post-Rebellion Granada

The shadow of Granada's recent turmoil appears in the first line. Latino's speaking subject calls out to Pedro de Deza, the Audiencia president whose problematic role in Granada's rebellion came into view repeatedly in chapter 2:

> Deza gravis meritis, pietate insignis avita,
> cui dotes animi reddit natura benigne,
> clarus ab officiis et regis munere praeses,
> Garnatae missus fato, civilia iura
> ut regere imperio, cives regnumque tueri,
> urbibus ut posses aequas concedere partes,
> patratus patriae nostris celebratus in oris,
> militibusque pater gratus tutorque bonorum,
> excellens ductor, Baetis tutela per orbem.

(*The Song of John of Austria*, hereafter *SJA*, ll. 1–9, pp. 288–9; Latino 1573, 2nd gathering, fol. 2r)[3]

(Deza, dignified by your service and marked by your ancestral piety, on whom nature generously bestowed all the gifts of mind and soul; renowned official and leader of the royal chancery: destiny sent you to Granada to administer civil law, to watch over the kingdom and its people, and to grant equal privileges to its cities. You are revered on our shores as the nation's emissary, a kindly father to the soldiers, protector of the virtuous, skilled commander, and world-renowned guardian of Baetis.)

These verses, arguably the most difficult in the poem, record some essential facts about Deza. A claim to Old Christian family heritage, stature as an inquisitor, and high judicial rank made him the most powerful crown official in Granada. The presidency of the two-pronged judiciary institution, the royal Audiencia and Chancillería, is attested in the lines above with the statement that Deza has authority over civil law by royal designation (ll. 1–6). Similarly, Deza's authority over military matters emerges in the final lines, with the Roman toponym Baetis (l. 9) encompassing Granada and southern Andalusia more generally. These verses also provide a subtle recollection of faction politics in the region. That is, by the time the poet penned these verses, Deza had wrested control over military affairs in Granada from the Marquis of Mondéjar, whose family had controlled such matters since 1492 in their capacity as holders of the *capitanía general* (captancy general).[4]

The poet registers the prestige Deza claimed based on his lineage as "ancestral piety" (pietate insignis avita). In general terms, Latino echoes Aeneas's signature virtue, drawing on the moment the Roman hero asks for admittance to the underworld (*Aeneid* 6.403). In the context of Spain in the later sixteenth century, ancestral piety was shorthand for Old Christian heritage, understood as being free of Jewish and Muslim ancestry. Further indices of how Deza's career advance pivoted on his mobilization of Old Christian identity animate a panegyric that prefaces the epic. The poetic voice draws readers' attention to Pedro de Deza's family ties to an avatar of Old Christian intransigence, Inquisitor General Diego de Deza (1498–1507), a pivotal figure in the expulsion of the Jews.[5] A more pointed allusion within the "pietate insignis avita" connects the praise of Deza to another passage from the *Aeneid*, calling to mind Virgil's evocation of a statesman whose dignified reputation can calm a mutinous mob ("tu pietate gravem ac meritis," *Aeneid* 1.151). These layered Virgilian allusions display a characteristic application of *imitatio* already seen in the elegy to Philip II, with the witty application of Suetonius's *cornix*, or black bird. Here, the poet digs deeper and adds solemnity, as he prepares to monumentalize the naval battle. But this lionization of Deza through the two-tiered reference to the *Aeneid* poses a special interpretive challenge. In structural terms, it recalls Jupiter in the first book of the *Aeneid,* as he looks down from Olympus and across the Mediterranean in the poem's opening passage. What does it mean, above, to watch Lepanto unfold through Deza's eyes?

Stated another way, why begin the epic of John of Austria's Lepanto victory with an exaltation of Deza in Granada? What links the memories of the drawn out war of attrition at home to the decisive morning of galley combat abroad? One of Juan Latino's own students or any other reader of ancient epics might have expected an opening sequence to telescope the entire story ahead in the manner of Virgil's "Arma virumque cano" (Wars and a man I sing, *Aeneid* 1.1). Alternately, the poet might have followed the Homeric opening, with the invocation of a muse. The call to Deza is an invocation, in that the poet asks for his approbation and support. But this passage situates the poet, not on a Parnassus of inspiration, but within the Spanish Monarchy's intertwining layers of judiciary bureaucracy that Deza had navigated to gain his office in Granada, while also enjoying the religious authority of an inquisitor. The question of why the poet begins with a call to this crown official redoubles when one takes into account the widespread distaste for his hard-line policies. Beyond the profound hatred Deza incited among the Morisco communities most directly harmed by his policies, he also provoked more guarded criticisms from John of Austria himself. Long-standing inter-family hatreds also pitted Deza against Granada's most influential noble family, the Counts of Tendilla, and its leader in the period of the Alpujarras revolt, the Marquis of Mondéjar. An idea of Deza's problematic image emerges in the investigation file that a crown auditor (*visitador*) was compiling even as Latino composed his *Song of John of Austria,* a turn of events explored in the closing section of chapter 2.[6] In fact, the controversies surrounding Deza in the aftermath of the Morisco rebellion and his own efforts to contradict the vocal criticism may have provided Latino with a special opportunity to publish his book of poems. A log of palace correspondence records how the Audiencia president sent Latino's Lepanto poem to Philip II's private secretary Antonio Gracián Dantisco just ten months after the Battle of Lepanto. Notably, this poem is a rare literary work that Gracián dispatched in this manner, suggesting a special point of access.[7]

Evidence of this alliance between Latino and Deza appears in an epilogue ("Peroratio") appended to *The Song of John of Austria.* The poet states that Granada's Audiencia president commissioned the epic:

Austriadae bellum navale, et proelia ponto
versibus et claris victricem dicere classem
iussisti nuper, vates num condere possem?
("Peroratio," Latino 1573, 2nd gathering [F1r], unnumbered folio)

(You recently bade me to recount the Austriad's naval battle and clash at sea and the victorious fleet in sonorous verses. How could I, the poet, begin to compose this?)

An accompanying margin gloss adds emphasis, noting that "Deza hoc opus componi iussit" (Deza ordered this work be written). Continuing, the epilogue celebrates the crown's resettlement program then underway under the official's supervision, in which settlers from northern realms such as Galicia and Asturias received grants of confiscated Morisco land. As I noted before, this effort to transform Granada's Hispano-Muslim heartland into an Old-Castilian farming community was a source of frustration as the poet composed the work.

This praise here for the controversial Audiencia president anticipates one of the defining dilemmas of Spain's Golden Age of literature. Time and again, literary culture would thrive on unsupported artists mired in quests for patronage. Alliances with powerful officials or aristocrats could bring financial support and prestige, but often required the writer to flatter notoriously flawed public figures, attack worthy rivals, and sometimes abase themselves. The awkward literary ring of Pedro de Deza's Olympian positioning anticipates the odd heroic architecture of Lope de Vega's epic *La Dragontea* (see Vega Carpio 2007 [1598]). This manifestly Virgilian epic, published a generation after Latino's *Song of John of Austria,* took sides in a bureaucratic dispute about who was the hero who foiled a 1596 attack by Francis Drake, proposing an obscure colonial official as the Spanish Aeneas who stops the dazzling "dragon" Drake. Like Juan Latino three decades before him, Lope probably made this artistically dubious decision because of a commission.[8] It is, therefore, particularly apt that Spain's most famous playwright would later invoke Juan Latino's legacy with mock self-abasement, citing the former slave's bond with the third Duke of Sessa as inspiration for his own "enslavement" to the sixth Duke of Sessa.[9]

For Juan Latino in the early 1570s, like Lope de Vega a generation later, publication obstacles intensified the need for alliances, even setting aside the issue of material support. Clearing official hurdles to publication was an arduous task, particularly with books that recounted the recent history of the Spanish Monarchy. The censorship of Lope's *Dragontea* on the grounds of its unauthorized discussion of recent events in the New World serves as a case in point.[10] Though the licensing dossier for Latino's Lepanto epic has yet to come to light, there are signs of this concern for access to print in the opening page of the volume. A theologian who contributed a prologue hails the freedman for winning over censors with his piety and erudition. He thus asks: "Censores videre pium, doctumque poema,/carpet quis merito nunc opus egregium?" (Censors have seen the pious and learned poem; who will now rightly attack the excellent work?)[11]

Contextual evidence about book publication at this time in Granada gives reasons to take the statement as much more than a commonplace denunciation of naysayers. It is instructive to compare the freedman's relatively fast track to publication – approximately ten months from the poem's completion to the final licence for publication – with the case of another book completed in Granada at this time: Luis del Mármol Carvajal's history of the Morisco revolt languished for over two decades, only appearing in print in 1600, even though the author had reported its publication was imminent in 1573.[12] Given the difficulties of gaining access to print in Philip II's Spain, Juan Latino's alliance with Deza may well have followed from a strategic necessity.

Exposure to censors, furthermore, would have been heightened by Latino's vulnerability in economic and professional terms. Since the new and underfunded University of Granada and Colegio Real did not have tenured teaching chairs, Latino depended on the sponsorship of patrons even in the best of times, as noted in the examination within Part I (chapters 1 and 2) of his social advancement in mid-sixteenth-century Granada. The city that emerged from the rebellion, moreover, likely offered further complications to earning a livelihood. Best available evidence indicates that the university and royal grammar school where Latino had gained his education and professional advancement were in turmoil. Latino's former master and some time sponsor, the Duke of Sessa, was contending with what would become unsustainable debts. Also, the grandee's tactics leading a royal battalion sent to quell the Morisco revolt had caused some loss of influence at court. Latino himself was involved in a long-running legal dispute about a levy of *censos* on his property in the Santa Ana neighbourhood, which pitted him against a crown-licensed tax collector.[13] Without losing sight of the manifest literary ambitions on display in the Lepanto epic, we can reasonably conclude from the context that Juan Latino needed access to

Deza, both for assuring continued material support and for navigating the channels of book censorship. For his part, Pedro de Deza likely commissioned Latino to write the Lepanto epic to counter the many damaging allegations against him.

The protagonism that Latino confers on Pedro de Deza demands reasoned examination in relation to the Granada in which the poet-and-educator composed the Lepanto epic. Earlier studies by V.B. Spratlin and José González Vázquez took note of how the poet deploys a rhetoric of militant Catholicism, but framed their assessments with condescension.[14] Recent considerations of Juan Latino's literary project have offered necessary theoretical rigour, but have emphasized the longer term literary horizons, a perspective that did not allow for the consideration of questions related to the poem's composition in post-civil war Granada. Most notably, Baltasar Fra Molinero has positioned Latino's reputation in the longer range history of Spanish literature of the Golden Age; J. Mira Seo, in turn, has examined the poet-and-educator with respect to classical tradition and African diaspora literature.[15] Missing until now is a detailed examination of the specific local alliances that inclined, or perhaps required the poet to monumentalize Deza and praise his controversial policies.

Going back once more to the opening invocation to Deza, we find an echo of the crown's racialization of Morisco identity. Note how the region's varied communities of Hispano-Muslim descent suffered broad-brushed official classification as a single caste of heretics:

Pervigil ipse diu cognosti cuncta parari,
haereticosque dolos, fraudes Maurosque moveri,
artes, insidias, simulatas ordine technas,
antiquum foedus, pactum caedesque piorum.
Secretum Mauris tunc alta mente repostum
iudicio mentis valuisti cernere princeps.

(*SJA*, ll. 17–22, pp. 288–9; Latino 1573, 2nd gathering, fol. 2r)

(Ever watchful, you knew to anticipate all manner of dangers: the deceit of the infidels, the betrayal of the Moors, their ruses and tricks, artifices masked as truth – all part of their age-old conspiracy to destroy the pious. Your mind's eye, great prince, was able to discern the plot then still buried deep in the minds of the Moors.)

These verses give voice to the accusations that Deza and his allies mobilized to justify the mass expulsions of Moriscos from Granada. These

Spaniards of Hispano-Muslim heritage become at once lapsed Christians (*hereticos*) – like Protestants – and a secretive fifth column affiliated to Spain's Muslim rivals (*dolos, fraudes, Mauros*) based in North Africa and the eastern Mediterranean. The radical simplification within these verses does accurately distil the racial terms with which hard-line officials massed together the region's varied Morisco population. As a result, isolated Arabic-speaking rural communities, urbane Granadinos with seats on the city council, and even a small number of prominent churchmen became objectified and amalgamated into an undifferentiated mass of Muslim enemies of the Spanish Monarchy. It bears repeating, once again, that all Moriscos were nominally Christians, having been required to undergo baptism from the beginning of the sixteenth century. As noted before, Juan Latino would have had numerous examples of such complexity from his own Granada neighbourhood, where significant numbers of Moriscos and Christian immigrants lived in close confines. Lacking other written statements or testimony – whether letters, a will, or other sworn statements – the line between sincere animus and formulaic rhetoric is impossible to draw in the passage above.

Continuing from the call to Deza, the speaking subject hails Deza for regaling John of Austria with his opulent hospitality when he arrived in Granada to quell the revolt (*SJA*, ll. 25–9, pp. 290–1; Latino 1573, 1st gathering, fol. 2v). The Audiencia president's wise council, the poetic voice notes, persuaded the young Habsburg commander to undertake the mass expulsion (*SJA*, ll. 68–73, pp. 292–3; Latino 1573, 1st gathering, fol. 3r). Viewed in light of the rebellion outlined in chapter 2, the poem seems to propose a calculated revisionism. After all, John of Austria's letters from Granada show a more nuanced if not entirely sympathetic view of Moriscos. In particular, he judged Deza's harsh treatment of them as a tactical error and expressed concerns about excessive violence unleashed by crown troops. In this respect, the sad irony underlying the region's history at this time follows from the extent to which an initially wary John of Austria would emerge as a ruthlessly efficient enforcer of the hard-line policy Deza proposed. The La Galera massacre discussed in chapter 2 is the most jarring instance of this tragic outcome.

In light of this recent history, there is a paradoxical appropriateness to the way that Juan Latino makes Granada's rebellion the starting point for Lepanto. In essence, the poet hands Deza the young Habsburg commander's naval victory. A possessive genitive (*tui Ioannis*) allows for a momentary appropriation of the victory at Lepanto for the crown official:

Audi gesta tui iam dantis vela Ioannis,
perlege victorem, quo non felicior alter
in bellum veniens Hispanos duxit ad arma.
(*SJA*, ll. 30–2, pp. 290–1; Latino 1573, 2nd gathering, fol. 2v)

(Listen now to the deeds of your John as he set sail: read about him in victory. No one more blessed than he has ever led the Spanish forces into battle.)

The *tui Ioannis*, in the context of the Spanish Monarchy, implies the relationship of an older advisor (Deza) and a young, high ranking commander (John of Austria).

But even as the lines above propose Deza as the intellectual architect of the recent victory, they also signal a shift in focus from post-rebellion Granada to the forming of battle lines at Lepanto. The direct, line-opening imperative verbs, *audi* (hear) and *perlege* (read), move away from the panegyric register that opens the poem. Now it is time for direct battle narration. Deza will reappear at pivotal moments, called to look upon the forming battle lines at Lepanto as if peering down from an Andalusian Olympus. But the bracing imperative verbs *audi* and *perlege* call the reader's attention to a place at the other side of the Mediterranean. As battle orders come into view, so do alternative conceptions of the people and nations of the *Mare Nostrum*.

Identities in Counterpoint

As if restarting the epic narrative, the poet inserts himself into the action about to unfold. In so doing, he also shifts the focus of his own patronage quest, from Pedro de Deza in Granada to Philip II:

Accipias vates orat supplexque Latinus
en petit, ut grandi tu princeps mente revolvas,
quae numquam saeclis poterit delere vetustas,
quamvis sustineas Augusta negotia solus.
(*SJA*, ll. 52–5, pp. 290–3; Latino 1573, 2nd gathering, fols. 2v–3r)

(The poet Latinus, your suppliant, prays that you receive and ponder in your mind, great prince, these events that time can never erase, even as you alone shoulder the burden of imperial affairs.)

The change in focus is double. First, the poet turns attention away from Deza onto himself. The verses now foreground Juan Latino, as the *vates* or poet who will commemorate the battle in verse. We return, in effect, to the position asserted in the elegy "On the Birth of Untroubled Times," in which Latino introduces himself to Philip II as the new poet that the auspicious new era demands. A second shift relates to the patronage relationship. The verses above refocus attention from Latino as suppliant before Deza to the poet standing before the king himself. Granted, as an Audiencia president, Deza – as reader – could have parsed the term *princeps* in line 53 above to signify his own rank as the foremost crown official in the region. But the Roman imperial lexicon within the passage inclines interpretation more decisively to Philip II. *Princeps*, after all, was the title Augustus Caesar used to emphasize his civilian duties.[16] The passage, in effect, grants the king the imperial title which he had been unable to inherit from his father, Charles V, due to unresolvable differences with the German branch of the Habsburgs.[17] Ear carefully tuned to the Spanish king's already legendary capacity for unceasing, hands-on labour, the poet cannily gives this kingly toil a decidedly imperial lexicon, as "Augusta negotia."

Continuing, Latino moves up the chain of authorities still further, redirecting his supplications to heaven. His prayer for inspiration tailors ancient-Roman polytheism to a Catholic world picture:

Aspiret coeptis ut nostris rector Olympi
et verus mentem dictis incendat Apollo,
iustitiae sol natus homo de virgine Iesus;
Catholicae Musae faveant Hispana canenti,
versibus ut plenum pietatis condere carmen
nunc valeam lotus Parnasi in gurgite sancto,
Romanae Ecclesae, dono virtutis aquarum,
virginis auspiciis narrabo et nomine Christi.

(*SJA*, ll. 56–63, pp. 292–3; Latino 1573, 2nd gathering, fol. 3r)

(May the ruler of Olympus breathe blessings on our undertakings. And may the true Apollo – Jesus, the sun of justice, born a man from a virgin – kindle my mind with eloquence. May the Catholic Muses look with favor on me as I sing of Spanish deeds, so that I might now be able to compose a song filled with pious verses; having bathed in the holy waters of Parnassus, by the grace of baptism in the Roman Catholic Church, I will begin to tell my story with the Virgin Mary's blessing and in Christ's name.)

These lines position Latino's epic at a true crux of Renaissance epic: how could the Christian poet integrate Christ, saints, and angels into the classical epic architecture?[18] This particular synthesis of pagan and Christian motifs shows the inspiration of the widely admired *De partu Virginis* (*The Virgin Birth*) by Jacopo Sannazaro (1458–1530). Like his Neapolitan predecessor, Latino conceives divine mysteries through a Christianized Mount Olympus, with inspiration coming from the Parnassus of baptismal waters and protection from the Virgin Mary's blessing.[19] Such blending of pagan and Christian elements, as Michael Putnam notes, would have been taken in stride by readers and other poets of the era, for whom "the world of Rome is not far distant, whether as a touchstone to highlight the higher morality of the new faith or as a continuing stimulus for the imagination."[20]

While echoing Sannazaro, Latino also adapts a Christianized astral image, the *sol iustitiae*, to conceive of the divine inspiration for literary eloquence. This "Sun of Justice" is most familiar today through Albrecht Dürer's engraving that shows Christ – head surrounded by a blazing halo – atop a lion, with a sword in one hand and the scales of justice in the other. The image emerged from patristic writings, which adapted the Roman god ("Sol Invictus"). The motif gained wide currency through sixteenth-century editions of Pierre Bersuire's repertory of biblical images. The solar and Apollonian imagery above also reveal that Latino was attune to iconographic programs favoured by Philip II, where exaltations and justifications of Spanish imperial power drew on intertwining solar and Apollonian references.[21]

Of particular interest here is how the freedman reaffirms that Catholic baptism has conferred access to a font of pious inspiration ("Catholicae Musae faveant ... Parnasi in gurgite sancto"). This sacramental grounding of Christian devotion offers an alternate conception of virtue to the earlier vision of inherited or ancestral piety, recorded through Pedro de Deza's *pietate avita*. Where Deza's signature virtue stems from his Old Christian lineage, the poet's portrait of his own religiosity comes through the individual embrace of baptism. This claim to piety allows for New Christian subjectivity.

In a manner akin to his self-assertion within the elegy for Philip II, "On the Birth of Untroubled Times," the poet's invocation here emphasizes his singular virtue as a baptized Christian, bypassing, if not explicitly negating, narratives of ancestral black Christianity. Chapter 3 noted how Latino could, at this point, have invoked the black magus, Prester John, or the Ethiopian baptized in the Acts of the Apostles to assert his own claim to Old-Christian identity. Instead, this affirmation of a Christian virtue conferred through baptism sets in motion an alternative conception of Spanish virtue. The opening strain praised Deza's policies against Moriscos, which had hinged on a denial of baptism based on classifications of ethnicity or caste. But here, soon after, the poet affirms a Christian piety nourished by baptismal waters, not blood inheritance.

Through which of these two subject positions should the reader interpret the forming battle lines at sea? Is the focal point of the narrative the Inquisitor's Olympus from which Deza is called to witness John of Austria's glory? Or is it the Parnassus of the baptismal font from which Juan Latino draws divine poetic inspiration, a position that leaves room for New Christian identity? These questions remain open as the poetic voice directs his focus to the battle front.

Christians and Muslims on the Front Line

Shifting from Granada, eastward to Lepanto, the narrative charts how the two massive coalition fleets encounter one another out in the eastern Mediterranean. First to come into view are the Muslim galleys as they navigate westward from Constantinople, here named with pre-Ottoman nomenclature, as the Bosphorus Straits of Byzantium:

> Ut iam Turca phalanx instructis navibus ibat
> per Graias urbes captivam ducere praedam
> coeperat et portus verrens per litora latos;
> saepe Corinthiaci spumas salis aere secabat.
> Tercentum longae rostris stridentibus agmen
> implerant magnum, scindentes aequora naves,
> quot prius in portu Bizantum viderat ingens
> Bosphorus angusto quas misit fervidus aestu.
> In caelum pini surgebant; marmore silva,
> arboribusque frequens fluctus percurrere visa est
> Hispanam versus classem …
>
> (*SJA*, ll. 93–103, pp. 294–5; Latino 1573, 2nd gathering, fol. 3v)

(As the Turkish attack force traveled in a fleet of galleys, it had begun seizing spoils from the Greek cities and sweeping the spacious seaports that lay along the shores, often cleaving the foam of the Corinthian sea with bronze. Three hundred warships with screeching prows filled out the great flotilla as it sliced the waves, the same number mighty Byzantium had seen in the harbor, when the choppy Bosphorus conveyed them through its narrow passage. The masts rose to the sky: a forest on the marble surface of the sea, crowded with trees, seemed to race across the waves toward the Spanish fleet.)

This vivid depiction of galleys as they plow through waves, in effect, transports the reader far from the palace headquarters of Granada's Audiencia, the setting of the Deza encomium that opens the poem. The resulting picture of the battle front balances historical, pedagogical, ideological, and artistic imperatives.

As maritime history, the verses accurately record the coastal raids that typified Mediterranean warfare at sea in the sixteenth century. Seasonal raiding blurred the lines between military action and commerce, between warship and merchant vessel.[22] These lines also convey how galley fleets clung to coastlines, relying on landmarks for basic orientation ("per litora latos"). This proximity, in turn, allowed for the coastal raids ("per Graias urbes ... coeperat") needed to replenish food, water and, most important, captive rowers. In geographic terms, the passage records the Ottoman navy's westward path from Constantinople to the Gulf of Corinth (Lepanto). From the perspective of pedagogy, margin glosses orient Latin apprentices, noting that the Corinthian Sea ("Corinthiaci") correlates in the vernacular to Coranto ("vulgo Coranto"; *SJA, princeps,* fol. 3v). Such basic explanations typify one dimension found within the annotations, which position the book as an extension of classroom teaching or even an interactive Latin lesson.

Beyond these intertwining goals of historiography and classroom pedagogy, however, the passage records how Lepanto resonated in terms of religious affiliation and sectarian conflict in the region. Here, the portrait of the Ottoman fleet blurs what was a decidedly cosmopolitan fighting force. One sees, instead, just one Turkish phalanx ("Turca phalanx") that the Bosphorus strait spews westward. Yet the poet's own sources would have contradicted this conception of a homogeneous enemy force. Detailed battle orders of the Ottoman armada that circulated in maps and news bulletins depicted a multinational fighting force (see figure 12).[23] Perhaps most challenging to the Spanish obsession with Old Christian purity, the Muslim military hierarchy embraced Catholic and Jewish converts to Islam. Kara Hodja ("Caracossa"), commanding a contingent on the right wing, was reputed to be a lapsed Dominican friar. Leading the North African contingent, Calabrian native Uluç Ali ("Luchalí" or "Occhiali") had already become a source of fascination to Spaniards. The ethnically diverse and meritocratic Ottoman command

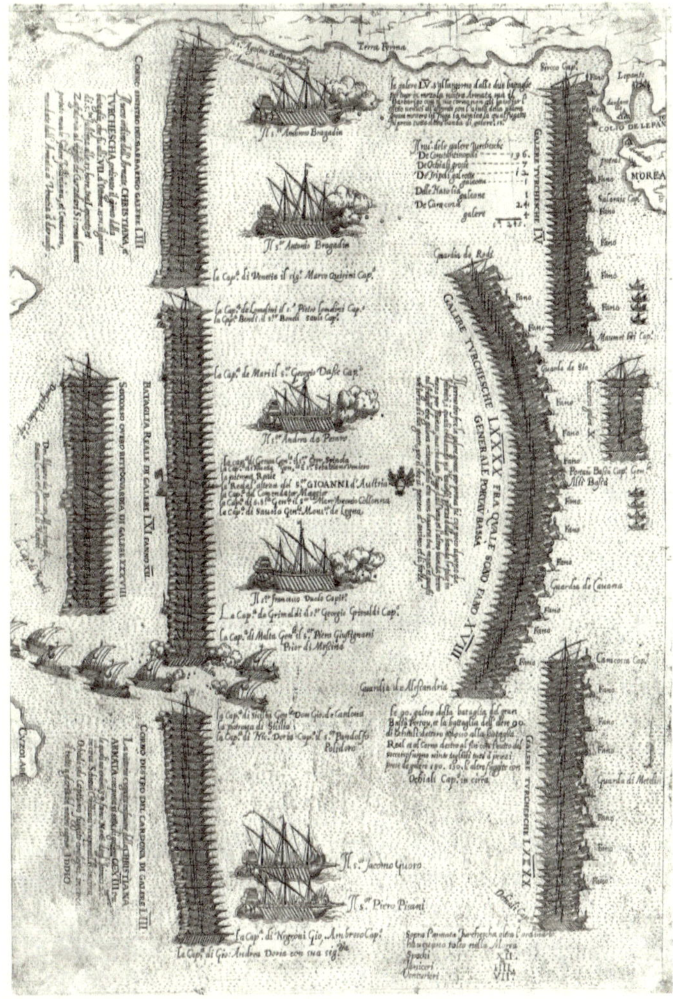

Figure 12 Diagram of Battle Orders at Lepanto, anonymous.

This unsigned map of battle orders records the first cannonade from the Venetian galleasses in the Holy League vanguard. It may be the work of Giovanni Francesco Camocio or a cartographer following a diagram he prepared in Venice.

Source: "Il vero ordine dell'Armate Christiana et Turchescha." From the Real Biblioteca, Madrid, Spain, Map Call # 455 (50). © Patrimonio Nacional.

contrasted with the leaders of the Holy League fleets.[24] Among them, high naval command followed from inherited prestige and titles. John of Austria led the fleet in his capacity as the son of Charles V and half-brother of Philip II; Genoese commander Giovanni Andrea Doria was the grand-nephew of the renowned Andrea Doria, Charles V's foremost naval commander. The papal fleet sailed under the command of Marco Antonio Colonna, scion of the exalted Roman dynasty.

The allusive architecture of *The Song of John of Austria* suggests the poet did grapple with the challenge posed by Ottoman identity. Appropriately, a Virgilian allusion alerts the reader to potential affinities with those sailing in this enemy fleet. The image of the Ottoman fleet slicing through the Corinthian sea ("saepe Corinthiaci spumas salis aere secabat") echoes the first live-action glimpse of the displaced Trojans in the opening sequence of the *Aeneid*:

> Vix e conspectu Siculae telluris in altum
> vela dabant laeti et *spumas salis aere ruebant*.
> (*Aeneid* 1.34–5, emphasis mine, translation below by Fagles p. 48)

> (Now, with the ridge of Sicily barely out of sight,
> they spread sail for the open sea, their spirits buoyant,
> their bronze beaks churning the waves to foam.)

From a literary perspective, Latino's Virgilian borrowing, the "spumas salis aere ruebant," pays homage to the Mantuan's poetics of seafaring. The rhythmic parallel, signalled with Latino's insertion of the citation in the same metric foot where it appears in Virgil, adds emphasis to the narrative parallel. But at the same time, viewed in terms of early modern ethnography, the Trojan reference calls to mind the long-standing association of the early modern Ottoman Turks with ancient Trojans. James Hankins argues that this association underpinned a current of humanist ethnography in which some scholars sought alternatives to the dominant crusader rhetoric.[25] Above, the Trojan connection posed with the "spumas salis aere" invites a similar inquiry as to who exactly are the adversaries at Lepanto. Are they the Muslims whom the opening sequence lumps into one undifferentiated race of enemies? Or, are they Trojan-like warriors, and as such, embodiments of ancestral values of military heroism? When the firing begins, such questions of identity come into still sharper focus.

Returning for now to the image of navigation, the direct citation of the first glimpse of sailing Trojans in *Aeneid* 1 also speaks to a different facet of the poet's Virgilian engagement. This aspect is one that Latino shares with other neo-Latin poets of Lepanto. The enticements of seafaring passages from the *Aeneid* – epitomized above with the "spumas salis aere" – arguably exceed even the allure of Virgil's view of the Battle of Actium in *Aeneid* 8, profound as that inspiration was.[26] In this respect, the view above of the Ottoman fleet sailing towards Lepanto speaks to a particular reverence for Virgil, construed as the consummate poet of navigation, viewed in all its aesthetic power, dangers, and in terms of technical points.

Indeed, as the narration moves ahead to the battle itself, the poem gives further testimony of Juan Latino's appreciation for the intricacies of Mediterranean navigation and of Virgil's position as a touchstone. In one particularly striking passage, as battle lines continue to take shape, Latino honours the nautical prowess of the oldest Holy League commander at Lepanto, Venetian commander Sebastiano Venier:

> Non ille exhorrens Turcas, non arma, procellas;
> ventorum flatus norat maturus et alto,
> murmura silvarum nautis quid prodere pergant,
> ortus, occasus, tacito surgentia caelo
> sidera cuncta, polos geminos, qui in vertice mundi.
> (*SJA*, ll. 601–5, pp. 324–7; Latino 1573, 2nd gathering, *princeps*, fols. 12v–13r)

> (He was not afraid of Turks or artillery or tempests; experienced on the sea, he understood the blasts of the winds, how murmurs of forests can mislead sailors, sunrise, sunset, all the stars that rise in the silent sky, and the twin poles that crown the world.)

The passage balances the demands of recent history and literary tradition. As historical record, the portrait pays special homage to Venier as the most seasoned of all Holy League commanders, drawing attention to his command of Venetian forces at age seventy-five.[27] Venier's ability to adjust his course at sea by listening to the wind murmuring amid treetops epitomizes the expert navigator. The commander listening for rustling leaves reminds us today of how Mediterranean navigation in the sixteenth century continued to depend on cabotage or sailing close to shore, as it had since antiquity.

No less significant here is how the portrait of Venier aboard the Venetian flagship engages Virgil's image of Aeneas and his men sailing to seek an alliance with King Evander in *Aeneid* 8.82–96. The personified Tiber River appears dappled with the reflection of the surrounding forest. Latino's image of stars rising in a silent sky to aid Venier's navigation ("tacito surgentia caelo") reconfigures Virgil's image of Rome's rising imperial power ("Romana potentia caelo"), with lexical echoes reinforced, yet again, by metrical parallels. Also, the vision of expert navigation proposes a metaliterary analogy. That is, Venier's course to Lepanto, guided through the sounds of forests and the positions of stars, figures Juan Latino's poetic navigation to Lepanto, where Virgil is the foremost guide. This sophisticated, textured *imitatio* did not register for influential twentieth-century scholars, who sometimes voiced condescension towards Latino as a black poet.[28]

Continuing his portrait of Venier, the poet does shift from the praise for navigational expertise to the rhetoric of holy war that impelled both the Christian and Muslim fleets towards the battle. The Venetian commander "fiercely hated the Moors and despotic Turks" (oderat infensus Mauros Turcasque tyrannos; *SJA* 608, pp. 326–7; Latino 1573, 2nd gathering, fol. 13r). The result is a marked duality. That is, examinations of less bellicose Mediterranean touchstones, seafaring foremost, mesh with the rhetoric of religious conflict that justifies the imminent naval clash. When the poet airs this crusading ideology, he does accurately capture the main impetus for the two fleets. Indeed, commanders of both the Catholic and Muslim armadas carried orders to destroy the enemy in God's name. Thus, the Ottoman sultan, Selim II, dispatched his lead admiral to "attack the fleet of the Infidels fully trusting in God and his Prophet." Similarly, Philip II reminded his commanders and soldiers that they would be fighting Turks in the name of all Christendom.[29]

A particularly striking visualization of this crusading discourse appears even before Venier's arrival above, at the moment when advancing Ottoman forces espy the Spanish contingent. Muslim adversaries recognize John of Austria's fleet by his standard, adorned with an image of Christ on the cross:

> Cum subito nostras cernunt adnare carinas,
> regalem remis ingenti mole sequentes
> vexillumque crucis celsas volitare sub auras,
> et niveum spargi, fulgere et ducere cursus.

Salvator mundi tendebat brachia fixus
monstrabatque latus cunctis adapertile ferro.
(*SJA*, ll. 114–19, pp. 294–5; Latino 1573, 2nd gathering, fol. 4r)

(Suddenly they see our galleys sailing under oars following behind the royal flagship in a giant mass. Then they see the standard of the cross flying in the air, glimmering like fallen snow to brighten and guide the way. The crucified Savior of the world hung with his outstretched arms, showing to all his spear-pierced side.)

In the *princeps*, a woodcut image of the Crucifixion reinforces the poetic evocation of Christ's passion. The only such illustration inserted into the poem, the woodcut envisions the moment enemy fighters catch sight of the battle standard on John of Austria's flagship.[30]

On their most basic level the Crucifixion image and accompanying verse description document the defining religious symbol for the Holy League fleets. Here, the unspoken point of contrast is the flag that flew opposite to this Crucifixion image. Ottoman admiral Muezzinzade Ali Pasha, John of Austria's counterpart, flew a sumptuous silk banner with thousands of individual panels embroidered with God's name.[31] Consequently, the battle front at Lepanto crystallized an iconographic divide that shaped religious identity across the Mediterranean, but had been a particular issue in the poet's home city of Granada. Images of the cross, unlike those of the Virgin Mary, were anathema to Muslims.[32] A reader of Latino's Lepanto epic who examined the woodcut image of the Crucifixion and parsed the ekphrastic description of that same passion scene within the corresponding verse – "salvator mundi tendebat brachia fixus" – focused his or her mind on a central point of contention at Lepanto. But this point of conflict is by no means the only reference point for Mediterranean identities as battle lines take shape.

Indeed, other reference points for religious affiliation and identity come into view even as the moment of firing draws nearer. Verses record how John of Austria exhorts his soldiers to follow his standard and fight in Christ's name. Fighters repeat his battle cry. But at this moment where the rhetoric of religious warfare is most overdetermined, the poetic voice literally veers away from the cheering Spaniards. In so doing, he reveals a perspective that differs sharply from other poets of Lepanto. Momentarily, Muslim galley slaves chained to the Spanish rowing bench come into view:

Sed remex Maurus captus vinctusque catenis,
inter spem timidus Turcas dum cernit amicos,
iratis ducibus mortem sibi quisque timere.
(*SJA*, ll. 400–2, pp. 312–13; Latino 1573, 2nd gathering, fol. 9r)

(Yet each Moorish rower, captured and bound in chains, is apprehensive even in the midst of his hope when he sees his Turkish comrades, and fears his own death if the commanders are angered.)

Grammar lends a tone of urgency to this passage. The *sed* interrupts the cheering, charging Spaniards with a reminder that some aboard the galleys suffer as soldiers celebrate. Momentarily, the cheering, charging Spanish forces that John of Austria rouses in the previous sequence have faded from view.

This brief but fraught view of a galley slave marks a more ambiguous conception of the fighting about to begin. In light of Juan Latino's own personal experience of the African slave diaspora, the passing evocation of one of the slaves rowing the Spanish galleys into combat carries a special resonance. However brief, the portrait conjures the subject position of a chained rower. In fact, it stands as the most direct depiction of a slave's subjectivity within Latino's published poetry. After all, the autobiographical statement analysed in chapter 1 and reproduced in figure 3 alludes to but does not expound on the experience of the poet and his kin, as one of untold numbers of families torn apart by the era's expanding slave trade.

This passing glimpse of a Muslim galley slave is also noteworthy within the corpus of Lepanto poetry. Latino's best known counterparts, whether writing in Latin or vernacular, do not pause to explore the subject position of the Muslim galley slaves whose steady rowing was a linchpin in the Holy League attack plan. In contrast, several poets of Lepanto evoke the subsequent testimony of Christian rowers who had been chained to Ottoman rowing benches. By way of comparison, the influential prose account of the battle by poet Fernando de Herrera records post-battle testimony of the Christian captives freed from the Muslim galley benches after the fighting, but does not highlight Muslim rowers. Juan Rufo's *Austriada* follows Herrera's lead, briefly hailing the freed Christian galley slaves. Alonso Ercilla's *Araucana* does not evoke enslaved rowers on either side, though his epic bears witness to the suffering of the Mapuche fighters who resist the Spanish conquerors.[33] Latino's perspective here is also unique when examined in relation to the twenty-one neo-Latin poets from Italy featured along with his *Song of John of Austria* in the I Tatti Renaissance Library's *The Battle of Lepanto*.

Shifting to the point of analysis to Latino's first readers, we confront a logical question at this juncture: how did the poet and his most immediate interlocutors construe the "Maurus captus." Plausibly, the chained Moorish rower could be a displaced Granadino of Hispano-Muslim origin. A number of the captive oarsmen chained to Spanish galleys at Lepanto were Moriscos consigned to the galleys as punishment for the revolt of 1568–70. Even as Juan Latino was preparing his epic for publication, his commissioning patron, Pedro de Deza, was working to capture any Moriscos still hiding in the region, after which they would be designated as galley slaves.[34] The logic aired in the verses above ("inter spem timidus Turcas dum cernit amicos") was the same reasoning that sealed the fate of Granada's Moriscos, including those who did not take up arms against the crown: officials averred that Moriscos were a secret fifth column who made Spain vulnerable to the expansionist aims of the Ottoman empire. "Amicos" distils such accusations, signifying not only friendship, but also partisanship and ties of clientage. A Virgilian allusion here would allow for an association of the "Maurus captus" with Granada's Moriscos as conceived by hostile crown officials. Maxim Rigaux draws attention here to the hemistich "sibi quisque timere," a direct echo of the elaborate lie the Greek fighter Sinon tells the Trojans to convince them to allow the wooden horse into their city.[35] His assessment of this scene reminds us of how the reference to a famously deceptive Greek soldier could support the prevailing Spanish views of deceptive Moors or Moriscos, an accusation used frequently to justify the indiscriminate punishment in Granada. This potentially negative allusion to Sinon, however, must be weighed against the strong emotional pathos of the hapless galley slave who wonders if he will ever see home again.

Notwithstanding potential echoes specific to Granada's violent civil war, a "Maurus captus" could also be a North African Muslim. *Maurus*, as an early modern ethnonym, pivoted on an ambiguity whose consequences were particularly dire for Spain's Hispano-Muslims. In this respect, the "Maurus captus" registers the tragedy of Spain's Moriscos, which played out after an influential coterie of church and crown officials essentially carried out a de facto reclassification of baptized Christians from Granada, rendering this native population as foreign agents. *Cristianos nuevos de moros* became increasingly viewed as *Mauros*, understood in vague terms as part of a cosmopolitan alliance of Muslim enemies of the Spanish Monarchy.

Whether one conceives the "Maurus captus" in precise material terms as an enslaved Granadino or in more general terms as a Moor, a tragic premonition emerges from the brief but searing glimpse of the galley slave. Discerning the captive rower's furtive backward glance, a nameless Spanish overseer orders him to keep his eyes forward and maintain the steady oar strokes needed to power the Spaniards into combat. Should John of Austria prevail, the slave might gain freedom. Failure to row steadily, in contrast, will bring summary execution:

"Quod si mendosus remum nunc pellere tentas
ut Turcis operam des iam victoribus, ipse
tardanti stricto hoc iugulum mucrone resolvam.
Proditor et salsas ibis iam truncus in undas."
(*SJA*, ll. 409–12, pp. 312–15; Latino 1573, 2nd gathering, fol. 9v)

("But if you treacherously strive to row the oars to assist the Turkish conquerors, I myself will sever your laggard's neck with this drawn sword. Then your body, traitor, will fall headless into the salty waves.")

This threat of summary execution at sea marks an emotional turning point. Earlier scenes of combat preparations depicted military regalia, intricate battle standards, and aired the formal oratory of the harangues through which commanders roused troops. But now, the poetic voice examines a more private moment of suffering. Defying the would-be executioner, the oarsman casts a furtive glance at the Ottoman standard. The sight sparks nostalgia for the "sweet fields" of his lost homeland ("impellens dulcis patriae reminiscitur agros"; *SJA*, l. 417, pp. 314–15; Latino 1573, 2nd gathering, fol. 9v). This brief reverie offers what will be, within the poem, a rare and fleeting glimpse of a private realm beyond either the maritime battle front itself or the palaces where leaders plot military strategy and await battle news. As a witness to a slave's yearning for his lost homeland, the verse carries the added poignancy that follows from Juan Latino's personal connection to the unfolding African diaspora. His own missing or unspoken family history, charted in chapter 1, was a casualty of the Atlantic slave trade as it expanded during the sixteenth century.

The view of the galley slave's suffering also signals the intensifying engagement with the *Aeneid*. For one, the captive's headless torso ("truncus"), conjured menacingly by the Spanish overseer, connects the *Song of John of Austria* to the vanquished Troy. Specifically, the profaned body wantonly discarded at sea by an executioner recalls King Priam's death by decapitation at the hands of the merciless, unrepentant Neoptolomus (*Aeneid* 2.549–68). In chapter 5, I will return to the echoes of Priam, when I analyse how the poet reflects on the human costs of the naval battle.

But for now, another literary connection within the "truncus" requires attention. This image of violent death speaks to Juan Latino's engagement with another revered classical predecessor, Lucan. Yet unlike the explicit and sometimes insistent engagement with Virgil, the Lucanian debt will remain unacknowledged even as it comes into sharper focus.

Lucan Implied

In narrative terms, the Spanish commander's menace – "salsas ibis iam truncus in undas" – retraces the steps of a terrifying premonition in Lucan's *De bellum civile* (*Civil War* or *Pharsalia*). Book 1 closes with a woman's dire prediction of Pompey's murder and decapitation: "Hunc ego, fluminea deformis truncus harena/qui iacet, agnosco" (Him I recognize, lying on the river sands, an unsightly headless corpse; Lucan, *De bellum civile* 1.685–6; Braund 1992, 21). Latino follows the narrative path of Lucan's premonition as he inserts the headless torso in a prediction of doom ("ibis iam truncus in undas"). To be sure, this allusion is more an evocation than the kind of direct citation of Virgil we see time and again in *The Song of John of Austria*. But the *truncus* as a harbinger of violent death for the unnamed Muslim galley slave points us to a decidedly Lucanian concern with the suffering of anonymous fighters.

Indeed, at many points, the emotional impact of Lucan's galley clash in *Civil War* Book 3 (ll. 509–762) stems from his devastating view of how common soldiers bear the brunt of galley warfare. Unnamed fighters fall overboard and flail helplessly in a vortex of blood and saltwater. Latino's emphasis on the *truncus* adrift serves as but a first marker of a Lucanian view of war within the descriptive fabric of *The Song of John of Austria*. Yet the debt remains unspoken, in contrast to the much-vaunted engagements with Virgil's *Aeneid*. Why the silence?

That Juan Latino would draw on Lucan, by itself, seems natural, even necessary. Spanish poets and theorists claimed Lucan as a "poeta español" given his birth in Roman Hispania. They also hailed his singular power to render "historia verdadera" (true history) in verse.[36] For Latino in particular, the natural Spanish attraction to Lucan would have intensified in light of their common ties to Córdoba. Notwithstanding their Neapolitan title, the Dukes of Sessa whom Juan Latino had served as a slave rooted their foremost claim to stature in the house of Córdoba, as attested in their surname, Fernández de Córdoba. A family history plausibly records Latino's birth in their Baena, Córdoba estate, a claim I assess in chapter 1. Even without the certainty of a birthplace, we know Latino's early childhood service to the third Duke of Sessa involved significant time in the family's Córdoban lands.[37] When Latino perfected the Roman language in late childhood and deepened his engagement with classical literature, Córdoba's own ancient epic poet would have been an example and inspiration.

Given the evident ties to Lucan, the reason for the silent engagement with the foremost epic poet of Roman Córdoba invites further reflection. One reason may follow from the unsettling subtext of civil war. Spanish commentators of Lucan's poem conceived Rome's civil war the "revuelta de Roma" (Roman revolt).[38] The ten books of his *Civil War* offered many scenes and statements that could have been applied to evoke Granada's own recent revolt. To cite just a few of the many eerily adaptable scenes, one could turn to the moment Romans tremble at how war will devastate their city (Book 1.257–65), or the poet's lament for the resources squandered in civil war instead of empire building abroad (Book 2.111–73), or in the depiction of the city's wealth plundered by Caesar's own troops (Book 3.154–68). The events that transpired in Granada after the Morisco revolt broke out featured many Lucanian settings, a point most evident in reading Hurtado de Mendoza's chronicle, with its strong classical inflections. Most disquieting of all, Lucan's poetic voice insists, time and again, that war waged at home is by definition unwinnable because it is by nature impious (*nefas*) and evil (*scelus*).[39]

It stands to reason that, for a poet writing an epic in post-rebellion Granada, Lucan is a predecessor best handled with delicacy. Virgil's *Aeneid* must have seemed a more manageable reference point, for all its many ambiguities and reservations, about which the next chapter will have more to say. Indeed, this negotiation between two epic models comes into still sharper focus as the narrative shifts from forming battle lines to the combat itself.

5 The Costs of Modern Warfare

Combat Examined

At the moment a Holy League fleet of unprecedented size prepares to fire on an equally formidable Muslim coalition navy, the stars seem to align for the epic sublime. John of Austria, son of the Holy Roman Emperor, was poised to take on Ali Pasha, the sultan's brother-in-law. At last, modern times had brought the would-be poet laureate an occasion of the magnitude of the great epic battles of antiquity, whether Hector against Achilles in the *Iliad* or Aeneas facing Turnus in the *Aeneid*. Also conferring epic dimensions, these two commanders found one another just south of the site where Octavian faced Mark Antony in the Battle of Actium. Latino, in tandem with scores of poets, chroniclers, and map makers, registered the historical and thematic parallels. But once combat actually begins in Book 2 of *The Song of John of Austria*, some questions emerge that complicate the task of moulding the chronicle of Lepanto into epic form. Here, Juan Latino's rigorous adherence to first-line reports and news bulletins for his battle narration introduces some tensions within the overall poetic agenda, of updating ancient epic to recount empire building in his own time. Clio, in effect, clashes with Calliope. In the pages ahead, I examine this tension between historical documentation and epic artistry. Analysis will scrutinize the poet's use of his source materials and his narrative sequencing, comparing such choices to other writers of the day who prepared Lepanto commemorations.

Following the first news bulletins of the battle, Latino captures the moment the battle begins. The six largest galleasses in the Venetian vanguard unleash a devastating cannonade on the Ottoman front line, a moment frozen in time in figure 12. I cite the complete sequence that captures the first volley of cannon fire, in order to highlight crucial artistic and ethical issues that come into play:

> Sulfura iamque globos spargebant picea fumo
> permixtos, crebris aether micat ignibus ingens.
> Tunc sonitu curva et resonabant litora late,
> fluctibus in mediis geminantia saepe fragorem.
> Non lapides iactos Turcae perferre valebant.
> Saxis nam crebris repetebat saepe procella;
> queis capita et dentes, oculos cerebrumque refringi,
> malas, mandibulas, resoluta et pectora cernas.
> Rupibus et nubes iam terque quaterque cadebat
> machina, nec colubri poterant, nec sulfura pelli.
> (*SJA*, ll. 1016–25, pp. 352–3; Latino 1573, 2nd gathering, fol. 20v)

> (And now the pitch-black sulfur discharges clouds mixed with smoke, as the mighty ether flashes with repeated fire. Then the curved shoreline resounds far and wide, sometimes echoing the din in the middle of the waves. The Turks are unable to endure the volley of stones. The storm is relentless, dense with rocks: you could see heads, teeth, eyes, and brains shattered by them, cheeks, jaws, and torsos gone limp. Three and four times the war engine dropped clouds of rock. Neither culverins nor artillery fire could be repelled.)

As a chronicle of the battle, these verses convey the astounding firepower of the Venetian merchant ships repurposed for war at sea with cannons whose size and weight exceeded the capacity of lighter Mediterranean galleys. The passage above also demonstrates that galley warfare in the era was not naval combat in the strictest sense, but rather amphibious warfare, with the relationship of a fleet to shore as critical as its position relative to the opposing fleet. In particular, the poet captures the proximity of land through the echoing shoreline.[1] In dramatizing the destruction in terms of bodies broken apart ("queis capita et dentes, oculos cerebrumque refringi,/malas, mandibulas, resoluta et pectora cernas"), he also follows closely the first reports and chronicles. This particular view of the destruction resembles the influential early chronicle from Venetian Giovanni Pietro Contarini, who also records the opening cannonade as an unprecedented destructive force and records the bodies and galley parts scattered across the waves.[2]

In artistic terms, the passage above is noteworthy on several issues. First, we see a careful avoidance of neologisms to describe the modern artillery. Note the last two lines of the passage above. The *coluber* (snake) signifies the cannon, *sulfur* becomes a synecdoche for the artillery fire, and the rocks (*rupes*) denote the ordnance spewed from heavy artillery. In effect, the poet marshals classical Latin to dramatize early modernity's most fearsome innovation – gunpowder weapons. Above, the concision and rhythm of Latin hexameters captures the indiscriminate mutilation that artillery fire unleashes. The cannon fire, after all, kills Turkish soldiers without engaging them in reciprocal combat, after which it erases their humanity, leaving a mass of distended body parts.

This poet's choice to examine artillery fire's impact in concrete terms contrasts with the abstraction or stylization that predominates in the poetry of Lepanto. Michael Murrin thus drew attention to how Alonso de Ercilla's *Araucana* and Juan Rufo's *Austriada* do not offer direct descriptions of Holy League firepower.[3] A particularly illuminating contrast to Latino's documentary approach is the prose chronicle of Lepanto by another poet of Andalusia, Seville native Fernando de Herrera. Like Latino, Herrera crafted his commemoration of the battle as soon as the news of the victory reached Spain. Dates of their respective licensing suggest the two poets worked in parallel, most likely without knowing the other's work given they were based in different cities.[4] Though in prose, his *Relación de la guerra de Chipre y suceso de la Batalla Naval de Lepanto* featured such vivid poetic language and stunning imagery that it quickly emerged as a touchstone for subsequent Castilian poetic accounts of the naval clash. The 1572 edition of the history culminated with a celebratory *canción* that stretches to 21 stanzas (*CODOIN* 21:375–82). Here, the poet distils the history of Lepanto into a broad-brush celebration of the battle as a clash of the Christian West, viewed as God's own army, confronting a Muslim East, construed as Pharoah's army ("Frente de Faraón"; *CODOIN* 21:375). The title and subtitle capture the poet's interpretation of the triumph as the work of Providence: "Canción en alabanza de la Divina Majestad por la vitoria del señor don Juan" (Song in praise of the Divine Majesty for the Victory of the Lord Don John).

In due course, both Ercilla and Rufo would emulate Herrera's prose chronicle, as would Portuguese poet Jerónimo de Corterreal. Mercedes Blanco has demonstrated, moreover, that the Guatemala-based Latinist Francisco de Pedrosa transposed a passage from Herrera into his hexameter poem on Lepanto, the *Naumachia* completed circa 1580.[5] A comparison between Herrera and Latino is illuminating since the two poets prepared accounts of Lepanto in parallel, but emerged with different notions of what constitutes an appropriate song of Lepanto.

Two Versions of Lepanto

In narrative terms, Herrera's prose history covers the same ground as Latino, recounting how an opening volley of cannon fire devastated the Ottoman vanguard. But compare Latino's noxious hail fire – cited above – to Herrera's view of the same opening cannonade:

> [Las] galeazas comenzaron a disparar con grandísima furia y priesa, levantando las balas por cima de la agua. Los turcos, sintiendo el daño que les hacían, porque ninguna defensa podía resistir a la violencia de su ímpetu, bogaron con mucha presteza por guardarse dellas sin embestillas. (*CODOIN* 21:356)
>
> (The galleasses began to fire with intense fury and speed, launching the artillery over the sea. The Turks, feeling the harm these weapons inflicted on them – because they had no power to resist the force of destruction – rowed swiftly to protect themselves without engaging them in combat [ramming into enemy galleys].)

We have the same moment Latino dramatized. But where Latino's verses literally unpack the cannonade to show sulphur, cannon balls, and fire, Herrera's prose conveys the violence of artillery fire with abstracting nouns, of fury, speed, damage, and violence. From their comparable initial perspectives of the first volley of fire from the Holy League vanguard, the two accounts diverge in focus. Herrera's narrator, in effect, flies overhead to offer a bird's-eye view of the unfolding battle. He takes note of a fleeing Turkish column that escapes the destruction in the centre to attack Venetians on the left flank. Moving on, he details events on the right flank. To conclude, Herrera does return to the question of the Holy League artillery. But here, his position might surprise readers familiar with condemnations of the "fraud" of gunfire that Miguel de Cervantes would distil in Don Quijote's speech, "Arms and Letters." The poet here avers that the new danger from gunpowder weapons makes modern war more heroic than the great battles from antiquity.[6]

In contrast to Herrera's panorama of the entire theatre of combat that characterizes both the lengthy prose history and the ensuing "Canción en alabanza de la Divina Majestad," Juan Latino's poetic voice dwells on the scene of the first cannonade. So doing, the *Song of John of Austria* retains its opening focus on the fighting in the centre where the two flagships clash. Here, the poet's fealty to the first news bulletins and eyewitness accounts yields potentially unsettling details about the victory. Though the preliminary verses and elegy for Philip II propose to "sing" of Lepanto as a great triumph and harbinger of imperial expansion ahead, some of the specifics of how the victory comes about invite questions about empire's ethical costs.

One such up-close exploration of heroism takes shape as the Ottoman admiral, Ali Pasha, enters the picture. Immediately after the opening volley of cannon fire, Ali comes into view, as if the black fog of gunpowder has momentarily cleared. As a counterpoint to the fire the galleasses unleash, the Ottoman admiral draws his bow and rallies the troops unnerved by the cannonade:

> Nunc Bassan gladio pugnat nunc flectit et arcum,
> bracchiaque extendens nunc mittit ab aure sagittas.
> (*SJA*, ll.1050–1, pp. 354–5; Latino 1573, 2nd gathering, fol. 21r).

> (Now the Pasha wields the sword, now he bends the bow, and extending his arms he launches arrows from ear level.)

This image of a seasoned warrior's raw strength, as he pulls back the stiff bow string ("flectit") and fires with outstretched muscles ("bracchiaque extendens nunc mittit"), brings forth a counterpoint to the opening view of firepower. Though Ali Pasha enters the action as an enemy commander who shouts the sultan's orders to destroy Spanish troops, some aspects of his leadership incline to a nostalgic position. With the increased importance of the cannon in contemporary warfare, Spanish poets and theorists exalted the *diestro brazo*, understood as the strong, experienced arm of an aristocratic military commander, a motif that Leah Middlebrook has illuminated in her examination of the courtly turn in lyric poetry.[7] Here, the notion of the commander's "battle-tested arm" drawing the bow revives the Castilian tradition of the *diestro brazo*, albeit through an enemy commander.

A margin gloss adds further emphasis to this portrayal of the Ottoman admiral preparing to fight, drawing attention to the image of "Bassan, et dux et miles" (the pasha, commander and soldier; Latino 1573, 2nd gathering, fol. 21r, margin). Like the portrait of the leader drawing his bow, the gloss momentarily extracts Ali Pasha from the rhetoric of religious warfare that opens the poem and reappears at key points. Yet here, Ali stands not so much as an avatar of an enemy religion as he does a practitioner of a storied military art. The interplay of text and margin suggests a pedagogical working of the kind Craig Kallendorf has analysed, in that the gloss points readers to a passage from which they can extract practical knowledge.[8] Viewed in isolation, the Ottoman commander embodies military virtue. Might there also be a hint of wistful longing for the soldier-rulers of eras past? For Juan Latino and any contemporaries with some knowledge of the inner workings of the high Spanish military command of the day, Ali's direct leadership in battle contrasts with the bureaucratization of Spain's high command. In fact, this development was a particularly sensitive issue for Latino's title hero. Both at Lepanto and in Granada two years before, John of Austria chaffed at the requirement that he vet all military decisions with the councillors his brother commissioned to supervise him.[9] Viewed in light of Philip II's imposition of a supervisory role for John of Austria in combat, the brief view of Ali Pasha rousing troops for combat and fighting alongside them harkens back to military leadership construed through action rather than managerial oversight.

Continuing with the unfolding combat, the poet closely follows the first news bulletins of the battle, as verses detail the bloody, hand-to-hand combat that transpires aboard Ali Pasha's command ship. With the Ottoman front line weakened by the opening cannonade, John of Austria's *Real* rams the Ottoman flagship, the *Sultana*. At this point, Latino could have followed other Lepanto poets, in using the clash of two fleets to name individual fighters. The epic catalogue offered a natural framework for such accounts. By way of comparison, we can return briefly to Herrera's narrative: having taken an overhead view of the different sections of the battlefield, he ultimately distils the battle's fury through dramatic cameos of individual aristocrats. Thus, he hails Pedro de Malta from Zaragoza, who bravely boards an enemy galley armed with only his sword and shield, striking down four enemy fighters. Likewise, he celebrates Antonio de Paredes, who boards an enemy galley despite the arrows lodged in his leg and side; there he fights to reach the mainmast and only then, succumbs to an arrow through his neck (Herrera, in *CODOIN* 21:360). The poet does not conceal the widespread destruction or horrors of war. But he calibrates the battle's epochal nature in terms of the individual heroic deeds of noble fighters armed with the traditional weapons of the high aristocracy.

Taking a different narrative strategy to transport the reader into the fog of war, Latino focuses the view of combat through nameless foot soldiers. Once galleys from opposing sides have rammed and boarded one another's boats, an undifferentiated mass of soldiers moves forward and back in deadly embrace. At this moment, the freedman presents a compressed and dramatic version of a moment that many of the first news bulletins agreed was a turning point: the three charges through which John of Austria's forces sought to capture the mainmast of the Ottoman flagship. Here, the poet uses the repetition of polyptoton to convey the lethal pile-up of men with both sound and syntax: "Virque viro certans infense./Pesque pedi stat" (Man vied fiercely against man. Foot treads on foot; *SJA*, l. 1060, pp. 354–5; Latino 1573, 2nd gathering, fol. 21r). The sense of extreme compression wrought through polyptoton captures the special danger of combat on the cramped galley decks, where the danger of falling overboard and drowning compounded the threat of enemy weapons. Dramatizing this peril, the poet marshals a simile to visualize the flailing of soldiers who have fallen overboard:

> Delphinum similes iuvenes immania cete,
> per fluctus videas timidos optare salutem.
> (*SJA*, ll. 1073–4, pp. 354–5; Latino 1573, 2nd gathering, fol. 21v)

> (You could see scared youths struggling for safety in the waves like dolphins alongside huge whales.)

On its own merits, the dolphin simile proposes an ingenious conceit. Doomed soldiers who have slipped or been pushed off galley decks become flapping dolphins, dwarfed by galleys as large as whales in comparison.

Powerful on its own, the image gains still more impact through allusion. Once again, Latino adapts an image from Virgil, who likens the young Trojans manoeuvring in the funeral games of *Aeneid* Book 5 to swimming dolphins. The hexameter to which Latino alludes thus reads:

> Impediunt texuntque fugas et proelia ludo
> *delphinum similes*, qui per maria umida nando.
> (*Aeneid* 5.593–4, emphasis added)

> (Weaving/their way through mock escapes and clashes all in sport/as swiftly as frisky dolphins skim the rolling surf.)
> (Fagles 2006, 173)

As before, a structural likeness accents the lexical repetition, with the comparative phrase "delphinum similes" in the same metrical position in Latino as it is in the corresponding passage from Virgil.

This choice of allusion might initially seem less apt than the echoes of Virgil's account of the Battle of Actium in *Aeneid* 8. Yet this citation points to another touchstone for neo-Latin poets of Lepanto, for whom the funeral games of *Aeneid* 5 are as rich a source of inspiration as is Virgil's Actium. Book 5 offered Juan Latino and other contemporary poets who commemorated Lepanto a different range of poetic settings. Specifically, the funeral games display young men in their prime pushing themselves to the limit of their strength and resilience, through boat races, the boxing match, a shooting contest, and the simulated battle.[10]

While honouring this facet of Virgil's legacy, Latino's dolphin simile departs from its Virgilian model in a crucial respect. That is, the freedman's comparison dwells on the suffering of anonymous soldiers who have fallen off galley decks in the heat of battle. This contrasts to Virgil's exaltation of elite Roman families in the athletic competition of their putative Trojan ancestors. Diverging in this key respect, Latino deploys the dolphin simile to memorialize the kinds of soldiers whose names do not figure in the news bulletins and chronicles that served as the freedman's sources. This concern with anonymous fighters attests, once again, to an unspoken debt to Lucan. The view of young men flailing in the water calls to mind Lucan's own scene of naval combat in *Civil War* 3, where unnamed soldiers fall from galley decks in the thick of battle.[11]

A connection here to the great epic poet of Roman Hispania brings to light the same duality chapter 4 revealed. That is, Latino's debt to Lucan goes unmentioned, in contrast to the repeated instances where the poet and his prologuists advertise the Virgilian connection. Again, this silence might stem from the sensitive nature of an ancient civil war, readily adaptable to the recent war that had devastated Latino's home city. Or, the silence might follow from long-standing literary hierarchies; that is, from late-antiquity to the Renaissance, hierarchically minded commentators ranked Virgil first among epic poets, with Lucan relegated to second.[12] That said, the two predecessors are not irreconcilable opposites who force the poet to choose one legacy over the other. Lucan, after all, composed his *Civil War* in dialogue with Virgil, as his most illustrious predecessor.

Latino maintains the stance between two predecessors as fighting continues from the dolphin simile. Suddenly, the seeming impasse of fierce combat breaks with an announcement that momentarily interrupts the chain of action verbs:

> Hic Bassan caesus fertur gladioque perisse,
> atque humilis miles truncum liquisse superbum.
> (*SJA*, ll. 1075–6, pp. 354–5; Latino 1573, 2nd gathering, fol. 21v)

> (At this moment, Ali Pasha is said to have been struck and to have perished by the sword. Some lowly foot soldier reportedly left nothing but a proud torso.)

The impersonal verb *fertur* (it is said) attributes the information of Ali's death to a vaguely defined oral tradition. This contrasts with the direct combat analysed above, where the subjunctive *videas* (you could see) situates the poetic voice and reader at the scene of the battle. But now, the *fertur* marks a degree of narrative and ethical distance by means of an Alexandrian footnote, understood as an attribution of information to source material.[13] In the passage above, the *fertur* moves away from the discursive markers of direct eyewitness (*videas*) to the register of an oral history.

Another notable feature in the scene of Ali Pasha's death is the asymmetry with respect to the heroic architecture of classical epic. Selim II's brother-in-law has succumbed, not to John of Austria, but to an unnamed Spanish foot soldier ("humilis miles"). Among the many questions Ali Pasha's death in combat raises, one is particularly Virgilian. Should John of Austria have spared the life of an admired enemy commander? This ethical crux of classical epic takes on the added freight of the epic environment specific to Habsburg imperialism, where a central justification for wars of conquest was the efficacious religious conversion of the vanquished.

A Battlefield Execution under Scrutiny

Questions that arise from Ali Pasha's death at the hands of an unnamed foot soldier redouble upon consideration of Latino's sources. Until this moment, Latino's narrative has rigorously adhered to the facts and narrative sequence offered in the earliest Venetian and Spanish battle reports. Yet in the account of Ali's death, the poet blurs agency, despite the fact that his sources attribute the enemy death to John of Austria. For instance, gentlemen-soldier Nicolás Augusto de Benavides described how one of John of Austria's bodyguards killed Ali Pasha after the Turk refused to surrender to the Habsburg. Then in a gesture as harsh as it was routine in early modern warfare, Spaniards cut off the Turkish admiral's head to display as a trophy.[14] From the moment of reckoning to the execution and subsequent desecration of the corpse, Benavides ascribes full agency to John of Austria. No statement of regret for the body's desecration emerges; this practice, after all, united Christian and Muslim armies across battle lines, as accounts of how Ottoman captors treated fighters captured in the sieges of Malta and Cyprus attest.

A similarly direct account of Ali Pasha's death anchors the Venetian report dispatched aboard the *Angelo Gabrieli*, first of the heralds of the victory in Holy League lands. Likewise, the first report that the Spanish command unit sent to Philip II offers the same basic account. In matter-of-fact prose, it states that Spaniards slit the throats of Ali Pasha and 500 other Turks: "fue Dios servido dar la victoria a la Real de su Magestad de la Real del Turco, degollando el Bassá con más de quinientos Turcos" (God's will was done granting victory to his majesty's flagship over that of the Turk, cutting the throats of the pasha and 500 other Turks). *Degollar* in this context could literally mean they decapitated the commander and hundreds of others with sword strikes, or more metaphorically, that they executed them.[15] As above, no intimations of regret emerge, whether for the Turkish commanders killed instead of captured alive, or for the subsequent defilement of a respected adversary's corpse. The mass slaughter of prisoners recorded in this passage follows from a grim protocol of Mediterranean warfare at sea: victors would have interviewed prisoners to identify and then summarily execute fighters with special skills in gunnery, archery, or other military arts that took years of practice to perfect.[16] Official dispatches from Lepanto record John of Austria in full command during the summary executions, with no indication of his discomfort with this routine practice.

As word travelled in the weeks and months ahead, the accounts of Ali's death split into diverging paths, where a key point of distinction was precisely the degree to which John of Austria was responsible for his Ottoman counterpart's fate. Earliest Italian chroniclers of Lepanto conceive the young Habsburg in direct command, gleefully striking down his adversary. Italians do not seem to register that Philip II had ordered his half-brother to refrain from direct combat and installed a troika of advisors to supervise him. Undeterred by the realities of this command structure, Gerolamo Diedo, a Venetian official in Corfu, portrayed a dazzling John of Austria waving a bloody sword.[17] Diedo's vivid picture of the commander's "gagliardezza incredibile" (wondrous bravery) gestures to the aesthetic pleasure associated with epic heroes engaged in single combat. Among the many Italian poets who followed on such heroic intimations, Giovanni Battista Arcucci, a jurist and theologian from Naples, envisioned a scene that harkens to Homer's Achilles. His John of Austria cuts a path of destruction across the Ottoman command unit, cutting down Ali Pasha, then slashing onward to strike down a series of enemies. This Achillean view of John of Austria would have staying power in Italian historiography, to the point that even Pope Pius V's first biographer succumbed to the epic temptation. His account of this moment at Lepanto emphasizes the heroic fury with which the Habsburg cuts down Turkish adversaries ("tagliando a pezzi"). In this telling, Spanish soldiers then present their commander with Ali Pasha's head, whereupon he joyfully displays it and cries victory.[18]

In light of these exaltations of John of Austria's heroic fury in the earliest Italian news bulletins, Latino's version of Ali Pasha's death reads, at a minimum, as a guarded recalibration of facts. Again, the verb *fertur* (it is said) deflects the event to other, unnamed sources. The executioner is not John of Austria or an officer accompanying him. Rather, it is an anonymous foot soldier ("humilis miles").

A telling detail in this narrative sequence is how Juan Latino's version juxtaposes Ali's post-mortem desecration with the Holy League's most prominent casualty, Venetian Agostino Barbarigo. In command of one contingent within the Serenissima's large fleet, Barbarigo managed a daring manoeuvre, pivoting his unit to better face the Ottoman right flank, withstanding a devastating hail of arrows from its elite Janissaries.[19] Just after this crucial pivot, the Venetian was mortally wounded by an arrow to the eye. The poet registers this sacrifice with two classical allusions:

> Barbarigo Venetus, perfosso lumine telo –
> Hannibalem referens – postquam victoria parta est
> magnanimus dixit: "Placida nunc morte quiescam."
>
> (*SJA*, ll. 1191–3, pp. 362–3; Latino 1573, 2nd gathering, fol. 23v)

(Barbarigo the Venetian, his eye pierced by an arrow – bringing to mind Hannibal – declared heroically after victory was assured, "I will now rest in a peaceful death.")

The first allusion seems particularly fitting as a testament to Barbarigo's tactical feat at Lepanto. That is, it compares him to the Carthaginian general regarded as the consummate military tactician; in particular, the passage recalls how Hannibal lost an eye during his Alpine crossing in the Second Punic War. This historical reference would have drawn on Livy's *History of Rome*. More unsettling, however, is the second classical allusion. Barbarigo's magnanimous last words echo the Trojan pilot Palinurus in *Aeneid* 6.371: "sedibus ut saltem placidis *in morte quiescam*" [emphasis added], that is, "at least in death/I'll find a peaceful haven" (Fagles 2006, 194). In common with other Virgilian references, a parallel metrical positioning accents the lexical repetition. On the face of it, the citation might seem a straightforward case in which the poet borrows a sonorous Virgilian phrase about resting in peace. As an example of bravery, Barbarigo's death and last words would be suitable material for extraction into commonplace books or for study as an example of bravery.[20]

Yet the story of Virgil's Palinurus, when viewed in its full narrative context, adds an unsettling note. The Trojan ship pilot had fallen overboard, unnoticed by his comrades, after falling asleep at the helm (*Aeneid* 5.830–71). He then drifted for three days and nights, until at last he caught sight of Italian shores. But when he finally managed to swim to land, savage coastal residents stabbed him to death and stripped him of valuables. Aeneas thus finds Palinurus languishing without a proper burial (*Aeneid* 6.359–61). The declaration Latino echoes ("*in morte quiescam*") repeats the pilot's plea to Aeneas, to take his hand to lead him across the river Styx into the underworld. But the Sibyl who guides the descent forbids it, consoling the doomed pilot with the promise that Italians will bury him and pay homage at the site.

At first glance, the tribulations of the unburied Palinurus begging in vain for deliverance might not seem problematic when cited to commemorate the heroic death of Barbarigo. After all, the mortally wounded Venetian would have received last rites administered by one of the friars aboard Venetian galleys. If studied in isolation as an exemplary military deed, Barbarigo's death presents a compelling case study of bravery. The unburied Palinurus seems not to signify. But for the reader who examines Barbarigo's death within the full narrative sequence, the dire fate of the pilot becomes highly pertinent.

To see how this occurs, we can follow the passage from Barbarigo's last words as the scene unfolds from there. Picking up from the final verse cited above, the passage continues:

... magnanimus dixit: "Placida nunc morte quiescam."
Iam Bassan truncus summas volitare per undas,
atque caput magnum praefixum cuspide acuta,
praelongo in pilo, magno clamore videntum.
Terribiles oculos nequeas adversa tueri,
ora viri tristi nigroque fluentia tabo.
(*SJA*, ll. 1193–8, pp. 362–3; Latino 1573, 2nd gathering, fol. 23v)

([Barbarrigo] declared heroically ... "I will now rest in a peaceful death." Now the mutilated Pasha drifts atop the waves, and his great head is displayed up high on the sharp tip of a long pike, with a great cry from those watching. You could hardly look at the fighter's terrifying eyes, his hostile face, oozing with miserable black gore.)

Viewed now in light of the complete passage, the epic sublime offered in the heroic death of Barbarigo clashes with the remembrance of an unburied Ali. As if Barbarigo's words still echo, the "iam Bassan" darkens the reflection on military heroism. Now, the poet's choice of citation becomes meaningful. That is, the vain hope of the unburied Trojan, that he might rest in peace ("morte quiescam"), speaks as much for Ali Pasha as it does for Barbarigo. Virgil's unburied Palinurus is the victim of a sacrilege. Might the same be said of the unburied Ali Pasha?

Ethical questions also come to light when this allusively dense passage evokes other violent deaths in classical epic. For one, a margin notation invites comparison of Ali's severed head with two particularly problematic deaths in the *Aeneid*:

Euriali, et Nisi sic capita Vergil[ius] cecinit.
(Latino 1573, 2nd gathering, fol. 23v, margin)

(Thus Virgil narrated in verse the deaths of Euryalus and Nisus.)

The gloss invites the reader to ponder this view of Ali's head displayed as a battle trophy in relation to one of Virgil's most ambiguous accounts of empire building, the raid by Nisus and Euryalus in *Aeneid* 9.[21] The two comrades, portrayed in homoerotic terms, conduct a brazen nighttime raid of the Rutulian camp, but they are ultimately doomed by the heavy weight of spoils they have seized from slaughtered enemy fighters. Weighed down by this plunder, the two Trojans are captured and killed by arriving enemy sentries. The margin citation above connects the gory sight of Ali Pasha's severed head with the severed heads of the two Trojan youths, hoisted high on pikes by avenging Rutulians. As before, lexical and metrical parallels tighten the proposed connection. The outcry ("magno clamore") prompted by Ali Pasha's severed head closely follows the "multo clamore" Virgil depicts at the sight of the two heads (*Aeneid* 9.466). The horrifying black fluid oozing from the Turk's severed head ("nigroque fluentia tabo") likewise calls to mind the "atroque fluentia tabo" (*Aeneid* 9.472).

The repeated echoes of the story of Nisus and Euryalus connect a decisive moment at Lepanto to a particularly complex episode in Virgil's chronicle of Rome's foundation. The two friends epitomize soldierly camaraderie, bravery, and sacrifice. For these virtues, Virgil promises transcendence in a rare authorial apostrophe that concludes the episode:

> Fortunati ambo! si quid mea carmina possunt,
> nulla dies umquam memori vos eximet aevo
> dum domus Aeneae Capitoli immobile saxum
> accolet imperiumque pater Romanus habebit. (*Aeneid* 9.446–9)

> (How fortunate, both at once! / If my songs have any power, the day will never dawn / that wipes you from the memory of the ages, not while / the house of Aeneas stands by the Capitol's rock unshaken, / not while the Roman Father rules the world.) (Fagles 2006, 281)

Latino's own margin gloss quoted above transcribes the Virgilian apostrophe into indirect discourse. But the raid that promises to bring lasting fame remains problematic, given that the two friends slaughter sleeping Rutulians, not armed adversaries. Further complicating the view of heroism, Nisus and Euryalus die, not in single combat, but because they are overburdened with plunder. The potentially discordant messages within this Virgilian episode have recently come to light in media debates in the United States in light of the use of this passage at the National September 11 Museum in New York.[22]

Returning to Latino's treatment of Ali Pasha's death, a further complexity arises from a second allusive layer built into the passage. That is, the Turk's defiled body deepens Latino's engagement with a decidedly Lucanian concern, the mistreatment of dead bodies. A view above of Ali Pasha's headless body adrift at sea ("Iam Bassan truncus summas volitare per undas") returns to an earlier point of intersection. As did the Spanish commander's threat to a Muslim galley slave – explored in chapter 4 – the headless body adrift recalls Lucan's premonition of Pompey's death by decapitation: "hunc ego, fluminea deformis truncus harena/qui iacet, agnosco" (him I recognize, lying on the river sands,/ an unsightly headless corpse; Lucan, *De bellum civile*, 1.685–6; Braund 1992, 21).[23] As before, Lucan's inspiration goes unremarked here.

Though this debt passes unmentioned, Juan Latino's disturbing, close-up view of Ali Pasha's death and defilement strikes a decidedly Lucanian posture in other respects. Notably, Latino's identification of Ali's executioner as a *humilis miles* calls to mind Lucan's condemnation addressed to Septimius, as *miles Romane* (Roman soldier), who lays a dying, defenceless Pompey across a bench and severs the head, after which he carries it away as a trophy. Lucan dwells on the gruesome task of severing muscles and veins, and then cries out in condemnation of the sacrilege (Lucan, *De bellum civile*, 8.662–78). If Latino's engagement with this scene is much more subtle, the implications of the proximity between Ali and Pompey's fates are profoundly unsettling.

On the issue of how Latino depicts Ali Pasha's death, it is once again instructive to compare *The Song of John of Austria* to battle commemorations by other Spanish poets of Lepanto. A degree of anxiety seems palpable as the best known poets steer clear of a direct narration of the Turkish commander's execution and desecration of his body. Latino's closest contemporary, Fernando de Herrera, sets aside the vivid prose he uses elsewhere, recording the death with studied indirection: "cuando mataron a Alí Bajá" (when they killed Ali Pasha). Herrera's third-person verb seems to incline the interpretation to Spanish fighters but makes no factual commitments. Continuing, his narrator avoids the sight of the severed head. When distilling the battle chronicle in the hendecasyllables of the "Canción en alabanza de la Divina Majestad," Herrera blurs the enemy commander's humanity still more, abstracting the vanquished Ottoman rivals in terms of "Babilonia y Egito" (Babylon and Egypt) or "la Luna" (the Crescent). Alonso de Ercilla, for his part, follows Herrera's prose account in terms of the narrative sequence, but ends his prophetic narration of Lepanto in Canto 24 of the *Araucana* just before Ali Pasha's death. Another poet who followed and adapted Herrera's account, Juan Rufo, transforms Ali Pasha's death in combat into a medical mystery. His *Austriada* portrays the Ottoman admiral as an ill-tempered choleric with blood-shot eyes, asking whether he died of an enemy sword or his own deadly rage.[24]

As Lepanto historiography evolved in the months and years after the battle, a definitive account of Ali Pasha's death would remain elusive.

Where initial reports of his death attributed it to a sword blow, some subsequent accounts stated he succumbed to a bullet from a harquebus. While doubt on this specific detail lingers even today, one supposition found in some recent studies of Lepanto is unsupported by reliable period sources: the allegation that John of Austria was outraged at the desecration of Ali Pasha's corpse.[25] Letters and dispatches sent just after the battle to Philip II and other court officials attest to all manner of second guessing over tactics and the distribution of war spoils. Yet none of these first responses and memoranda that reached Spain from Lepanto reveals discomfort or anxiety about the treatment of Ali Pasha. Nor do the battlefield dispatches or first reports register any expression of regret or anger by John of Austria on account of the post-mortem mutilation.

Latino thus stands as one of the first voices of regret for how Ali Pasha was treated upon capture and death. This sense of loss intensifies when, as the battle continues, the poetic voice cites testimony of freed Christian galley slaves. They lament Ali Pasha's death, noting he might have converted to Christianity:

> Quod si inter pugnam captus vir forte fuisset,
> ille fidem mira Christi virtute bibisset,
> quem remex noster captivus semper amarat
> optaratque crucem Bassani in fronte videre.
> Sunt etiam Turcis quamvis sua praemia laudi.
>
> (*SJA*, ll. 1207–11, pp. 364–5; Latino 1573, 2nd gathering, fol. 24r)

> (Yet if by chance the man had been captured while fighting, he would have imbibed the Christian faith because of his wondrous virtue. Our captive rowers had always revered the Pasha and hoped to see him wear the cross on his forehead. Even among Turks honor has its rewards.)

Appropriately, the last verse replays Aeneas's exclamation on seeing Priam commemorated in Dido's Palace: "Sunt hic etiam sua praemia laudi" (even here, merit will have its true reward; *Aeneid* 1.461; Fagles 2006, 63). A significant implication follows from this lineage. After all, the poet memorializes the death in combat of the Ottoman admiral with reference to a particularly solemn homage to the fallen king of Troy.

Moreover, the hypothetical conversion narrative suggested in the *sunt etiam* passage above refutes the racial argument for indelible Muslim identity. Verses above, after all, contemplate an efficacious conversion from Islam to Christianity. To be sure, the lament remains firmly anchored in imperialist ideology, with a logic that calibrates a Muslim's virtue with reference to his suitability for Christian conversion. But the ideal of assimilation, at least, stops short of extermination or exclusion.

The emotional pull of the near conversion becomes stronger still when connected to the poet's earlier evocations of his own New Christian identity. Ali's hypothetical conversion, above, returns to the poem, momentarily, to the baptismal font. This was also the location for the poet's opening invocation, which situates his own literary vocation at the "holy waters of Parnassus" (Parnasi in gurgite sancto; *SJA*, ll. 56–63, pp. 292–3; Latino 1573, 2nd gathering, fol. 3r). In the same metaphorical terrain, the verb *bibisset* (from *bibo*) that dramatizes a frustrated chance at Christian baptism for Ali is rooted in a patristic lexicon, which conveys a convert's embrace of Christianity as the imbibing of Christ deep in his or her heart.[26]

But if the imagined conversion of Ali finds ample justification in a long view of church history, the idea appears more nostalgic than plausible within the closer context of post-rebellion Granada where the poet crafted these verses. Church and crown officials, after all, had championed and then ruthlessly carried out the expulsion and enslavement of tens of thousands of baptized New Christians of Hispano-Muslim descent. This process I detail in chapter 2 negated untold numbers of Christian conversions en masse, without regard to individual merits. The longed-for reconciliation in which Ali Pasha the enemy commander joins the Spanish fold as a captive-turned-Christian convert is a much less plausible narrative in post-rebellion Granada.

Ali's death, when viewed as a frustrated conversion, also undercuts the epic's underlying notion that Lepanto marks a new milestone for the Spanish Monarchy's global expansion. From the dawn of Spain's imperial expansion in the late fifteenth century, the basic impetus for and justification of conquest was the promise of efficacious Catholic conversion. No matter how routine the practice of slaughtering enemy commanders and defiling their corpses had become in sixteenth-century warfare, such violence undermined a fundamental justification for Spain's empire building: the propagation of the Catholic faith.

In fact, Latino's narrative of a frustrated conversion in captivity calls to mind a particularly resonant myth of a frustrated Christian conversion – the notion that the Aztec ruler Moctezuma was about to embrace Christianity when he was killed, most likely by Spanish invaders under the command of Hernán Cortés. In the later sixteenth century, chroniclers pondering the 1519–20 conquest of Mexico contended with the sensitive issue of the Mexican ruler's death in captivity. In the decades that followed the event, allegations of wanton Spanish cruelty took hold, as did efforts to deflect them. Jesuit Juan de Tovar, drawing on both Spanish and native-Mexican sources in the 1580s, recorded the story that a dying Moctezuma requested baptism. Reportedly, the priest who should have performed the sacrament was distracted by his involvement in looting. A particularly detailed account of the frustrated conversion appears in the *Historia verdadera de la conquista de Nueva España* by Bernal Díaz, though the soldier-chronicler deflects blame from Spaniards.[27]

The allegations that Spain's conquering armies were actually harming the faith by killing suitable converts would gain a worldwide audience through the hyperbolic accounts of massacres in Bartolomé de Las Casas's *Brevísima relación de la destrucción de las Indias*, which had appeared in print two decades before Latino composed his Lepanto epic. The central premise of this polemic addressed to Philip II is that greed and excessive cruelty prevent the king from fulfilling his God-given duty to Christianize Amerindians. As Latino wrote his poem, the Las Casas treatise had not yet gained the wide international audience that would come, a half decade later, with the translations printed in Protestant realms of northern Europe. But the Dominican was already a voice to be reckoned with in Spain, particularly since the 1560s, when he abandoned earlier proposals for salvaging the imperial project. By this point, a disillusioned Las Casas came to advocate the more radical position that Spain should abandon its overseas empire and return sovereignty to native people.[28] Such questions about American colonies were not as removed from memory of Mediterranean wars as one might think today. In juridical terms, the Spanish Monarchy considered Amerindians and Granadinos subjects of the Crown of Castile. Rolena Adorno draws attention, in this respect, to the fact that the efforts to eradicate Arabic in Granada in the 1560s coincided with the suppression of Franciscan Bernardino de Sahagún's compilation of Nahua history. In terms of court politics of the time, the faction led by Cardinal Diego de Espinosa – the sponsor of Granada's controversial Audiencia president Pedro de Deza – promoted the hard-line posture towards Moriscos in Granada and the establishment of Inquisition tribunals in the Americas.[29] In short, the fates of Moriscos of Granada and Amerindians were intertwined when matters of life or death were debated in the highest reaches of the court.

Returning our focus once again to the specific narrative sweep of the Lepanto epic, we can see how the fate of Ali Pasha marks a turning point in *The Song of John of Austria*, much as it does in the first reports of the battle. Yet here genre proves decisive. Initial letters and bulletins view this moment in tactical terms. But in the literary recollection, Ali Pasha's death takes on added moral dimensions related to a fundamental dilemma of ancient epic: revenge versus magnanimity.

On this point, one of *The Song of John of Austria's* key points of divergence from other Lepanto epics is how it dwells on the plight of Ali Pasha's bereft sons, Saïd and Mohammed, who had travelled with him into battle. Latino could have drawn here on any number of battle dispatches that described how Spaniards captured the two young Ottoman princes. For instance, the letter Nicolás Augusto de Benavides penned the day after the battle offers a dramatic account of their capture by John of Austria, describing how they wept upon seeing their father's severed head on display as a Spanish battle trophy. Mohammed died in captivity, but in the year after the battle, Saïd's captivity became a point of fascination across Europe.[30]

Latino adds the force of funeral elegy to the story of how Ali's captive sons see their father's severed head. Their grief momentarily transports the poem from the militaristic realm of a battle scene to the future awaiting the bereft survivors. The poet conjures their abjection in a stirring lamentation that is the epic's longest speech. As with the great Spanish elegiac poetry Bruce Wardropper illuminated in his classic study, the passage records the emotional maelstrom of a personal loss, giving voice to anger, denial, and endurance.[31] The grieving Ottoman princes protest that their father let them survive his death. They then speak of their pending captivity at the hands of vengeful enemies. Finally, they lament that their own heads are not displayed alongside their father's. So doing, the princes reprise the nostalgia for a lost homeland, the sentiment featured in the poet's earlier glimpse of a Muslim galley slave who steals a backward glance at the Ottoman fleet, a scene contemplated in the preceding chapter. The lengthy excerpt that follows, of the Ottoman princes' lament for Ali Pasha, warrants special consideration within the Spanish canon of elegies, alongside such renowned scenes as Pleberio's lament before the dead Melibea in the *Celestina*:

"Scilicet ut Veneti nostri potirentur et arma,
tot reges victos disiectaque corpora ponto,
captivam classem cernant? Fraterque Philippi

ut geminos ductet puppi victosque triumpho?
Sordidus ut miles iugulum regale feriret?
Regnatorque pater truncus videaris in undis?
Quo ferimur miseri servi ad fastidia regum?
Non iterum campos Byzanti, et regia castra
visuri, et caros materna in sede penates?
At vos Hispani nostri miserescite duri:
spargite nos fluctu, vasto hoc immergite ponto [...]
In nos ardenter mites convertite ferrum.
Porrectum iugulum mucrone en solvite nostrum.
Figite iamque caput geminum sic puppibus altis.
At patris digno nostri mandate sepulchro."
(*SJA* ll. 1238–48, 1252–5, pp. 366–7; Latino 1573, 2nd gathering, fol. 24v)

("Can it really be that Venetians have gotten the better of us, and now look on our artillery, scores of conquered rulers, sea-strewn corpses, and our captive fleet? That Philip's brother leads your two bound sons on his ship in triumph? That a vile soldier has slit a royal throat? And that you, admiral and father, are seen as a trunk on the waves? Where are we bound, miserable slaves to endure the scorn of kings? Will we ever again see the fields and royal fortresses of Byzantium, or the cherished hearths of our maternal home? Fierce Spaniards, have mercy on us! Scatter us over the water, submerge us in the deep sea [...] Be kind, and turn your sword zealously against us. Come now, sever our exposed necks with your sharp blade. Display our twin heads up high on your stern. But then grant us a burial worthy of our father.")

At first, the passage gives voice to European stereotypes of overweening Turkish pride.[32] Speaking in this vein, the brothers air their shock that Venetians and Spaniards defeated their father.

But their lament then gestures to more universal questions of filial piety, reprising earlier dilemmas of wartime ethics. The brothers thus condemn their father's executioner as a "sordidus miles," echoing the "humilis miles" (l. 1076) from before. They then envision their father's body adrift, as a "truncus," reprising earlier allusions to the headless bodies of Virgil's Priam and Lucan's Pompey. This nostalgia for a lost homeland, the "campos Byzanti," recalls the mournful reverie of the Muslim galley slave in Book 1 (l. 417). Finally, their plea that their Spanish captors mercifully execute them; "in nos ardenter mites convertite ferrum," echoes the vain plea with which Nisus offers himself to save the doomed Euryalus: "in me convertite ferrum" (*Aeneid* 9.427; "turn your blades on me," Fagles 2006, 280).

Adding force to this lament is the fact that the two brothers mourning their father stand as the *Song of John of Austria*'s sole representatives of an intact family. A marked contrast sets them apart from their captor, Latino's title hero. John of Austria, as the illegitimate son of Charles V, endured humiliating slights when Philip II refused to instate him as a member of Spain's royal family. This was a contentious issue during Don John's stay in Granada, as it was in preparation for Lepanto. In light of the fundamental importance of family and lineage within epic architecture, the family of Ali Pasha, at least momentarily, transcends the rhetoric of a Holy War between Christians and Muslims. Instead, the bereft sons epitomize filial piety, one of the core virtues that epic poetry explores and models.

In the end, the very problems with Spain's naval victory attested in the brothers' lament signal what is arguably Juan Latino's most meaningful Virgilian engagement. As classics scholars have shown, the *Aeneid*'s exaltation of Rome's emergence as an empire coexists with voices of regret.[33] Something analogous occurs with *The Song of John of Austria*. Yes, the poet celebrates imperial expansion. But the contemplation of Ali Pasha's fate adds regret to the forming memory of the naval victory. I would propose that from here, Latino's version of events swerves away from the imperial teleology that shapes the exultant elegy "On the Birth of Untroubled Times" that prefaces the epic as well as from the poem's opening justification for the collective punishment of Moriscos in Granada. Once the poetic voice dwells on Ali Pasha's fate and his bereft sons, the idea of the heroic poem expands to encompass the mourning for what is lost in wars for imperial expansion. A more expansive and questioning conception of the form likewise informs the poem's account of Lepanto's denouement. As with the death of Ali Pasha that emerges as the battle's climax, the vision of what happens once victory is at hand diverges sharply from the other epics commemorating the naval battle of 1571.

A Soldiers' Mutiny and an Enemy's Escape

Departing from the letters and bulletins that served as his primary sources as well as from the dominant narrative focus found among other poets of Lepanto, Juan Latino dwells on the most unseemly side of Spain's great victory at sea. With surprising directness, the poetic voice recounts how the victorious Spaniards begin to fight among themselves for the choicest plunder. Convinced that officers are cheating them of their due portion, soldiers threaten to mutiny:

Certabat miles prædam cognoscere captam,
atque suas iuste partes sibi tradier inde,
qui pro rege suo Turcas invaserat hostes,
pectoreque averso monstrabat vulnera passus.
Ductores avidi totom de more volebant.
Incertum vulgus studia in contraria fertur;
seditione levis populus consurgere visus.
Iamque furor gentis commotis arma ferebat.

(*SJA*, ll. 1296–1303, pp. 370–1; Latino 1573, 2nd gathering, fol. 25v)

(Each soldier, striving to assess the captured loot and ensure that his share of it was fairly handed over to him, displayed the wounds he suffered on his exposed chest when he had attacked the Turkish enemy for his king. Greedy commanders, as usual, wanted everything. The unsettled crowd is drawn into conflict; the fickle throng seems on the verge of mutiny. Now the men's wrath brought weapons into the heated disputes.)

In essence, a new battle arises. Spaniards fight among themselves for shares of the seized Ottoman treasures, as well as enemy prisoners to ransom or sell as slaves. Potential condemnation in this passage mitigates with the mention of the soldiers' battle scars, a signal that the claim to loot follows from battle service. Indeed, this routine compensation mechanism was particularly critical for the Spanish soldiers at Lepanto, given that the salary payments from the king were so far in arrears that many lacked adequate clothing and food.[34] Taking note of this discord, the poetic voice reports that the threat of mutiny prompts John of Austria to appoint a judge to supervise the division of spoils. That the poet states his name, Nabbas, attests to Juan Latino's access to privileged information, since the crown official he names, Doctor Navas de Puebla, does not appear in published accounts of the battle.[35]

This near-mutiny adds yet another layer to the poet's engagement with Virgil's *Aeneid*. The tumult of rebellious soldiers replays the first simile of the Roman epic (*Aeneid* 1.143–53). Juno, trying to prevent Aeneas and his men from reaching Italy, unleashes a deadly tempest, giving rise to the first of a series of storms within the poem. Upon learning of this usurpation, Neptune takes action to calm the winds. Virgil conveys the scene with the poem's first simile, which likens the god's power to calm the sea to a revered elder statesman's capacity to stop a sedition-stoked uprising with wise words. Latino, for his part, transposes the simile to direct narration. The swirl of rumours, "seditione levis," that provoke soldierly violence echoes Virgil's "seditio" (*Aeneid* 1.149), and the "furor ... arma ferebat" replays the Mantuan's "furor arma ministrat" (*Aeneid* 1.150; "rage finds them arms," Fagles 2006, 52). Continuing from here, John of Austria's soothing words calm the rebellious soldiers: "Austriades animos dictis et pectora mulcet" (John of Austria calms their minds and hearts with his words; *SJA*, ll. 1306, pp. 370–1; Latino 1573, 2nd gathering, fol. 25v). This verse cites Virgil's evocation in the storm simile of a wise statesman's calming words: "ille regit dictis animos et pectora mulcet" (*Aeneid* 1.153; "he rules their furor with his words and calms their passion," Fagles 2006, 52). In contrast to the earlier allusion to the raid of Nisus and Euryalus, which the poet identifies with a margin citation, no gloss draws attention to this reference. Thus, we get a sense of the eclectic pedagogical strategies built into the Lepanto volume. Where the poet identifies the potentially less accessible reference to an episode in Book 9, the Latin apprentice here must recognize the allusion to the opening storm.

In terms of military ethics and tactics, the looting scene contrasts to the more muted accounts of the same moment found in roughly contemporary chronicles or poems. For instance, Venetian chronicler Giovanni Pietro Contarini distils the frenetic rush to seize war spoils with one dense sentence: "Since all the Turkish galleys were vanquished by Christian force, all turned to sacking and looting widely to claim enemy spoils until nightfall, so that all that remained was in their hands."[36] Moving on quickly, the Venetian changes the subject, offering the long-range historical judgment that the Holy League victory at Lepanto equalled Actium.

The most common position among poets of Lepanto is to avoid the looting at the battle site. In *De bello turcico*, Bernardino Leo, a poet from the Lazio region of Italy, chronicles an orderly division of war spoils among the Holy League contingents that return to Corfu several days after the battle, but avoids recounting the on-site plunder.[37] For their part, Fernando de Herrera and Alonso de Ercilla bypass Spanish looting altogether. Drawing attention to the fact that neither Herrera nor Alonso de Ercilla after him detail the plundering at Lepanto, Elizabeth Davis raised the question of the sources for poet Juan Rufo's lament of the tactical and ethical pitfalls of looting, aired in his circa 1584 Lepanto epic, the *Austriada*.[38] The possibility that Rufo draws on Latino's poem or a shared source lies outside the scope of this study, but remains an issue for later examination.

Taking stock of the emphasis given to accounts of looting and near-mutiny, the impression that results is that plunder derails significant military objectives. Two telling artistic choices here are the actions that constitute the battle's denouement and the narrative sequencing. Specifically, the poet recounts the intense looting and trading among Holy League troops and then immediately details the one significant setback in the decisive victory – the intrepid escape of Calabrian renegade Uluç Ali. First, the poetic voice reveals how plundering soldiers transform the maritime battlefield into an improvised trading post:

> Quid referam Venetos, rapientes magna Liburnos,
> Illyrici captos Turcas quos inde tulerunt?
> Atque Italus, Tuscus redeuntes, nauta redemptor
> advectasque sibi merces quas emerit illinc?
> Captivosque duces, dandos puerosque parenti,
> ingenti pretio redimendos undique Turcis?
> (*SJA* 1333–8, pp. 372–3; Latino 1573, 2nd gathering, fol. 26r)

> (Why should I speak of the Venetians and Liburnians as they seized great spoils? Or the captive Turks that the Illyrians carried away? And what of the goods that the Italian or Tuscan merchant seaman acquired from there and took for himself as he returned? Or the captive leaders and youths that will be returned to their family after being ransomed at a great price from the Turks?)

Terminology here is striking. The "nauta redemptor" becomes the new guise of the soldier, who acts as a merchant, seizing and trading plunder. Such a figure of a soldier-turned-merchant reveals an essential facet of Mediterranean warfare at sea, with no clear distinction between merchant- and war-ships.[39] This duality, moreover, had shown itself to be a driving motivation for the same Spanish *tercios* present at Lepanto when they fought, two years earlier, to suppress the Morisco uprising in Granada, an issue explored at some length in chapter 2.

But what is common to military practice is not necessarily compatible with epic poetry that proposes to memorialize deeds in wartime. Above, the personalization of the narrative, with the first person subjunctive "quid referam" (why should I speak) asks, in essence, whether the looting and bartering of soldiers belong in an epic narration. An idea of the tension between historical veracity and poetic decorum emerges, once more, in a comparison with the freedman's contemporaries who also viewed Lepanto in epic terms. Where Latino, above, presents the aligned Holy League forces – Venetians, Liburnians, Illyrians, Italians, and Tuscans – as they transform into merchants, Neapolitan jurist Giovanni Battista Arcucci adheres to a staple of epic narration, culminating his account of the battle with a celebration of the noblemen from across the Catholic lands of the Mediterranean who triumphed at Lepanto. Though in prose, Fernando de Herrera's account draws on the epic catalogue to culminate the narration of the battle with a list of the illustrious dead on the Holy League side. A case in point, in this respect, is Herrera's distillation of Italian fighters in such summarizing statements as "great fortitude in combat took place on the flagships of the Colonna [the Papacy], Savoy, and Venice, with particular heroism among Venetians on that of Canaleto."[40] Such lionization seems a far cry from Latino's depiction of rapacious Venetians and Liburnians above ("Venetos ... rapientes Liburnos"), the bartering Tuscans, or the mutinying Spanish troops.

Having recorded the intense looting, the poetic voice turns to Uluç Ali. Verses describe how he evades the Genoese fleet, overwhelms the small contingent of the Knights of Malta, and then escapes the devastation. Notably, the poet positions the wily escape of this nemesis of Spain's imperial aspirations in the Mediterranean right after the *quid referam* sequence cited above. Having just asked, rhetorically, how words could describe the intense looting and trading of victorious Holy League fighters, the poetic voice shifts to follow the flight of Uluç Ali. He sees:

> Regulus aufugit timidis inglorius armis,
> non ausus nostris pelago concurrere, caute,
> quos iam victores cernebat sorte superbos ...
> (SJA, ll. 1339–41, pp. 372–3; Latino 1573, 2nd gathering, fol. 26r)

> (The pirate king Uluj Ali flees in dishonor with his cowardly
> forces, not daring in his caution to confront our men at sea, having
> already determined that the victors were exultant in their fate.)

The disparaging treatment of Uluç Ali here contrasts to the reverence shown to Ali Pasha ("Bassan, et dux et miles"), as a magnanimous and dignified admiral. "Regulus ... inglorious" demystifies the commander

Spaniards knew from his deeds as corsair governor of Algiers, signalling him as an ignominious warlord. Intriguingly, Juan Latino's *regulus* correlates to the *reyezuelo* with which Ginés Pérez de Hita names the leader of Morisco rebels in Granada, Fernando de Válor.[41] Yet much as the term "regulus ... inglorious" diminishes Uluç Ali, the poet's account of his escape gives full notice of the blend of fear and fascination he stirred in Spaniards of the later sixteenth century.[42] However cowardly the poet might construe the decision to flee instead of fight, some of the scene's tactical implications cast a shadow on Holy League fighters. Might the intensity of the looting chronicled just before have allowed for Uluç Ali to devastate the contingent from the Knights of Malta and then escape? Could Spanish soldiers and officers, fighting among themselves for plunder, have transformed a decisive victory into a tactical defeat?

In fact, the Calabrian renegade's escape would soon prove a notorious shortcoming to an otherwise decisive victory, given that he supervised the rebuilding of the Ottoman fleet. By the time Juan Latino completed the *Song of John of Austria* in the summer of 1572, Uluç Ali was in command of a renewed fighting force of some two hundred galleys.[43]

Whether or not Juan Latino had word of this rebuilding as he penned his epic of Lepanto, there is little doubt he intimated a limitation of the victory at sea in October 1571 when he chose to relate Uluç Ali's escape. Though the Calabrian actually fled to Constantinople, Latino here conjures a stealthy return to Algiers: "Puppibus et tacitis nocturnus venit" (with his ships sailing stealthily in the night, he reaches Algiers; *SJA*, ll. 1348, pp. 372–3, Latino 1573, 2nd gathering, fol. 26v). This North African stronghold was frightfully real for Latino and his Spanish readers, since thousands had suffered long enslavement there. Algiers was also the place where Charles V's goal of North African domination stalled definitively after a disastrous attack of 1541.

Once more, a comparison of the same episode in Latino and Fernando de Herrera is revealing. The poet from Seville does not include an Algerian interlude in his account of the naval battle's conclusion, though he refers to the devastation inflicted on the Knights of St John. On a related note, the lyric poem that Herrera appends to his prose chronicle, the "Canción en alabanza de la Divina Majestad," concedes no tactical setbacks to the victory. Rather, the poetic voice hails the complete destruction and humiliation of the enemy, without conceding that a major adversary escaped. Herrera's lyric commemoration thus closes with praise to God for shattering the enemy ("Rompiste al enemigo") and a wish that Spain's adversaries might burn in hell ("Padezca en bravas llamas abrasada"). These are, in short, two divergent interpretations of Lepanto. Herrera's prose chronicle and accompanying "Canción" garnered a wider audience than did Latino's epic, attaining notable artistic influence in the decade that followed. But in the longer term, Spain's literary history would follow a path more akin to Latino's view of Lepanto, as an epochal naval victory undercut by some tactical errors and ethical questions. Those problems would often become acutely visible to Spaniards in Uluç Ali's Algerian redoubt. Most famous, Cervantes's long odyssey after the naval battle would take him to the very slave dungeons Latino evokes in this passage. Cervantes's literary career would thereafter pivot at key moments on efforts to give artistic life to the irony that heroism at Lepanto gave way to abjection in Algiers.[44]

From the vantage point of the narrative discourse within the *Song of John of Austria*, Uluç Ali's flight from Lepanto also signals a shift within the poem, from the real-time chronicle of the battle itself back to the metapoetic exploration of the battle as a news story unfolding in the late fall of 1571. Latino opened his poem by allegorizing the spreading battle news, with Fama carrying word of Lepanto to war-torn Granada. Now, with the battle ended and the rush for spoils underway, the poet returns to the same personification allegory. Thus, when Uluç Ali reaches Algiers, Fama has already passed through, reporting the battle's outcome to Christian captives in the *bagnios* of Algiers (*SJA* ll. 1352–3; pp. 372–3; Latino 1573, 2nd gathering, fol. 26v).

From here, Fama's flight steers the poem to completion as her course traces the arc of Lepanto as a breaking news story. The winged messenger travels from Lepanto to the pope in Rome, over the Alps, and then crosses the Pyrenees. After spreading word among northern realms of Iberia, Fama takes the news to Philip II in the Escorial, and then flies south to the poet's home city. Continuing, she heads south into the Nile region, Ethiopia, and then eastward to Arabia and India (*SJA* ll. 1644–52, pp. 392–3, Latino 1573, 2nd gathering, fol. 32r). In terms of the Lepanto historiography, the personification allegory solves one fundamental poetic challenge that news of the event posed: how to record the seeming rapid-fire travel of the news itself.[45]

The closing passage redoubles the metaliterary reflection of how the battle becomes etched in collective memory. With the city of Granada rejoicing over the news of Lepanto, another bulletin arrives: the queen, Anna of Austria, has given birth to a new royal heir, Prince Ferdinand:

Haec Garnata ducis dum cantat gesta Ioannis,
ecce tibi rumor sparsus iam moenia complet.
Annam Reginam natum peperisse Philippo
omnibus est princeps concessus caelitus almus,
haec sors Hispanos victores una manebat,
solamenque viris, multorum causa bonorum
ventura. Hinc pratis fundetur copia rerum,
mollibus hinc flavus gaudebit campus aristis,
militiae spes magna ducum columenque salutis,
gentibus Hispanis virtus et robur avorum.
(*SJA*, ll. 1821–30, pp. 402–4; Latino 1573, 2nd gathering, fol. 35r–v)

(While Granada sings of the deeds of John of Austria, look, the news spreads to you and now fills the city walls: Queen Anne has born a son for Philip – a beloved prince granted from heaven for all. This singular good fortune awaited the triumphant Spaniards, a comfort for men, and a promise of abundant blessings ahead. Now bounty will spring forth from pastures, golden fields will rejoice in soft grain, the commanders' great hope for the military, the mainstay of our salvation, a source of strength for the Spanish people, and his forefathers' might.)

The auspicious birth of a crown prince becomes a news story that intertwines with the spreading chronicle of Lepanto. This convergence inspires the poet to restate the opening prophecy of new imperial horizons, in conjunction with new times of plenty and prosperity in Granada. Continuing to the closing lines, the jubilant city becomes a vantage point for looking ahead to Philip II's expanding global empire:

Iam regnis pax magna tuis, Auguste Philippe,
princeps Fernandus consurgit clarus in orbe.
Hic tibi felici revocabit sorte triumphos,
victrices ducet nostras in bella phalanges.
Hic Christi nomen defendet victor et armis,
ut gentes unum Christum per saecula regem
cognoscant victae Fernandi et Marte Philippi.
(*SJA*, ll. 1831–7, pp. 404–5; Latino 1573, 2nd gathering, fol. 35v)

(Emperor Philip, great peace is at hand in your realms, as resplendent Prince Ferdinand comes into the world. It will be his good fortune to win great conquests for you and lead our triumphant troops in battle. He will defend

> the name of Christ, a victor in arms, so that the nations, tamed by the military might of Ferdinand and Philip, will come to know Christ, the one and eternal king.)

Strategically, the verses above cast the panegyric to Philip II in a Roman lexicon, as *Auguste Philippe*. Once more, the poet confers an imperial designation on the ruler who had been stymied in his attempt to secure the title of Holy Roman Emperor. At the same time, the vision of new conquests is resolutely Christian ("unum Christum per saecula regem"), hewing the portrait of a Philip *imperator* with reference to the specifications of Habsburg piety.

In this closing prophecy of prosperous days at hand, the dissonant notes aired in the chronicle of the battle go quiet. Set aside in this closing scene are questions about the cost of empire raised within the account of the battle itself, whether relating to the indiscriminately destructive artillery weapons, the lack of magnanimity shown in desecrating the body of the slain Ottoman admiral, or in the ravenous plunder and slave trading among victors. At least here, when news of a great victory overseas reaches Granada, the *Song of John of Austria* is an exultant Habsburg song. A scene analogous to Titian's view of a winged allegory of Victory heralding more imperial expansion for Philip II comes into focus. Fixed at least for this moment on the printed page is a vision of prosperity at home, the *pax* of a world empire abroad, and lasting fame for the poet himself. These are soaring ambitions, both for the freedman and the international polity he would serve as poet laureate.

Conclusion: Song of the Black Swan

Post-Script to Lepanto

We have seen how a literary sleight-of-hand gives *The Song of John of Austria* its remarkable immediacy. To offer a lasting remembrance of the moment in late 1571 when Granadinos broke open dispatches from Madrid and then read together the news of a decisive victory overseas, the poet tamed Virgil's monstrous Fama. Juan Latino redraws the flying messenger with hundreds of wings, eyes, and ears of *Aeneid* 4; now she is a bearer of good tidings. Her breaking news reports that John of Austria and his Spanish forces matched the most celebrated *gesta* of antiquity. At different points, the epic likens the Holy League commander to Scipio Africanus; Hannibal crossing the Alps; and most decisively, to Octavian in the Battle of Actium. Juan Latino's artistic feat here is also memorable. Censors' statements printed in the front-matter of *The Song of John of Austria* reveal that the educator-turned-poet completed the densely allusive, erudite epic of almost 2,000 verses within about ten months. This short time span for the technically demanding hexameter verse suggests that the poet toiled to complete his epic before the battle's symbolically important first anniversary.

While paying tribute to John of Austria, Juan Latino calibrates his panegyric verses to speak to the manifest imperial aims of Philip II. Ambitions rekindled by the resounding victory at Lepanto, the king's advisors were debating how to harness the momentum to foment new eastward empire building. The goal was to retake Constantinople and Jerusalem, thereby restoring Rome's eastern empire for western Christendom and claiming that imperial title for Philip II. Charting Fama's flight to speak to these lofty goals, Latino's *Song of John of Austria* follows the winged messenger from the battle site off the coast of Greece to Italy, then Spain, after which she veers south to the Nile. On reaching the Ethiopians, she crosses eastward to Arabia and India. This course, westward to Spain then southeastward into Africa, briefly adheres to a medieval cartographic paradigm that retained a hold on imaginations in sixteenth-century Europe. In this older conception of space, the uncharted regions of sub-Saharan Africa were part of the East, in contrast to the emerging continental organization that was construing Africa as a separate entity.[1] Juan Latino, in keeping with the euphoria after Lepanto, offers the king a map of new realms and subjects found to the east and southeast of Iberia.

Yet as we have seen, this literary tribute to Spain's house of Austria bears a pointed admonition. Chapter 3 explored a highly personal statement of Latino's literary agenda, "On the Birth of Untroubled Times." This elegy for Philip II insisted that the desired eastward imperial expansion would require a more inclusive attitude towards the blacks who live in the distant lands that he aspires to rule. Anticipating as well the white courtiers who might reject him because of his skin colour, the poet reminds the king that in such distant lands, there are black courtiers who will look down on a white visitor. This warning evokes an illumination found in the *Libros de ajedrez, dados, y tablas* of Alfonso X (figure 11). This bibliographic treasure had been passed down to Philip II within the library of Isabel I of Castile, still held, as Latino wrote, in Granada's Capilla Real. To conclude this elegy for new, auspicious times, the poet renders himself a black raven (*cornix*). This shapeshifting is a witty adaptation of a well-known verse from Suetonius. Adapting the revered historian of the ancient Roman emperors is especially appropriate for the poet seeking a voice in Spain's early modern empire.

In a crucial respect, this call for access was heard. I documented in chapter 4 how Latino's Lepanto volume reached the desk of Philip II's private secretary, Antonio Gracián Dantisco. This gatekeeper's dispatches focused on diplomacy and the procurement of books and relics for the Escorial Palace complex still under construction. That Latino's volume of commemorative poetry on Lepanto reached this rarified echelon of the court attests to his ability to capitalize on patronage ties at the highest level. The price of such access was an alliance with the controversial president of Granada's Audiencia, Pedro de Deza. Chapter 4 addresses the dilemmas this alliance presents in the context of Granada's violent recent history. When we ponder Deza's role in sealing the tragic fate of the region's Moriscos, a range of ethical problems emerge from Latino's dependence on him for access to high officials at court. This official oversaw the collective punishment that the crown visited on these native Granadinos, spearheading the mass expulsion and enslavement that even many contemporaries found unjust and heavy-handed. But without such an alliance, Juan Latino's work would have only obtained publication licence with great difficulty, if at all. By way of comparison, a Latin professor in Guatemala and native of Madrid, Francisco de Pedrosa, sent his Latin epic on Lepanto to court with a request for publication licence that was ultimately not granted. Another writer preparing a work for publication in Granada, Luis Mármol Carvajal, took over two decades to publish his history of the Second Revolt of the Alpujarras.[2] In light of the labyrinthine permission channels, the short period from the time Latino sent his completed Lepanto volume to court to the book's appearance in print hinged on special access for the educator-and-poet. As a result, his Lepanto epic appeared in print when the naval battle was still very recent history.

Even so, the political and diplomatic winds had shifted quite dramatically by the spring of 1573 when the press of Hugo Mena in Granada issued Latino's finished volume. From many angles, Mediterranean geopolitics seemed more attune to Latino's engagement with Virgil's cautionary stories of empire building that I examine in chapter 5 than to the tamed allegory of Fama we find in the panegyric opening and closing passages. Even before Juan Latino finished the poem, Pope Pius V died. The Holy League alliance of the most powerful Catholic fleets in the Mediterranean was scarcely longer lived than this crusading pope. Crucially, the Republic of Venice negotiated its own peace with the Ottomans, conceding its former island colony of Cyprus to the sultan in exchange for reviving lucrative eastern trade networks.

Turning from the Mediterranean east to the poet's home city of Granada, we can see that the new era of bounty heralded in the closing passage of the *Song of John of Austria* was also proving elusive. As noted earlier, Granada's leaders tied the hope for economic revitalization to the recolonization program designed to replace expelled Moriscos with settlers from northern parts of Castile. But in the short term, the resettlement initiative attracted mostly impoverished immigrants from Galicia and other northern parts of Castile who could not match the ancestral knowledge of water management and horticulture of the expelled Moriscos.[3] Ironically, the new settlers initially conjured as industrious Castilians of Old Christian origins would soon be disdained as *advenedizos* (strangers) by one of Granada's most influential chroniclers, Francisco Bermúdez de Pedraza. Though the term most commonly signifies a foreigner with the decided connotation of social inferiority, in sixteenth-century usage it also referred disparagingly to new converts from Islam or "pagan" cultures.[4] A paradox emerges in this slippage of terminology. One oppressed minority, Moriscos dwelling in small mountain villages, is driven away and replaced with landless peasants from the north. But these new arrivals, in turn, become objects of scorn from the same elite, expressed with the same ethno-religious epithet (*advenedizos*).

Even in the more privileged confines of the city centre where Juan Latino lived and taught, we find signs of tension. Here, however, the issue of racial and religious bias is impossible to separate from more mundane internecine disputes. The university, underfunded even in better times, emerged from the civil war and ensuing ethnic cleansing campaign in still more fragile state, with particular devastation in the medical faculty, a traditional Morisco stronghold. Juan Latino was not part of this worst-affected collective, but nonetheless suffered a challenge to his own position. Surviving faculty senate minutes of the University of Granada from the early 1570s record an effort to oust him from the prime classroom space he had occupied for some four decades. Here, though Juan Latino was repeatedly called a *catedrático*, the informality of his affiliation to the university may have become a liability. As I noted in chapter 1, he taught under the auspices of the royal grammar school (Colegio Real), but in practice came to be viewed as an integral part of the university faculty. His popularity as a Latin teacher compensated for the fledgling university's lack of an endowed Latin chair. The crown's publication licences also refer to him as *catedrático* in the university, as do litigation records of the royal treasury (*hacienda*). Yet faculty senate minutes in the mid-1570s begin to speak of his Latin class in the Colegio Real as a "usurper" of valuable university space. The idea of usurpation is noteworthy, given that documents from previous decades do not make such distinctions between Latino's de jure ties to the grammar school and his de facto role in the university. A memorandum Antonio Marín Ocete transcribed records how the archbishop, Pedro de Guerrero, intervened on Latino's behalf to defend his continued access to his traditional classroom space.[5]

What to make of these problems at work that faced the poet-and-educator just after his publication debut in 1573? The conflict over classroom space may reflect university faction politics, disciplinary rivalries, or just an acute shortage of space. It might even signal efforts to push out a teacher getting on in years. But bias against a black man cannot be ruled out entirely, particularly given the document's lexicon of untoward intrusion, with the term "usurpation" appearing repeatedly. Nonetheless, any interpretation of this controversy in relation to minority identity would need to tread carefully and consider other explanations.

A more direct statement of differentiation based on minority status emerges from remembrances of Granada's literary establishment in these later years. One story that gained wide currency in a printed poetry anthology is revealing for how it describes the poet and cathedral musician Gregorio Silvestre (1520–70) presiding over a literary academy. He greeted arriving comrades but pointedly ignored Juan Latino. When the schoolmaster protested, Silvestre replied: "Pardon me *maestro,* but I thought you were the shadow of one of these gentlemen."[6] A low-comic jest about different skin colour mixes with an assertion of the inferior standing of a black man in a gathering of poets, as the *sombra* or shadow of the others.

An irony of the joke is that a gathering of Granada's best poets in the mid-sixteenth century would probably have included talented versifiers who had honed their skills in the language arts in Juan Latino's own classroom. Here, Brian Vickers's comments on the same period in English letters are pertinent, in that he notes that "credit for the ability of so many Renaissance writers to use the full expressive resources of language must be given to the humanist school-system and to the masters who so energetically enforced it."[7] Indeed, one promising angle for future inquiries as scholars recover Juan Latino's story is precisely the search for information about the students he taught. With known documents, we cannot gauge whether Silvestre's alleged quip was indeed exclusionary or insulting, or whether it was a record of witty banter among fellow poets.

Yet we do know that Juan Latino had occasion to ponder on his own terms the delineations between insider and outsider in these later years. Two years after Lepanto transpired and less than a year after Latino's *Song of John of Austria* appeared in print, Philip II ordered that his immediate family members buried in Granada's Capilla Real be disinterred and transferred to the new Escorial Palace complex just outside Madrid. Juan Latino provided commemorative epitaphs, chronicling the ceremony held 25 January 1574. Royal chapel workers disinterred the king's deceased family members in preparation for their transfer to the Escorial Palace, with a large cortège of high ranking nobles and churchmen arrayed as witnesses.[8] Chapter 1 began with an examination of the lapidary self-portrait Latino appended as a preface to the volume commemorating the *Traslación* ceremony, *Epitaphs on the Solemn, Memorable, and Catholic Transfer* (abbreviated as *De Translatione*). To conclude, I return to a different passage of the same volume, this time to consider one more avian wonder through which Juan Latino claims a voice in the Spanish Monarchy.

A Song for a World Empire

Once again, the educator-turned-poet directs himself to the powerful royal secretary who shepherded the Lepanto volume through the court's process of publication licence. A prefatory elegy addressed to Antonio Gracián Dantisco begins by expressing gratitude for the support he gave the Lepanto epic. Then he hails Gracián Dantisco's honour that stems from his family's long tradition of secretarial service to the Habsburg Monarchy, dating back from the service of his father Diego Gracián de Alderete to Charles V. Finally, he beseeches the younger Gracián for protection once more. Verses affirm that favour from so respected a court official would bring the acclaim of the grudging crowd. Up to this point, the rhetoric adheres to the tradition of prologues. But the poet veers towards a more personal terrain that seems apt in a book honouring Philip II's ritual of family piety. Attuned to the solemnity of the occasion, the poet frames his request for crown access within an intimation of his own pending mortality:

> Spiritus iste tuus sublimen pellet in auras,
> ignibus incendet frigida corda seni. (*De Translatione*, fol. 34v)

> (Your own life-giving breath will reach high into the winds, breathing warmth to kindle the sluggish mind of the old man.)

Note how the freedman harnesses the different nuances of *spiritus*, a term denoting life-giving air and poetic inspiration. This duality conveys the extraordinary power conferred on the private secretary who regulated communications with Philip II. Support from the official could breathe new life into a poet who, at fifty-eight, was an old man (*senex*) by the standards of the times and in comparison to Antonio Gracián, the scion of a secretarial dynasty who was two decades his junior.

Continuing, the poetic voice builds on the concept of Gracián Dantisco's power to give life-nourishing air (*spiritus*), essentially launching the freedman in flight. To sing of Lepanto, Latino presented himself as a black raven who sings of new, auspicious times. In this later foray into print, the poet undergoes another metamorphosis – into a black swan:

> Dulcia qui Aethiopum moduletur carmina lingua,
> sed quae Romanos exprimat ore sonos.
> Ut niger ipse tuo volitat dum flamine Cygnus,
> rara suo caelum vertice signet avis. (*De Translatione*, fol. 34v)[9]

> (He [the old man] shall be able to measure forth sweet songs in the language of Aethiopians, but he emits these [poems] in Roman sounds from his voice. For as long as the black swan flies with your favouring wind, a rare bird will mark out the sky with his tufted head.)

These verses naturalize the patron-client alliance, with the royal secretary's support conceived as the favouring wind that allows the black swan to soar heavenward. For his part, the poet draws himself as a literary craftsman who will measure out eloquent verses. Just as *The Song of John of Austria* displays the freedman's mastery of epic versifying through emulation of Virgil and Lucan, this portrait of the artist as a black swan claims a connection to Martial and Juvenal, masters of the social commentary expressed in the concision of epigrams built on elegiac couplets (Martial) or hexameters (Juvenal).

Artful imitation of Martial allows Latino to metaphorize this new foray into print publication as a swan song. The first of the two couplets replays a celebrated passage from this Roman poet born in Hispania, *Epigrammata* 13,77: "Dulcia defecta modulatur carmina lingua/cantator cycnus funeris ipse sui" (the swan gives forth its sweet measured song with failing tongue, itself the minstrel of its own death). Poets of the Spanish Renaissance had expanded the classical topos of a paradoxically sweet death song to signify the life-long literary vocation of a poet or orator who strives to expand his output of rhyming sounds and mathematically calibrated verses. The detailed gloss from Covarrubias to *cisne* records this figurative conception of the words of an aging poet as a swan song: "and thus those who in old age have exerted themselves in their writings, not only poets but also orators – who do not lack for meter and rhyme."[10] The intimation of mortality within Latino's particular swan song is twofold. He is a poet full of years at age fifty-eight when he signs off on this volume. At the same time, he commemorates a ceremony honouring the departed members of the king's own immediate family.

Layering his adaptation of Martial, the poet also alters Juvenal's famous aphorism, "rara avis in terris nigroque simillima cycno" (a rare bird on this earth, exactly like a black swan, Juvenal, *Satire* 2.6.165). The maxim would provide European letters with an expression for the ultimate impossibility, something not refuted until English explorers saw black swans in Australia in the eighteenth century.[11] In Spanish letters, we have seen how chroniclers invoked the familiar verse to appropriate Latino's success for the Duke of Sessa's greater glory. The grandee reportedly hailed Latino as "rara avis in terra, corvo simillima negro" ([my] black raven is a rare bird on earth). The alleged quip from his former master speaks to the fashion that emerged among European elites in the sixteenth century, who employed black servants or slaves for ostentation and to make jests about contrasting skin colour. In Italy, where members of the Sessa family served the Spanish crown at decisive moments in the sixteenth century, Ludovico Sforza of Milan earned the epithet "Il Moro" because of his frequent portrayal with black Africans. When Latino was studying at Granada's new university, Nicholus Clenardus arrived in the city with Antonius Nigrinus, one of three young black men whom he purchased in Portugal and then trained to serve as unpaid classroom assistants. Repeatedly, the Flemish humanist used these young men to make demeaning classroom jokes about black servitude and thus add levity to Latin learning.[12]

But in Latino's adaptation, Juvenal's maxim becomes a figure of self-affirmation as a black swan who has mastered the literary forms of Renaissance Europe. Now his singularity is not a testament to a grandee's wealth or a humanist's wit, but a credential the poet controls and mobilizes on his own terms to secure court sponsorship and claim a voice in Spanish society. Along the way, the poet alters an axiom of poetic imagery – that a swan is, by necessity, white. María Rosa Lida de Malkiel has shown how poets from Garcilaso de la Vega onward drew profound inspiration echoing and building on Virgil's "candidior cycnis" (whiter than swans) from *Eclogue* 7.37. Sebastián de Covarrubias turns to such literary models to offer the swan as a "white bird with lightest feathers with which no other colour is mixed; only the beak and feet are coloured."[13] Finally, Latino's self-portrait as a black swan also features a pointed echo – with the metrical parallel drawing attention to the classical intertext – of Virgil's striking image of white swans grazing in grassy streams: "Pascentem niveos herboso flumine cycnos" (*Georgics* 2.199).

As with his earlier self-portrait as an auspicious raven, Latino's black swan carries a pointed political message. Adopting it as an emblem, the freedman renders himself the voice of the multi-ethnic and multilingual global empire Philip II envisioned after Lepanto. Returning to the pair of couplets quoted above, the pleasing songs ("dulcia ... carmina") emerge from a poet whose native tongue, *lingua,* is Ethiopian, understood as a black African. But the sounds – that is, the finished literary product – are Roman ("sed quae Romanos exprimat ore sonos"). Artful literary creation results from a labour of cross-cultural translation and transformation. Far from being an impediment, the poet's alterity, as one whose native language is from Ethiopia or sub-Saharan Africa, is part of the singularity that merits lasting fame and court sponsorship.

A linchpin of Juan Latino's song for a multi-ethnic, cosmopolitan empire is Philip II's standing as the Catholic Monarch. As he did with the 1573 Lepanto volume, Latino addresses *De Translatione* to "the Catholic King" (ad Catholicum ... Regem). In so doing, the poet underscores the implications of the honorific that Philip II inherited from Ferdinand and Isabel. *Catholicus* denotes *universal (universalis*). In his own invocation as poet, Latino identifies himself as Poeta Catholicus.[14] Following the lexical thread from Nebrija's seminal Latin dictionary to Covarrubias, *universal* stands for one who "is aware of many different things and speaks about them knowledgeably."[15] This universality is brought to life in sound and sight through the black swan. We have, in short, a stunning emblem of self-affirmation wrought through a skilful adaptation of illustrious Roman predecessors. Alas, Juan Latino's "Catholic song" would not ring out for long in the coming era of crown expansion. What happened?

Granted, the book of epigrams on the *Traslación* did gain print licence from the crown and appeared in 1576. But unspooling fate would soon change the terrain in which the poet had envisioned his rise to greater prestige and lasting fame. For one, the supposedly tired, aging poet would outlive a succession of mostly younger patrons. Antonio Gracián Dantisco, his point of entry to the court of Philip II, died in 1576. The same year, two other some-time benefactors also died, Archbishop Pedro de Guerrero and the Duke of Sessa. In fact, the one ally who seemed to enjoy both unalloyed good fortune and a long life was the least sympathetic. In 1577, Pedro de Deza left his position as Audiencia president under the cloud of accusations of cruelty and corruption I detailed in concluding chapter 2. But he left having been promoted to cardinal. Elevated to prince of the church, he relocated to Rome. Belatedly, Deza received a particularly dazzling version of the face-saving ecclesiastical promotion that John of Austria had indeed recommended to Philip II at a time when the official had seemed to be the main obstacle to ending the war in Granada. In Rome, Deza garnered immense prestige and wealth, becoming a pillar of what Thomas Dandelet calls Spanish Rome.[16]

In contrast, John of Austria himself never fulfilled the lofty imperial aspirations expressed in Latino's epic. Less than a year after the naval battle, John of Austria led a campaign to corner the one Muslim naval commander who escaped unscathed from the destruction at Lepanto, Uluç Ali. Though Don John seemed poised to trap the Calabrian convert to Islam at the Balkan port of Navarino, Uluç Ali took shelter under the rocky fortress of Modon and escaped once again. In Constantinople, he supervised the reconstruction of the Ottoman fleets.[17] The following year, John of Austria set his sights on the recapture of Tunis, hoping to recover Charles V's celebrated 1535 conquest and, in turn, secure a royal title for himself. He briefly did take the North African port city, but the Spanish garrison fell in less than a year to forces under Uluç Ali. After a chain of disappointments, John of Austria succumbed to disease in 1578 during a military campaign in the Low Countries. In death, his half-brother honoured him with space in the royal crypt of the Escorial, giving him the full recognition as a member of Spain's royal family that he had pointedly refused to grant him in life.[18]

Philip II, for his part, did ultimately extend his rule to eastern realms, though not as poets and chroniclers had envisioned after Lepanto. Instead of gaining new realms through conquering armies marching eastward behind the Habsburg standard, Philip II came to rule distant eastern lands as the result of the death of King Sebastian of Portugal without successors in the Battle of Alcazarquivir (1578). This debacle, as Ruth MacKay shows, was the tragic culmination of a campaign in North Africa that the Portuguese king had devised with the explicit aim of matching John of Austria's exploits at Lepanto.[19]

Another irony emerges from the very nature of the *Traslación* ceremony Juan Latino commemorated. When Philip II ordered his deceased family members to be taken out of Granada's Capilla Real and sent for reburial to the Escorial, he essentially deprived the city of its tangible claim to symbolic centrality within Habsburg Spain. Not long after he ordered the royal bodies moved to the new palace complex, Philip also sent for most of Isabel I's personal library. Shipments of books from Granada to the Escorial would eventually include Alfonso X of Castile's *Libros de ajedrez, dados, y tablas*, whose depiction of a black-ruled court came to life in Juan Latino's elegy "On the Birth of Untroubled Times."[20] The Capilla Real would still guard the tombs of the Catholic Monarchs and their daughter Queen Juana, but no longer tend the graves and prized relics of members of the ruling Habsburg dynasty.

Granada's loss of symbolic centrality in Habsburg Spain matched the city's diminished economic and cultural stature in the decade after the end of the civil war. Taking note of the ultimate consequences of the civil war of 1568–70 and the ensuing mass expulsion of Moriscos, A. Katie Harris notes that "though still an important urban center, Granada – the treasure of the Catholic Monarchs, the symbol of the ascendant Habsburgs and Charles V – increasingly found itself relegated to the status of regional capital of eastern Andalusia."[21] A range of initiatives sought to reclaim the lost prominence within the Spanish Monarchy. For instance, a group of nobles received crown licence to form a chivalric brotherhood designed to develop the military skills needed for "this frontier city," alleging that with its depleted population, the city required noblemen and residents who could wield arms. This initiative shows how jousting tournaments endured as a means of elite self-expression and training. It also points to one tactic through which Granada's elite would ultimately seek to recover its economic vibrancy in the first part of the seventeenth century.[22]

But during the shorter time frame of Juan Latino's mature years, the most enduring initiative to reassert Granada's stature within imperial Spain would be the work, not of gallant jousters, but of secretive counterfeiters. Falsified ancient Christian relics and writings appeared, first amid the ruins of a minaret repurposed into a church bell tower, the Torre Turpiana (1588), and then just outside the city at the Sacromonte (1595). Initially, the blatant fabrications of ancient Christian scriptures might seem a world away from Juan Latino's humanistically inclined textual practice. But on closer inspection, the forgeries which most historians attribute to Morisco intellectuals speak to some of the same dilemmas of race and religion we find in Juan Latino's literary self-fashioning. In both cases, we find a quandary about how to secure honour in a society increasingly fixated on signifiers of Old Christian lineage.[23] We have seen how Juan Latino issued a discrete challenge to the premise that Christian virtue is by necessity Old Christian. In the *Song of John of Austria*, he introduces himself as a poet whose muse resides in the "Parnassus" of Christian baptism. Before the same basic predicament, the counterfeiters of the parchments and leaden books concocted an ancient Christian lineage for Moriscos and the city of Granada.

The excitement and devotional activities that would emerge from the "sacred treasures" unearthed at the Torre Turpiana and Sacromonte probably came too late in Juan Latino's life to change his course of actions. His last documented attendance of a university faculty senate meeting dates from 1587, at which point he would have been seventy years old.[24] One chronicler from the seventeenth century recorded his death in 1590, though there is reason to believe he lived through the middle of that decade. It is unlikely that he reached age ninety as recorded in the now-lost Alcazar portrait of "a black man [...] with a label that says he was ninety years old."[25] More plausibly, the portrait's inscription records a memory that Latino was extraordinarily long-lived for the era. Lacking parish records of the freedman's death, Marín Ocete gives a plausible estimate of the period between 1594 and 1597.[26] Granada's patchwork of parish archives likely hold records to allow the subsequent tracing of surviving members of the Carlobal-Latino family and their eventual assimilation into the general population, though extremely limited hours and the arduous process of gaining permission from the archdiocese will require funding for a prolonged stay or work by scholars based in the city.

Best evidence now available suggests Latino outlived most if not all of his four or five children and his wife Ana Carlobal. A seventeenth-century chronicler identifies a grandson, Francisco Latino de Sandoval, as his heir. There are signs of a family legacy tied to Latino's decades as an educator. In 1599, university faculty deliberating on the conferral of a degree in canon law proposed leniency towards his widowed son-in-law, identified only as the Licenciado Fuentes. Though the would-be graduate was weak, faculty members proposed "benevolence taking into account the service his father-in-law the Maestro Juan Latino had given this university."[27] Admittedly, a claim to nepotism falls well short of the poet's own lofty vision of lasting Fama as a poet laureate for the Spanish empire. But in the context of early modern society, the ability to establish a legacy of family honour tied to his capacity as a respected educator was no small accomplishment for one who endured the destruction of family ties in the early Atlantic slave trade and who celebrated his origins outside Europe and – as best we can tell – refrained from the fabrication of a claim of Christian ancestry from time immemorial.

In time, church officials in Granada would also marshal Juan Latino's life as an example of how new education opportunities transformed Spanish society. In a manuscript history of the archdiocese completed circa 1611, Justino Antolínez de Burgos celebrated how Joan Méndez de

Salvatierra rose from humble origins in Extremadura to high rank as Granada's ninth archbishop. The prelate reportedly told Juan Latino to "note the power of letters, without which, you would never escape tending horses in a stable nor would I get from behind a plough in the fields."[28] This recollection brings *The Epic of Juan Latino* full circle. In life, Juan Latino's ability to mobilize new educational initiatives at critical junctures became the motor for claiming freedom and full membership in Granada's society. After his death, his remarkable advancement became part of a broader narrative about the transformative impact of education on Spanish society.

In terms of Latino's legacy within the literature of the African diaspora, a full assessment awaits further inquiries from specialists. My aim here has been to provide a multifaceted examination of the Spanish cultural context that shaped his life and informed his work, thereby laying the ground for examinations by scholars from related fields. Certainly, Juan Latino's claim to a voice anticipates pivotal figures in the diaspora. Frederick Douglass's resolve to become a newspaperman, "wielding my pen, as well as my voice" comes immediately to mind, as does the epiphany he experiences when first standing to speak to a gathering of abolitionists.[29] In *The Epic of Juan Latino*, we find this claim of a voice emerged in the earliest phase of the Atlantic slave trade itself.

Yet a full recovery of Latino's story will require a refutation of the distorted image of the poet-and-educator that emerged through a process of canonization in caricature during the seventeenth century. Shortly after his death, a series of writers reimagined his upward mobility, teaching career, and interracial marriage in comic terms that reflect a solidifying colour prejudice against blacks, as well as anxieties about Granada's Muslim heritage. The most influential distortion within early modern Spanish studies would be the *comedia* of circa 1615 by Diego Ximénez de Enciso, *Juan Latino*. Studies by Baltasar Fra Molinero, John Beusterien, and Emily Weissbourd have shown what this drama reveals about emerging discourses of race in Spain and early modern Europe. But whatever its value as a record of a broader cultural current, it has been a detriment to recovering the story of the poet-and-educator from Granada, given the stickiness of its racially charged plot points that are not supported by sources from the poet-and-educator's own life.[30] Other recollections from the same point in the early seventeenth century would be even more damaging. Notably, Ambrosio Salazar tapped into the most insidious representations of black men, narrating Latino's interracial marriage – given no particular emphasis in surviving period documents – as the result of his rape of Ana Carlobal.[31] Though the other posthumous fictions about Juan Latino retain a comic register, Salazar's fictional account of the marriage follows from a penchant for attributing sexual transgression to black Africans in Europe.

For most readers of the last four centuries, the first contact with Juan Latino has been the parodic poem that Cervantes inserted as a preface to his 1605 *Don Quijote*. The laudatory poem, from Urganda la Desconocida, praises the novel in the "broken end" verses ("versos de cabo roto") in which the poet elides the unstressed last syllable of Castilian octosyllables. Consequently, the schoolmaster and erudite Latin poet speaks a broken Castilian, in verses that gesture to the stock theatrical character of the captured black African, *esclavo bozal,* who is not yet fluent (*ladino*) in an Iberian language. In my translation below, I try to approximate the sonorous effect of the broken end Castilian verses:

> Pues al cielo no le plu-
> que salieses tan ladi-
> como el negro Juan Latin-,
> hablar latines rehu-
>
> (Lest it the heavens it might discommmm
> should you emerge so converrrrr
> as the black Juan Latiiiii,
> to speak Latins you must refuuu).[32]

The schoolmaster who inculcated generations of aspiring diplomats, churchmen, and crown officials in the language arts is portrayed as a kidnapped black African just arrived in Spain. It is true that the targets of Cervantes's parody are his contemporaries who lard their books with pedantic encomiastic poems. But the comic evocation of the voice of a *bozal* would distort and conceal Juan Latino's actual literary accomplishments.

A more benign reason that Juan Latino's career as a poet-and-educator receded from view in the seventeenth century was, of course, the gradual shift in elite linguistic culture. The dominance of Castilian as the de facto official language of the Spanish Monarchy made the poet's Latinate literary vocation seem less relevant than it did at the time he crafted his *Song of John of Austria*. In this sense, Juan Latino's books would become part of what James Hankins calls a "Lost Atlantis" of literature, submerged out of sight of most readers as the study of literature became divided into fields defined within the boundaries of the official languages of modern nation-states.[33]

Even as Latino receded into a marginal position in Spanish literary histories, his voice as a poet-and-educator would remain audible to bibliophiles. Thus, a compilation of Spanish feast days published in Lyon over seven decades after the *princeps* appeared selected *The Song of John of Austria* to mark the increasingly popular devotion to Our Lady of the Victory, a Marian devotion promoted in the wake of the Battle of Lepanto.[34] In the later seventeenth century, bibliographer Nicolás Antonio listed Juan Latino in his *Bibliotheca Hispana Nova*, recording his social advancement, honourable marriage, and prominence as a schoolmaster. He also lists his known literary works. Notable here is that Latino belongs to the *new* library of Hispania, understood as the library of modern Spanish writers. As Joannes Latinus, he stands in this canon as the equal of Ambrosio de Salazar, Francisco Bermúdez de Pedraza, Lope de Vega Carpio, and Miguel de Cervantes Saavedra, some of the seventeenth-century writers who had reimagined his teaching vocation, family life, and literary career through jests and comic scenes.[35]

Memory of the poet and educator of Granada was thus kept alive for three centuries in two seemingly incompatible guises. One was the fictional stereotype deeded from these Golden Age writers. The second is the Juan Latino this study has sought to recover and recontextualize: the erudite schoolmaster whose life unfolded in the crosscurrents of Spanish imperialism. There, he drew inspiration from its expanding intellectual and geographic horizons, but also found limits and contradictions.

Epilogue: Juan Latino in the Harlem Renaissance

With the proceeds from the sale of his extensive book collection on black culture to the New York Public Library, Arthur (Arturo) Schomburg (1874–1938) sailed from New York to Spain in 1926. His goal was to find evidence about black painters and confraternities from early modern Seville and search for traces of Juan Latino's life in Granada. The bibliophile had first discovered the poet-and-educator of Granada in his school days in his native Puerto Rico, when he and his classmates memorized the verses about "el negro Juan Latin-" found in the burlesque prefatory poem in *Don Quijote*. As I noted in the conclusion, this literary recollection of Latino, published about a decade after his likely death (ca. 1594), reimagined the erudite poet-and-educator of Granada as a stuttering black man who is not yet conversant in Castilian. In so doing, Cervantes drew on a comic language already codified in Iberian theater. Schomburg would be a fitting scholar to correct the record. After moving to New York, he had sought to find the truth about Latino by compiling the (scarce) secondary sources. He balanced this query with avid book collecting, research on other artists of the black diaspora, and political activism, while working as the supervisor of the mail room at Bankers' Trust.

Retirement from the bank and proceeds from his book sale allowed Schomburg to travel to Spain to unearth "facts and information" about Juan Latino. He arrived in the freedman's home city on a train named – with paradoxical appropriateness – the Rocinante Express. He noted: "I had crossed the Atlantic because I was personally satisfied that there was no better place to uncover this information than in Latino's own home and under his own vine and fig tree."[1] At the university, he was delighted to meet Antonio Marín Ocete, who had recently completed a doctoral dissertation on Juan Latino. The terms with which Schomburg hails the study of 1923–4 speak to the scholarly ethos of the Harlem Renaissance, in that the visitor praises his host's revelations that resulted from an "exhaustive search, gathered from fragmentary facts, and buttressed with trustworthy references."[2]

But where Marín Ocete, echoing Cervantes, titled his study "El negro Juan Latino," the title of Schomburg's article restores the double name with which the schoolmaster of Granada himself signed legal documents – "Juan Latino, Magister Latinus."[3] As the Harlem polymath would have been particularly well placed to grasp, this double signature captures the broad range of social, vocational, and intellectual affiliations. "Juan Latino" is a Granadino, husband, head-of-household, and *vecino* of the Santa Ana parish. "Magister Latinus" is the erudite and innovative schoolmaster who inculcated generations of young Granadinos in the language arts they needed for university studies.

Schomburg's concise field note appeared in *Ebony and Topaz: A Collectanea,* compiled by the sociologist Charles S. Johnson. The Urban League–sponsored journal culled scholarly notes from different authors that likewise sought to find, evaluate, and connect the scattered evidence about the careers of artists and writers of the black diaspora. Johnson's editorial statement deploys the same archaeological discourse we find in Schomburg's field note, presenting the issue as a compilation of the "rare and curiously interesting fragments of careers and art which constitute that absorbing field of the past now being revealed through the zeal and industry of Negro scholars."[4] A similar testimony to the joy of diligent research stands out in the brief forward in which L. Hollingsworth Wood invites the *Collectanea*'s reader to "follow with zest the explorations of appraising eyes which have been made available to us in attractive form on these pages."[5]

Despite the three centuries that separated Schomburg from Latino, his historiographic framework would have been readily intelligible for the author who claimed a voice in sixteenth-century Spain as a black poet-and-educator. Appropriately, the note "Juan Latino, Magister Latinus" appears in the journal's pages just before portraits of three path-breaking artists from the ensuing centuries. After the note on Latino, the editor placed a pen drawing of poet Phillis Wheatley by W.E. Braxton, with the text of her poem "To a Gentleman, on his Voyage to Great Britain for the Recovery of his Health." Turning the page, we find a mezzo-tint of Ignatius Sancho, a noted literary figure in eighteenth-century London, rendered from a painting by Thomas Gainsborough.

Then, there is a likeness of Francis Barber, who was servant, research assistant, and literary executor to lexicographer Samuel Johnson.[6] This gallery in miniature spans the African diaspora. Latino – in his telling, born in sub-Saharan Africa and transported to Andalusia – stands in the company of Wheatley, born in Senegambia; Sancho, born on a slave ship; and Barber, from a plantation in Jamaica.

Schomburg would not be able to carry out the recovery of Juan Latino that he presages. In the decade that followed, he devoted his time to a wide-ranging agenda of cultural and political advocacy. He collected African art, campaigned against lynching, supported benevolent organizations for black performers, worked to build the library collections at Fisk University in Nashville, and served as the curator of the Negro Historical Society headquartered in the 135th Street branch of the New York Public Library. This was the collection he started while still working at Bankers' Trust and the nucleus of the vibrant research centre that now honours him, as the Schomburg Center for Research in Black Culture. It is among his research notes and papers that we find an outline of a scholarly agenda for recovering the first known black writer from the slave diaspora. May it continue.

Appendix 1 Elegy for Philip II, "On the Birth of Untroubled Times" (De natali serenissimi ad Catholicum et Invictissimum Regem Philippum Elegia)

(In *Ad catholicum … Epigrammatum liber*, fols. 9v–11r, 1st gathering, B1v–B3r), prose translation by Elizabeth R. Wright and Andrew Lemons. Margin notes from *princeps* are transcribed and translated in the endnotes, coinciding with their original placement.[1]

Autorem res magna petit, nascique poeta
debuerat fratri, Summe Philippe, tuo.
Unicus est victor, scriptorem quaeritat unum,
res nova vult vatem regibus esse novum.
Auribus alme tuis non haec victoria ponto est
audita, hic scriptor nec fuit orbe satus,
Aethiopum terris venit, qui gesta Latinus
Austriadae mira carminis arte canat.
Is genibus flexis orat te, invicte Philippe,
Cantator fratris possit ut esse tui.
Nam si nobilitant Austriadae bella poetam,
Phoenicem Austriadam, quod niger, ille facit.
Terribilis classis gentes motura Philippi,
orbi portentum tunc erit Austriades.
Prodigiosa viros turbabit fama poeta, [10r, B2r]
volventes fastis haec monumenta tuis.
Aurora hunc peperit, Reges Arabumque beatos,
primitias gentum quos dedit illa Deo.
Quod si nostra tuis facies Rex nigra ministris
displicet, Aethiopum non placet alba viris.
Illic Auroram, sordet, qui viserit albus,
suntque duces nigri, rex quoque fuscus adest.

Candace Regina genus, nigrumque ministrum
  vel curru Christo miserat illa suum.
Legerat ille genus non enarrabile Christi,
  Austriadae pugnas non canet iste tui?
Obvius Aethiopem Christum docet ore Philippus,
  discipulum Christus mittit ad Aethiopem:
non temere Aethiopi caelo datus ergo Philippus,
  ne Aethiopi haec forte Philippe neges.
Quid quod et Austriades exactor gentis iniquae
  Garnatae vatem viderat esse suum.
Et dixit, fratri narrabo mira Philippo
  de te, qui scriptor diceris esse novus.
Consuevere pii reges miranda tenere
  Aulis, ostentum regibus ut facerent.
Secula regnantum, nigrum Romana potestas
  invideat vatem iure Philippe tibi.
Filius ecclesae vives Auguste Philippe, [10v, B2v]
  si pateant cunctis ad pia vota fores.
Nec rerum est Dominus, qui non admiserit omnes,
  gentem ne excludat regia forte meam.
Dignetur regnis hominem donare Philippus,
  scriptorem fratris iam velit esse sui.
Si Christus vitae fuscos non despicit autor,
  Catholicus vatem respice iure tuum.
Ludicra, nec levia haec scribuntur gesta poetae,
  Roma ducem similem non tulit Austriadae.
Candidus hic lector cursus, puppesque tuorum,
  Victorem norit, fluctibus Austriadam.
Devictos Turcas cernet, classemque superbam,
  et Parthos fratrem vincere magnanimum.
Consilium pelagi, regis navale Tyranni
  imperium fractum, captaque signa sciet.
Omnia quae Latio scribit sermone Latinus,
  versibus et veris, arma ducesque canit.
Regnatura diu maiestas summa Philippi,
  scripta typis cudi haec imperet ipsa novis:
ut vivat carmen gestorum fratris in orbe,
  posteritasque legat Regia facta viri.
Qui nunc esta nobis belli spes altera ponto,
  auspiciis nomen tollet ad astra tuum.

Est cultor Christi magnus, Matrisque beatae [11r, B3r]
  Virginis, Ecclesae tutor, ad arma pius.
Magnanimus, fortis, felix, ductorque benignus,
  cui labor assiduus Martis, honorque placet.
Et miles pugnat, ceptis fit Caesar in armis,
  prudens consilio crescit et ingenio.
Dum natus princeps paulatim surgit in hostes,
  conficiet frater grandia bella tibi.
Fernandusque tuus, spes nostri, et gloria saecli
  res gerere, et Martem discet amare suum.
Virtute et patrem referens nil linquet inausum,
  sub iuga Turcarum mittet et imperium:
sub te iam Christi reddet pietate sepulchrum,
  regibus et fato debita regna tuis.
Haec tibi certa suo promittit carmine cornix,
    felix cuncta bene et prospera, dixit, erunt.

[The prose translation below retains the format of the elegiac couplets to facilitate a comparison with the Latin, though readability has, in some cases, necessitated the rearrangement of words between the hexameter and pentameter. Line numbers in paretheses coincide with the transcription above, appearing at the end of the corresponding passage.]

A great event seeks an author, and a poet
  had to be born for your brother, great Philip.[2]
The victor is unique, he demands a unique writer;
  a new event requires a new bard for kings. (1–4)
Such a naval triumph, benevolent one, has never reached your ears;
  this writer was not engendered in this world:
he came from lands of Aethiopia, Latinus,
  who sings the Austriad's wondrous deeds with his skill in song.[3] (5–8)
He beseeches you on bended knee, invincible Philip,
  so he can be singer for your brother.
Now if the wars of the Austriad ennoble the poet,
  he, as a black, renders the Austrian a Phoenix.[4] (9–12)
Philip's awe-inspiring fleet poised to strike nations,
  at which time the Austriad will be a portent to the world.
The astounding fame of the poet will stun men
  as they consider these momentous deeds in your annals.[5] (13–16)

Aurora begat him, and thus brought forth for God
those sainted kings of Arabia and offerings of nations.[6]
For if our black face, oh king, displeases your emissaries,
a white one does not please men of Aethiopia. (17–20)
There, a white man who visits the East is considered vile,
and there are black leaders, and there is even a dark-skinned king.[7]
Queen Candace sent her people
and black emissary to Christ in a chariot. (21–4)
He had read of the ineffable people of Christ;
will this man not sing the battles of your Austriad?[8]
En route Philip teaches the Aethiopian face-to-face about Christ,
Christ sends a disciple to the Aethiopian, (25–8)
not by chance, therefore, Philip was brought under Aethiopian sky,
nor, o Philip, should you, by accident, deny these just reasons.[9]
And what of the fact that the Austriad, banisher of the iniquitous race,
had considered him to be his bard in Granada.[10] (29–32)
He said, moreover, I will recount wondrous things to brother Philip
about you, who are called a new writer.
Pious kings grew accustomed to harbor wonders
in courts, so they might display them to kings.[11] (33–6)
For the years they rule, let Roman power, with reason
envy your black bard, o Philip.
You shall live as son of the church,
should the doors open to everyone for their pious offerings.[12] (37–40)
There is no lord of states who has not admitted everyone,
nor monarchy that would exclude my race capriciously.
May Philip deign to give this man to his realms,
may he now wish him to be his brother's writer. (41–4)
If Christ, giver of life, did not disdain blacks,
as a Catholic, justly turn your eyes to your bard.
Not light, frivolous, these deeds are written by the poet,
Rome has not brought forth a leader equal to the Austriad.[13] (45–8)
Here the enlightened reader will learn of the charges, and the galleys of your men,
the Austrian victor on the waves.[14]
He will see the great brother vanquish
humbled Turks, the proud fleet and Parthians. (49–52)
He will learn of the council at sea, the shattered naval empire
of the Tyrant king and the captured standard.
Latinus writes all these things in Latin speech,

and with true verses he will sing of arms and leaders. (53–6)
Let the supreme majesty of Philip – long may he rule –
demand these writings be stamped in a new medium,[15]
so the song of the brother's exploits shall come alive the world over,
and posterity shall read of the royal deeds of the man. (57–60)
He who is now a new hope for us in battle at sea,
will raise your name to the stars through auspicious things.
He is a great worshipper of Christ, and the holy Virgin Mother
protector of the Church, pious in battles,[16] (61–4)
a magnanimous, strong, fortunate, and kind leader,
who takes pleasure in assiduous toil and martial deeds.
And as soldier he fights, becomes a Caesar in battles waged,
prudent, matures through council and intelligence. (65–8)
As born leader he rises against enemies,
the brother will carry out great battles for you.
And your Ferdinand, our hope, and glory of ages,
will learn to govern affairs and love Mars himself.[17] (69–72)
Recalling the father in virtue, he will leave nothing undared,
he will submit the empire of the Turks under the yoke:
he will piously restore the sepulcher of Christ to you,
and the realms destined by fate to your rulers.[18] (73–6)
A raven promises you in his song these things are certain,
auspicious, he announced all will be well and prosperous.[19]

Appendix 2 Chronology

	The life of Juan Latino	Historical backdrop
1491		November: agreement (*Capitulaciones*) for Nasrid king, Abi Abdilehi (Boabdil), to surrender Granada to King Ferdinand II of Aragon and Queen Isabel I of Castile.
1492		January: Catholic Monarchs officially take possession of Granada. March: Edict of Expulsion against Jews.
1499–1500		First Revolt of the Alpujarras
1502		Religious tolerance for Muslims stipulated in the 1491 *Capitulaciones* ends. All who wish to remain in the region are required to undergo baptism.
1515	Death of the Gran Capitán (Gonzalo Fernández de Córdoba, first Duke of Sessa)	
circa 1517	Juan Latino's birth	
1520	Birth of the third Duke of Sessa (Gonzalo Fernández de Córdoba).	
circa 1525	Residency in Granada in the household of the Duchess of Terranova, widow of the Gran Capitán.	

	The life of Juan Latino	Historical backdrop
1526	Duke of Sessa, age 6, inherits his title upon the death of his father. Latino secretly begins his education, following the in-home lessons intended for his young master.	Charles V visits Granada. Foundation of Granada's Colegio Real (grammar school) and Studium Generale (University of Granada).
1536	The Duke of Sessa leaves Andalusia for the royal court.	
1546	Latino awarded the *bachiller* (baccalaureate) degree from the University of Granada.	Pedro de Guerrero becomes Archbishop of Granada.
1549	Latino and wife Ana Carlobal purchase a home in Granada's Santa Ana neighbourhood. Between 1549 and 1559, parish archives record four children baptized.	
1558	Latino listed in university faculty senate minutes as Maestro Juan Latino	
Jan. 1567		Five edicts prohibit an array of practices associated with Granada's Muslim heritage.
1568		Christmas Eve: the Second Revolt of the Alpujarras ignites.
1569–70		The expulsion and enslavement of Moriscos of Granada takes place as collective punishment for the revolt.
1571		Battle of Lepanto (7 October), Birth of a royal heir, Don Fernando (4 December)
1572		Fernando de Herrera, *Relación de la guerra de Cipre y suceso de la Batalla Naval de Lepanto.*
1573	Juan Latino's Lepanto commemoration appears in print, including the *Song of John of Austria (Austrias Carmen or Austriadis)* and Elegy for Philip II ("On the Birth of Untroubled Times").	
ca. 1576	Juan Latino's *De Translatione*	

	The life of Juan Latino	Historical backdrop
1578		Alonso de Ercilla publishes the 2nd part of *La Araucana*, which narrates Lepanto in canto 24 through ekphrastic prophecy. Deaths of Don Juan de Austria and the Infante Don Fernando.
1583	Marín Ocete (1924, 32, 58) states that Latino published an elegy to honour the recently deceased Duke of Sessa. No textual witnesses are currently known.	
1587	Last recorded mention of Juan Latino's attendance at University of Granada faculty senate.	
ca. 1597	likely death	
1602		Francisco Bermúdez de Pedraza completes his *Antigüedad y excelencias* de Granada in Valladolid. Published in 1608, the city history recalls Latino as one of "three famous black men" in Granada's history, offering a fictionalized account of his social advancement and marriage. This distorted record of Latino's career and family paves the way for the subsequent fictionalized recollections by Cervantes, Lope de Vega, Ximénez de Enciso, Ambrosio de Salazar and others.
1672		Nicolás Antonio's *Bibliotheca Hispana Nova* (first published in 1783) lists Latino's life and works in the company of other major writers.

Notes

1 Introduction: A Lost Portrait and a Forgotten Name

1 I give more detailed citations for Latino's biography in notes to chapters 1 and 2 and for Lepanto in chapter 3, noting as well problems related to period sources. An ideal point of departure for the vast Lepanto bibliography is Guilmartin 2003, 235–68. My outline of Latino's early life here draws on an early seventeenth-century chronicle of the family whom he served as a slave in childhood; see Fernández de Córdoba (Abbot of Rute), ca. 1620, fol. 174r. See Douglass (2014, 115–18) on the famed abolitionist and orator's struggle to gain literacy despite the prohibitions against teaching slaves to read.

2 Latino's Lepanto volume reached royal secretary Antonio Gracián Dantisco in August of 1572, sent by the president of Granada's Audiencia y Chancillería; see the log transcribed by Andrés 1962, 47–8.

3 On the Columbus "scene setting" before the Alhambra, see Colón 1986 [1492], 43, as well as the analysis of Columbus's alterations of the sequence of events in 1492 in Zamora 1993, 32–4. Harris (2007, 8) situates Ferdinand and Isabel's designation as the "Catholic Monarchs" in terms of Granada's transformation from a Muslim to a Christian city. For Cortés's "pivot" to Granada, see "Segunda carta de relación," in Cortés 1993 [1521], 184–5.

4 See, for example, the analysis of the Moro Wars in the Philippines in Seijas 2014, 61–7.

5 Essential sources for Granada's transformation from a Muslim to a Christian city are Cortes Peña and Vincent 1986; Coleman 2003; and Harris 2007.

6 On self-fashioning, see Greenblatt 1980. Laura Bass 2013 and Jorge Cañizares-Esguerra 2013 explore this conception of subject formation in Spain and Latin America, respectively. On *limpieza de sangre* in relation to

identity formation, see Nirenberg 2002 for the impact of mass conversions of Jews in the early fifteenth century, and for applications later in Spain and Spanish America, see Martínez 2008.

7 On the "genealogical turn" that elevated family lineage to the main form of communal memory in early modern Spain, see Nirenberg 2002.

8 Records on Latino's family life are gathered in Marín Ocete 1923–4, with additional information in Martín Casares 2000, 137, 388–90. On the activities associated with freedmen in Spain, see Stella 2000, 132, and Blumenthal 2009, 239–65, esp. 243.

9 On *artes liberales*, see Lewis and Short, as well as Cicero, *De Oratore* 3.32.127. The association of enslaved blacks in Granada with hard manual labour is registered by Morisco defender Francisco Núñez Muley 2007 [1567] 91: "Let them [enslaved blacks] bring the water pitcher on their backs, or carry burdens, or handle the plow." On the concentration of free blacks in more marginal sectors of Spanish society with focus on hard labour, see Stella 2000, 132.

10 The Duke of Sessa is cited in Bermúdez de Pedraza 1608, fol. 138v. Juvenal's *Satire* 2.6.165 reads: "rara avis in terris nigroque simillima cycno" (a rare bird on this earth, exactly like a black swan). Kaplan 2010, 94–107 traces the emergence in sixteenth-century Italy of elite portraits with black slaves or servants, documenting in parallel how racist humour sometimes informed the staffing of aristocratic households.

11 On Latino's posthumous canonization in caricature, see Fra Molinero 1995; Beusterien 2006, 106–14; and from a comparative Spanish-English perspective, Weissbourd 2013.

12 *Revealing the African Presence in Renaissance Europe*, Exhibition, Walters Art Museum, Baltimore, MD, curated by Joaneath Spicer, 14 October 2012 to 21 January 2013. The published catalogue does not include a photograph of the blank frame next to Juan Latino's name.

13 The royal palace inventory is transcribed in Martínez Leiva and Rodríguez Rebollo 2007, 74, entry #89 ("retrato de los pechos arriba de un negro, que es Juan Latino, con un letrero que dice de edad de 90 años").

14 Martínez Leiva and Rodríguez Rebollo 2007, 74, entries #90 ("retrato de un hombre armado") and #91 ("una mujer vestida de negro").

15 See Lowe 2012, 17.

16 For an analysis of how the ethnonym "Moor" was used to denote black Africans and the implications that resulted, see Devisse 2010, 77–81. Mercado's condemnation of the many illegalities and deceptions reads "violencia y dos mil engaños, y se hacen mil robos, y se cometen mil fuerzas" (Mercado 1571, fol. 101v). The Dominican nonetheless stands

with the majority of the theologians of his time in accepting the legality of slave-owning that conforms to just war doctrine (fol. 102v). For statistical documentation, see *Voyages: The Trans-Atlantic Slave Trade Database* (http://www.slavevoyages.org/).

17 Spicer (2012, 46) offers a cogent assessment of Dürer's project and its ultimate limitations from the artist's own vantage point.

18 Gilroy 1993, 49.

19 See Caro Baroja 2000 on the consequences for Moriscos of Granada's dramatic changes after 1492. Details of the urban transformation are provided in Cortes Peña and Vincent 1986, 18–38. The final "tragic" denouement of the Morisco expulsion is detailed in Domínguez Ortiz and Vincent 1978; a synthesis with detailed bibliography appears in Amelang 2011, 35–85.

20 On the role of Gonzalo Fernández de Córdoba (later the Gran Capitán) in the conquest of Granada, see Harvey 1990, 307.

21 On the greater quotidian interaction in daily life across ethnic lines in Granada, see Coleman 2003, 50; García Ballester 1984, 52–3 examines the impact of Moriscos on the university, with particular emphasis on the medicine faculty.

22 The Covarrubias entry reads: "Raza en los linajes se toma en mala parte como tener alguna raza de moro o judío." A particularly illuminating gloss of this definition appears in Harvey 2005, 6–9; see esp. 7 n4.

23 See Greer, Mignolo, and Quilligan 2007, 12–13 and 71–246, in addition to Paul Gilroy's aforementioned critique of scholarship on the Enlightenment and modernity (1993, 41–71).

24 The prefatory poem addressed to Philip II titled "De natali serenissimi ad Catholicum et Invictissimum Regem Philippum Elegia" ("Elegy On the Birth of Untroubled Times") appeared in Latinus 1573. Citations here and throughout will give the line number of the transcription and translation included here as Appendix 1, which I prepared with Andrew Lemons. I also give the folio number of the *princeps* (Latino 1573), now available on Google books, where the elegy for Philip II is in the first of two separate foliated gatherings of the volume (search under "Ad catholicum, pariter et invictissimum Philippum Dei gratia Hispaniarum regem, de felicissima serenissimi Ferdinandi Principis nativitate, epigrammatum liber … Austrias Carmen"). See also Holt Parker 2013 for an online edition.

25 Sweet 1997, 165. For the contours of the debate about racism and the question of how much we can situate its emergence in early modern Spain, see Blumenthal 2009, 269–77. Martínez (2008, 58–60) offers a compelling argument for a guarded use of the term "race" in the early-modern Spanish world.

26 Ronsard 2010, 25; see the gloss by editor-and-translator Phillip John Usher (ibid., 37 n58).

27 See Latino, *Song of John of Austria*, ll. 65, 292–3 (Latino 1573, 1st gathering, fol. 3r). To facilitate consultation, parenthetical citations of the Lepanto epic will give line and page numbers from Wright, Spence, and Lemons 2014. I also give the folio number of the *princeps* (Latino 1573), now available on Google books, where the Lepanto epic is in the second of two separate foliated gatherings of the volume (search under "Ad catholicum, pariter et invictissimum Philippum Dei gratia Hispaniarum regem, de felicissima serenissimi Ferdinandi Principis nativitate, epigrammatum liber … Austrias Carmen").

28 See Fra Molinero 1995, 125–62 and 2005.

29 Wright, Spence, and Lemons, 2014.

30 Coroleu, Caruso, and Laird 2012, IV.

31 See Marín Ocete 1923 and 1924. I have been able to corroborate most but not all the archival documents that he transcribes. Notes will draw attention to archival sources for which I have not been able to follow the scholar's tracks.

32 Sánchez Marín 1981.

33 See Fra Molinero 1995, 125–62 and 2005; Gates Jr and Wolff 1998; Gates Jr 2014 [1988]; and Smith 2015.

34 Studies on Latino, in the order mentioned, are Maurer 1993; Seo 2011 and 2012; Lemons, forthcoming; and Beusterien 2006, 106–14. Analysis of Latino's mobilization of Europe's Latinate literary tradition anchors the masters' thesis by Rigaux 2013. See also Soler Fiérrez 2014.

35 See Martín Casares 2000. This study is also indebted to Martín Casares's opening remarks to the 2012 colloquium, Esclavitud, mestizaje y abolicionismo en el mundo hispánico: Horizontes socio-culturales (University of Granada, 28 May 2012), expanded into a magisterial assessment of the state-of-the-art and scholarly methodologies in Martín Casares 2014a, 7–38.

36 Gilroy 1993, 17–18, draws attention to the motif of travel and relocation in the trajectories of Wheatley, Douglass, and other black "travellers." For Equiano, see Carretta 2005.

1 Latin Lessons amid the Remnants of Al-Andalus

1 An account of the transfer of Philip II's deceased family members appears in Siguënza 1986 [ca. 1602], 46–52. For the king's instructions, dated 30 November 1573, see AMG, legajo 1930, document 38; a scribe's account of the ceremony appears in the same legajo, document 40–1.

2 On Habsburg traditions of *pietas austriaca* that Philip II embraced with special zeal, see Coreth 2004 [1959, rev. ed. 1982]; and Río Barredo 2003.

3 See Snowden Jr 1983, 105–7, on the baptism of the Ethiopian eunuch by Philip. On the durability of the Prester John myth, see Fra Molinero 1995, 5–6; Scafi 2006, 219; Betz 2007, 28–30; and Relaño 2000, 81–95. Portuguese encounters with Ethiopian (Abyssinian) Christians are recorded in the chronicle of Francisco Álvares 1557, fols. 1–8.

4 On the Greek ethnonym, *Aithiops* (Αἰθίοψ, οπος), see *A Greek-English Lexicon* (1996) and Herodotus, Book IV, ch. 197.

5 Ortelius's atlas first appeared in Latin in Antwerp 1570, and was re-edited and translated numerous times (see Van den Broecke 1998). On "spacialization," see Padrón 2004. Considering Latino's use of the term Aethiops, Fra Molinero (2005, 344) proposes that a "medieval" world view is at work. The Ortelius map is available online through the Library of Congress Map Collection, at http://memory.loc.gov/ammem/gmdhtml/gmdhome.html (see under Ortelius in the "Creator Index," *Theatrum Orbis Terrarum*).

6 The reader annotation appears in Mela 1498, John Carter Brown Library, A498 M517c.

7 For instance, the triumphal arch the city of Messina (Sicily) erected for Don Juan de Austria after Lepanto referenced his Granada military campaign through the classicizing *Baetica*. See Cesare Valentino, "Proyecto de puente conmemorativo en Mesina."

8 Leo Africanus (al-Hassan al-Wazzan) 1563 reads "incogniti et lontanti dal comercio nostro" (fols. 1v–2r); and "quei della terra negra sono huomini bestialissimi, huomini senza ragione, senza ingengo, et senza practica: non hanno veruna informatione di che sia. Le meretrice tra loro sono molte, et per conseguente i becchi: da alcuni in fuori, che habitano nelle città grandi essi in fine hanno poco piu del sentimento humano" (fol. 11). Natalie Zemon Davis (2006, 94–5, 145–8) notes that Ramusio's edition alters the original manuscript to heighten the negative characterization of black Africans. On the tradition of Islamic geographers alleging the uncivilized savagery of black Africans, see Sweet 1997, 147–9; on Africanus in relation to the emerging European textualization of sub-Saharan Africa, see Curran 2011, 36–8.

9 See Saunders 1982, 39. Curran 2011, 37–8 gives the example of Leo Africanus's more nuanced examination of the Melli people.

10 Mármol Carvajal 1573, fol. 15v. On this chronicler's life, see Castillo Fernández 2015, XXII–XXVII. Puglisi 2008, 144, documents how Latino sought Mármol Carvajal's services as an agent at court, but misidentifies

the former as a Morisco. On Mármol Carvajal as a reader of Leo Africanus, see Rodríguez Mediano 2009.

11 "son todos idólatras, y muchos de ellos son tan bestiales que propiamente se pueden llamar monstruos de la naturaleza" (Mármol Carvajal 1573, fol. 44r–v).

12 On the enslavement of Hispano-Muslims of Malaga and Canary Islanders, see Phillips 2014, 36. German humanist Hieronymous Münzer (1920, 24–5) describes men and women from Tenerife (Canary Islands) who were sold at auction in Valencia in late 1594.

13 On the contributions of enslaved men and women to Granada in particular and Andalusia more generally, see Martín Casares 2000, 19–53; and for Seville, Fernández Chaves and Pérez García 2005. On slave labour at the Cromberger print shop, see Griffin 1988, 32, 78, 87–8. For the slave-soldier who saves his master from an ambush, see the early seventeenth-century chronicle of Luis Cabrera de Córdoba 1998, 1:487. See Clénard (Clenardus) 1940 [1536], 1:110, on the purchase of three black boys to serve as classroom assistants. For analysis of slaves working in artists' studios, see Méndez Rodríguez 2011, 119–53, with guild restrictions discussed 128–30. Juan Pareja's service to Diego de Velázquez is discussed in Stoichita 2010, 225–34, esp. 229.

14 See Adorno 2007, 64–8. The seminal study of 1952 by Domínguez Ortiz (2003 [1952], 39–49) pauses to assess why early modern intellectuals accepted the growing slave trade.

15 The advice and reservations about using slave labour appear in the seventh Duke of Medina Sidonia's letter (ca. December 1586) to Philip II, legajo 2400 Archive, Palace of Medina Sidonia. The 1507 inventory of his grandfather (the third duke) records 216 slaves; see Martín Casares 2000, 325.

16 For an indication of the Gran Capitán's fame, see Navagero 1754 [1563], 338. On the Gran Capitán's relatively disadvantaged early years, see Nader 1979, 140.

17 Douglass 2014, 30–1. On his choice of surname, see Gilroy 1993, 58–63.

18 Marín Ocete 1923, 106.

19 See Pike 1967, 354; and Clénard (Clenardus) 1940, 1:114–15 and 3:67 (letter of 10 January 1537). Clenardus's exhortation reads, "audi nomina, ut rideas magis."

20 On Galindo, see Muñoz-Fernández 2000, 127; and Márquez de la Plata and Ferrándiz 2005, 19–78, 112–18.

21 See Nirenberg 2002; and Elliott 1990 [1963], 220–4. For the impact on literary practices of the obsession with blood purity, see Bass 2008, 63–77.

22 Martínez 2008, 60. On the particular issues pertaining to *limpieza de sangre* in Granada specifically, see Amelang 2011, 113–23.

23 See Cruz 1996, 41.

24 See Marín Ocete 1923, 105; and Sánchez Marín 1981, 18.

25 The story of the Granadino who rejected bacon was disseminated in the anonymous *Casos notables de la ciudad de Córdoba* [2003, ca. 1618, 238–9]. Rebecca Earle (2012, 50–2, 209–11) traces such anxieties to as far back as Vincent de Beauvais's widely disseminated *Speculum doctrinale* and documents many manifestations in Spain's overseas colonies. See also Jean E. Feerick's (2010, 55–77) analysis of racial anxieties related to Irish wet nurses.

26 See Fernández de Córdoba (Abbot of Rute), ca. 1620, fol. 174r.

27 See Scott and Hébrard 2012, 7–8. On the connection of Guinea to Portuguese slave trading in the early sixteenth century, see Wey-Gómez 2008, 86–8; for analysis of the geographic origins of slaves transported to Andalusia, see Martín Casares 2000, 14, and the expansion on this research in Martín Casares 2014b.

28 Martín Casares 2000, 388–90. A late nineteenth-century collection of Granada legends would report that the Gran Capitán was Latino's father (Morell y Terry 1997 [1892], 37–8).

29 Stella (2000, 167–86) ponders the *mestizaje* attested in notarial archives, noting that some scribal documents label newborn children black in cases of mixed-race parentage (167). For a broad examination in the societies shaped by Spanish and Portuguese imperial expansion, see the essays in Ares Queija and Stella 2000.

30 See Bermúdez de Pedraza 1608, fol. 138r.

31 Vincent Carretta 2005, 320.

32 "Contra la voluntad de los que gobernaban la temprana edad del duque, viniendo él consigo ocupaba en estudiar cuantos ratos podía hurtar a la diligencia de los que se lo impedían," Fernández de Córdoba (Abbot of Rute), ca. 1620, fol. 174r.

33 Frederick Douglass 2014 [1855], 115–18. On Pareja's career as a painter in his own right, see Stoichita 2010, 231.

34 On the *paedagogi*, see Quintilian, *The Orator's Education* 1.1, 8–12. See also Wallace 2010, 28.

35 Fernández de Córdoba (Abbot of Rute), ca. 1620, fol. 173v.

36 David Rubio [1934, 39–40] discusses the arrival in Spain of the two Italian humanists in *Classical Scholarship in Spain*. See also Nader 1979, 79–80. For a specific case of a nobleman's education in the mid-sixteenth century, see Martínez Hernández 2004, 66–9. An explanation of how changing

aristocratic education fits into the broader "education revolution" appears in Kagan 1974, 10–11.

37 Liang 2011, esp. 5–63.

38 See Quintanilla Raso 1980, 348–55. For assessments of the likely editions owned, see the author's detailed footnotes, 370–82. Of the titles listed in the inventory, only works by Cicero, Ovid, Livy, Seneca, Plutarch, Valerius Maximus, and Aristotle had been published in Castilian translation circa 1518 (see Beardsley 1970, 3–4).

39 On the embrace of classical learning by Castilian nobles of the later fifteenth century, see Rubio 1934, 26–40.

40 See Callejón Peláez 2008, 199–248.

41 Callejón Peláez 2008, 1–72.

42 Callejón Peláez 2008, 30.

43 The scant documents about the Casa del Gran Capitán suggest it was a one-time Nasrid palace, though we lack conclusive proof (see Gallego Burín 1961, 263–5).The house was sold to the Discalced Carmelites in 1590 and torn down in the seventeenth century. A Carmelite nun who prepared a history of the subsequent convent speaks as well of Nasrid origins but also notes the lack of documents about the Gran Capitán's original palace (Corazón de María, 2005, 95–102).

44 See Greene 1982, 93–100.

45 See Harris 2007, 52–3 and 87. Verifiable traces of a Roman Iliberia would eventually turn up, two decades later, at a site outside the city.

46 See Fuchs 2009, esp. 63–5, 89, on how the Moorish silk cushions, *estrados*, epitomize the "hybridization" of quotidian life. On church officials' efforts to replace *estrados* with chairs, see Amelang 2011, 69.

47 See Hieronymous Münzer 1920 [1494–5], for the tally of mosques, 44; for the "ineffable" Alhambra and conversation with Tendilla 46–7; for *juegos de caña*, 64. For a Castilian translation, see García Mercadal 1999 [1951], 329–32.

48 Münzer 1920 [1494–5], 61–2.

49 On Clenardus's machinations to purchase an Arabic tutor as slave, see Clénard (Clenardus) 1940, 1:153 (letter of 12 July 1539); on his inability to find Arabic codices to copy or purchase, see 1:161 (letter of 7 April 1540). It is not clear from the Flemish humanist's letters from Granada whether two other young black men trained in Latin – Sebastian and Michael – had died, escaped, or been sold between his time in Braga and his arrival in Andalusia.

50 See Barletta (2005, ix–xxvi) on the shift in Arabic literary culture in Spain from Granada to Castile and Aragon. For Morisco traditions of medicine, see García Ballester (1984, 50–4).

51 On Granada's enduring Muslim appearance in the early sixteenth century, see Caro Baroja 2000 [1976], 149–74, as well as Barrios Aguilera 2002, 284–7.

52 On official perceptions that the city looked too Islamic, see García-Arenal and Rodríguez-Mediano 2010a, 51. See also Coleman 2003, 1–24. Barrios Aguilera 2002, 1–74, distils the causes and consequences of the first rebellion, while also offering population estimates of the city's Muslim population for this period. On the destruction of sacred Muslim locales, including the building over of cemeteries and the construction of churches over mosques, see Cortes Peña and Vincent 1986, 17–43 (see esp. Chart A, p. 28).

53 See Pereda 2007, 259–63.

54 García-Arenal and Rodríguez Mediano 2010a, 624.

55 Caro Baroja 2000 [1976], 161–3.

56 See the examples of slave labour that Martín Casares (2000, 321–7) has gleaned from estate inventories.

57 On the Calle Zacatín and environs, see Antonio Gallego Burín 1961, 309–10. For the Hispano-Arabic origins of the term Zacatín, see Real Academia, *Diccionario*, and Covarrubias. Granada's lower Zacatín, where the rag trade concentrated, was later removed to make way for the modern thoroughfare, Calle de los Reyes Católicos.

58 Antonio Gallego Burín 1961, 316–19. The main mosque was torn down gradually, beginning in 1588. The madrasa was still standing until the eighteenth century. See also Cortes Peña and Vincent 1986, 27.

59 The Sicilian humanist-educator Lucio Marineo Sículo (1533, fol. 172r) characterized Granada's silk market as a city within the city. On the centrality of the silk trade to Morisco livelihoods and culture, see Garrad 1956, 75–7. Harvey (2005, 150) ponders the extent that Sufi spiritual traditions survived within the guilds of the Alcaicería.

60 García-Arenal and Fernando Rodríguez-Mediano 2010b, 57–60.

61 See Covarrubias, *Tesoro*, as well as Dopico and Lezra 2001.

62 The story that King Philip II was conceived in Granada appears in the chronicle of Prudencio de Sandoval 1955 [ca. 1603], 174; the same chronicle describes the daring *leilas* with which Moriscas entertained the court in the welcome ceremony, 173–3. The meeting between Boscán and Navagero would be a staple of the earliest literary histories (see, for example, Velázquez 1797, 53). Navarrete (1994, 38–72) illuminates the impact of this encounter on poetry and poetics. Irigoyen-García (2014, 15–16) offers a particularly pertinent analysis of how recollections of the encounter positioned a Castilian ethnocentrism against Iberia's Arabic heritage.

63 Navagero's 1754 [1563] observations, in the order mentioned, are waterworks (330–1), fruit orchards (338), and setting for a humanist life of

contemplation (332). The latter echoes other highly literate travellers before him, most notably Peter Martyr's March 1492 "Letter to Pedro González de Mendoza, archbishop of Toledo" (Martyr 1530).

64 David Coleman [2003, 32–5] documents the diversity of Granada's Morisco population in *Creating Christian Granada*. Navagero's assessment of Moriscos reads: "Parlano i *Moreschi* la lor antica, e natia lingua *Moresca*, e pochi sono quelli che vogliono imparar lo *Spagnolo*. Sono Cristiani mezzo per forza, ma sono sì poco instrutti nelle cose della nostra Fede" (the Moriscos speak their old and native language, Moorish, and few seek to learn Spanish. They are Christian half by force, but are so little instructed in the aspects of our Faith) (Navagero 1754 [1563], 339).

65 On the crown *visita*, see Sandoval 1955 [ca. 1603], 173.

66 For an analysis of the decrees of 1526, see Domínguez Ortiz and Vincent 1978, 22.

67 A transcription of the founding *cédula* appears in Calero Palacios 1995, 48–55. The passage cited reads: "buenas personas para que prediquen y enseñen la dicha doctrina evangélica y para que informen a los fieles cristianos, mayormente a los nuevamente convertidos en los que han de hacer y obrar."

68 See Elliot van Liere 2003, esp. 1081.

69 The ceremony took place in December 1533: Universidad de Granada, Archivo Universitario. *Primer libro de actas de Claustro y Grados (1532–1560)*, 80. Marín Ocete states that Latino accompanied Sessa here, but offers no corroboration (Marín Ocete 1923, 110). This assertion follows the account in the seventeenth-century play, *Juan Latino* by Ximénez de Enciso.

70 In Fernández de Córdoba (Abbot of Rute), ca. 1620, fol. 174r.

71 The historian Antonio Álvarez-Ossorio states that Latinus was manumitted around 1538, though he does not cite any corroborating documents (see Álvarez-Ossorio Alvariño 2001, 76).

72 On Lope de Vega's patronage ties, see Wright 2001. An October 1615 letter from the playwright to the sixth Duke of Sessa requests specific kinds of clothing and discusses the symbolic value to the writer of such public displays of material support from the grandee (Vega Carpio 1989 [1941], 212).

73 Universidad de Granada, Archivo Universitario. *Primer libro de actas de Claustro y Grados (1532–1560)*, 196.

74 On the assumption that Latino was still a slave when he attended the university, see Marín Ocete 1923, 111. Marín Ocete (1923, 118) reports on Latino's public oration for the licentiate degree in 1557 by following Rodríguez Marín 1903, 36n. Following the trail from this note to the graduation records in the *Primer libro de actas de Claustro y Grados (1532–1560)*

of the Archivo Universitario (fol. 245) does not support the claim. The year 1557 is missing from the minutes.

75 "Quiso estudiar medicina, y por consejo de sus amigos lo dejó: por lo cual se aplicó a leer Gramática" (Bermúdez de Pedraza 1608, fol. 138v).

76 On the political sensitivity of medicine in Granada, see García Ballester 1984, 53–4; and Harvey 2005, 169.

77 On the large informal student population, see Kagan 1974, 166; Clénard (Clenardus) 1940, 1:147 reports on having black slaves in his Latin class in a letter of 6 December 1537.

78 Coleman (2003, 145–76) discusses Guerrero in Granada.

79 Pliny, *Natural History* (Preface 7): Cicero is "extra omnem ingenii aleam positus."

80 On the university neighbourhood, see Calero Palacios 1978, 185.

81 "Ad fugandas infidelium tenebras haec domus literaria fundata est"; transcribed in Calero Palacios 1995, 15.

82 Juan Latino's presence in the faculty senate is recorded in the Universidad de Granada, Archivo Universitario, *Primer libro de actas de Claustro y Grados (1532–1560)* on the following folios of the original bound "book of minutes": 364, 372, 383, 387, 391–2.

83 On the extent to which traditional university hierarchies still applied in Spain during the sixteenth century, see Elliot van Liere 2000, 57–8.

84 Covarrubias defines the *maestro* as "El que es docto en cualquiera facultad de ciencia, disciplina o arte, y la enseña a otros dando razón della" (he who is expert in some realm of science, an academic discipline, or [language] arts, and who imparts knowledge of it to others).

85 Censor report by royal secretary Antonio de Eraso, dated 30 October 1572. In Latino 1573, fol. 2r of the first of two separately foliated gatherings. Whenever I cite from this volume, I will include folio numbers that correspond to the digitized witness available on Google Books (from the Biblioteca Histórica "Marqués de Valdecilla" of the Universidad Complutense de Madrid, FLL 11,641). Litigation about a tax levy (*censo*) appears in AGS, Expedientes de Hacienda legajo 734, document 4. The Abbot of Rute's summation of Latino's career reads: "alcanzando por excelencia el sobrenombre de Latino mereció la cátedra de prima de latinidad, y retórica en la Universidad de Granada, y ser admitido (sin embargo de su color) por maestro de artes y decano en el tiempo de aquella facultad" [parenthesis in original]. In Fernández de Córdoba (Abbot of Rute), ca. 1620, fol. 174r. On the technical issue of the history of the chair in grammar, see Marín Ocete 1923, 115–17.

86 Sánchez Marín and Muñoz Martín 2009, 247–8.

87 López 1982, 19. Minutes of the faculty senate I have examined corroborate Bernardino de Carlobal's graduation in 1534, but not the Sessa connection (Universidad de Granada, Archivo Universitario, *Primer libro de actas de Claustro y Grados*, 88).
88 Martín Casares (2000, 160) and Stella (2000, 140) discuss the relative rarity of interracial marriages.
89 Latino's home purchase is documented in Martín Casares 2000, 387–8. Marín Ocete transcribed baptismal certificates for a daughter Juana in 1549, a son Bernardino in 1552, a daughter Ana in 1556, and a son Juan in 1559; Marín Ocete, 1924, 74–5. I corroborated these records in the same parish archive.
90 Cortes Peña and Vincent (1986, 29) document the building of the Santa Ana church over a mosque. For the Plaza Nueva's construction, see Antonio Gallego Burín 1961, 462–8.
91 See AGS Expedientes de Hacienda legajo 734, document 4. On the anxieties related to an emerging credit economy with the *censos,* see Vilches 2010, 252–3.
92 Hurtado de Mendoza's classification of social ranks reads, "gente media entre los grandes y pequeños" (1970 [ca. 1570], 105). On the upwardly mobile population of Latino's neighbourhood, see Cortes Peña and Vincent, 1986, 190; specific families who pass as old Christians are documented in Coleman 2003, 23 and 32, for the conversos from Toledo and the Moriscos-turned-Milanese, respectively.
93 For the census results themselves, see *Vecindario de Granada,* fols. 101r–22r (Juan Latino's household, fol. 101r). On the broader confessional context plus a statistical analysis of the city's slave population, see Martín Casares 2000, 101–10.
94 Henríquez de Jorquera 1987 [1643], 533, describes Latino's family, though it is not clear whether his posthumous account follows from eyewitness or documentary sources.
95 Coleman 2003, 52–9.
96 Menéndez y Pelayo 1927, 174, credits Latino's marriage and social status to "su nativo ingenio y a la cristiana caridad de nuestros antepasados" (his natural intellect and the Christian charity of our forebearers). Cuban scholar Calixto C. Masó (1973, 2, 60) offered the freedman as evidence of the positive interracial relations in the Hispanic world. Martín Casares (2000, 389) convincingly refutes this assessment of more benevolent Spanish attitudes towards blacks in the context of imperial expansion.
97 See *Vecindario de Granada*, fols. 124r, 152v.
98 The epithet *esclavo bozal* appears in the *Vecindario de Granada* to denote black-African slaves, though its uneven application makes it difficult to

judge the precise connotation (see, for example, fol. 220v). Covarrubias defines *bozal* as a "negro que no sabe otra lengua que la suya" (black who knows no other language save his own), but *Autoridades* registers a semantic drift by which the term refers to blacks more generally: "Es epiteto que ordinariamente se da a los negros, en especial cuando están recién venidos de sus tierras" (it is an epithet normally applied to blacks, particularly when they are just arrived from their lands).

99 The Hernández family is in the San Matías neighbourhood, *Vecindario de Granada*, fol. 244r; the likely couple of Francisca and Pedro are in San Miguel, fol. 337v.

100 In *Vecindario de Granada*, fol. 70r.

101 *Vecindario de Granada*, fols. 336v–7r. Juan, of course, was a relatively common name overall, though the frequency with which enslaved men are thus named does suggest type casting.

102 On the emergence of a professional royal judiciary and its labyrinthine nature, see Kagan 1981, 1–78; Byrne 2012, 45–51; and from a first-hand perspective of an observer of the time, Hurtado de Mendoza 1970 [ca. 1570], 105. Caro Baroja (2000 [1976], 155) follows Hurtado de Mendoza, capturing the most fateful dimension of Deza's legacy. Barrios Aguilera 2009 offers a concise biography of Deza.

2 Civil War, Shattered *Convivencia*

1 Harris 2007, 88–90.

2 My account of the decrees' proclamation on 1 January 1567 as well as the official deliberations and preparations in the preceding years follows Mármol Carvajal 2015 [1600]. For the proclamations as printed in a broadside edition in 1567, see *Pregmáticas* [sic] *y provisiones* 1567 This rare surviving imprint of the five decrees features unnumbered folios, so I cite as Decree 1, 2, etc.

3 "que ansí se pueden llamar [civiles guerras], pues fueron cristianos contra cristianos, y todos dentro de una ciudad y un reino" (Pérez de Hita 1998 [1619], 10). Though the first known edition dates from 1619, the author signed off on his chronicle in 1597.

4 See *Pregmáticas* [sic] *y provisiones*, Decree 1: "para que en todo ansí en lo interior como en lo exterior, se conformasen con los verdaderos cristianos."

5 "La diferencia y distinción del hábito en lo exterior ha sido y es gran causa para que ansí mesmo la haya en lo interior, de que Dios nuestro señor ha sido muy ofendido" (*Pregmáticas* [sic] *y provisiones*, Decree 1). I retain the archaic English term "habit" in translation, in order to capture the ambiguity of *hábito* in early-modern Castilian usage, which denotes both

the distinctive costume of a nation as well as the uniform of a religious or military order (see *Autoridades*).

6 On the issue of Morisco ownership of black slaves, see Martín Casares 2000, 279–83; and Phillips 2014, 38. For the fiscal and economic pressures already underway against Moriscos, see Garrad 1956.

7 See Devisse 2010, 77–81.

8 Martín Casares 2000, 414–15.

9 Mármol Carvajal 2015 [1600], 108: "[el] daño que se seguía de que los Moriscos del reino de Granada tuviesen esclavos negros de Guinea en su servicio, porque los compraban bozales para servirse de ellos, y teniéndolos en sus casas les enseñaban la secta de Mahoma, y los hacían a sus costumbres, y demás de perderse aquellas almas, crecía cada hora la nación morisca con menos confianza de fidelidad." On the documentary basis for allegations of Moriscos' ties to the Ottoman empire, see Hess 1968.

10 See Caro Baroja 2000 [1976], 215 for analysis of the discursive inversion, where habits construed as Castilian virtues are treated as Morisco vices. On the conceptions of *nación* in early modern Spain, see Gil Pujol 2004.

11 Universidad de Granada, Archivo Universitario, *Primer libro de actas de Claustro y Grados (1532–1560)*, 374–8 ("pues estando antes de agora este reino poblado de clérigos que sabían poco y idiotas, agora está el más adelantado que en to[do]s los reinos de su majestad hay pues para cada beneficiado en el Alpujarra y valle y costa y en todo el reino hay tantos opositores, todos graduados de licenciados, maestros y doctores en teología y artes y también en cánones.")

12 On the destruction of the baths, see Mármol Carvajal 2015 [1600], 122. The erotic scene of a concubine's bath is imagined in Münzer 1920 (1494–5), 47.

13 On the careers of Deza and Espinosa, as well as the orthodox policies they championed, see Martínez Millán and de Carlos Morales 1998, 362–3 (Deza) and 101–31, 371 (Espinosa). See also Elliott 1990 [1963], 238–9.

14 Mármol Carvajal 2015 [1600], 122–3.

15 The Núñez Muley petition is transcribed in Gallego Burín and Gamir Sandoval 1996 [1968], 275–9; the statement on "provincial dress" appears on 276–7. My citations are based on the English translation by Vincent Barletta (Núñez Muley 2007 [1567]). Barletta's introduction analyses the dilemma of a colonized subject in Granada as elsewhere (ibid., 1–55, esp. 27–9).

16 Núñez Muley 2007 [1567] 88, 91; see Barletta's analysis of Morisco slavery, 44–6.

17 The anticipation of a rebellion is detailed in Mármol Carvajal (2015 [1600], 141–56); on the prophecies (*jofores*), see García-Arenal and Rodríguez

Mediano 2010b, 32. Mármol Carvajal (2015 [1600], 165–7) details the false alarm about an Easter rebellion.

18 Mármol Carvajal 2015 [1600], 6–8. See also the novelistic account of the "dagger incident" in Granada's city hall in Pérez de Hita 1998 [1619], 8–10.

19 Caro Baroja 2000 [1976], 163.

20 Quoted by Mármol Carvajal (2015 [1600], 191), the rebel commander called out, "no hay más que Dios y Mahoma."

21 Documentation of Mármol Carvajal's military service during the rebellion appears in Castillo-Fernández 2015, XXV, while Puglisi 2008 draws attention to how the soldier-chronicler's own ambitions for advancement inform his interpretation of events.

22 Quinn 2013, 25.

23 On the rebel leaders' geopolitical and tactical calculations, see Hurtado de Mendoza 1970 [ca. 1570], 119–25; for the diplomat-and-chronicler's background and family ties, see Spivakovsky 1970, 368–96. On Pérez de Hita's literary agenda, see Quinn 2013, 79–100.

24 See Harvey 2005, 204–37; as well as Domínguez Ortiz and Vincent 1978, 35–6.

25 Testimony of how such martyr chronicles were etched into Spanish memory emerges in Cabrera de Córdoba 1998 [1619], 1:461–2; see also Mármol Carvajal 2015 [1600], 213–16.

26 Mármol Carvajal (2015 [1600], 380–2) recounts the commission on slavery.

27 The Válor debacle is recounted in Hurtado de Mendoza 1970 [ca. 1570], 190–5. Other accounts of voracious looting by crown forces appear in Hurtado de Mendoza 1970 [ca. 1570], 177–9, 244–9, and 259–60; the allotment of spoils is discussed in Mármol Carvajal 2015 [1600], 628.

28 "que había hombres que hasta los gatos se traían, calderas, cedazos, artesas, aspas, devanaderas, cencerros, hazadores, y otras vagezas semejante, y esto por no perder el uso de hurtar. Yo no digo aquí qué gente lo hazía señaladamente, que todos en común eran ladrones y yo el primero" (Pérez de Hita 1998 [1619], 63).

29 Hurtado de Mendoza 1970 [ca. 1570], 122–5 suggests not an inch of arable land in the Alpujarras was wasted. An eloquent assessment of this industry appears in Barrios Aguilera 2002, 92–100.

30 "movido a creer y afirmar fácilmente sin diferencia lo verdadero y lo falso; publicar nuevas o perjudiciales o favorables, seguirlas con pertinacia: ciudad nueva, cuerpo compuesto de pobladores de diversas pares, que fueron pobres y desacomodados en sus tierras, o movidos a venir a ésta por la ganancia" (Hurtado de Mendoza 1970 [ca. 1570], 279).

31 Sessa's forced temporary retirement inspires a wry aside by Hurtado de Mendoza 1970 [ca. 1570], 219; see also Domínguez Ortiz and Vincent 1978,

38–9. Álvarez Ossorio Alvariño [2001, 117–61] details the broader historical context for Sessa's military career. On his life-long sponsorship of Latino's teaching position, see Fernández de Córdoba (Abbot of Rute), ca. 1620, fol. 174r.

32 On the annual cycle for silk production and population estimates, see Garrad 1956, 78–9. Census and baptismal records alike demonstrate the industry's footprint in Latino's neighbourhood. Baptisms from 1543–69 in the Parroquia de Santa Ana (Granada), *Libro I*, are often recorded with the father's trade, allowing us to gauge how the cloth business remained a part of the neighbourhood's lifeblood before the revolt. The census of 1561 likewise shows the importance of silk production (*Vecindario de Granada* 1561, fols. 101–221r).

33 See Mármol Carvajal 2015 [1600], 318–19.

34 Baptisms of children born to enslaved women from the mountain communities are recorded in the parish registry of Parroquia de Santa Ana (Granada), *Libro I*, fol. 209v. For the city's changed population mix, see Martín Casares 2000, 113–15.

35 The years 1569–73 are missing in the book of faculty senate minutes (Universidad de Granada, Archivo Universitario, *Segundo libro de actas de Claustro y Grados, 1562–1600*, Legajo 1450). The volume's surviving pages do show fire damage on the edges, but other years escaped unscathed. The history by Montells y Nadal 2000 [1870] predates the 1877 fire; from the perspective of a nineteenth-century liberal, he decries how church interference defined the early years, but does not directly address how ecclesiastical control played out during the revolt. Setting out to contradict Montells y Nadal's negative reading, a celebratory history of the early years of the university by Orozco Díaz and Bermúdez Pareja [1958] stops at the rebellion. Calero Palacios [1997, 39–42] discusses the diminished operations in the rebellion's wake, but does not directly discuss what happened during the conflict.

36 García Ballester [1984, 55] speaks of the university's "collapse"; see also, García-Arenal and Rodríguez Mediano 2010b, 116.

37 Mármol Carvajal 2015 [1600], 396–9.

38 An account of the ceremonial entry appears in Mármol Carvajal 2015 [1600], 411–14. See also Hurtado de Mendoza 1970 [ca. 1570], 217–18.

39 Parroquia de Santa Ana (Granada), *Libro I* documents the 10 June 1569 baptism of Beatriz, daughter of Don Diego de Mexía and Doña Ana de Córdoba (fol. 210v).

40 The deliberations are detailed in Mármol Carvajal 2015 [1600], 418–22; he documents John of Austria's residence in Deza's Audiencia palace on p. 414.

41 In using the term "ethnic cleansing," I follow historian Geoffrey Parker (Parker 2010, 533–7).
42 On San Juan traditions, see Caro Baroja 1979.
43 I follow the accounts of the expulsion of Moriscos from Granada in Mármol Carvajal 2015 [1600], 474–9; and Hurtado de Mendoza 1970 [ca. 1570], 228–31.
44 Diego Hurtado de Mendoza 1970 [ca. 1570], 229.
45 See John of Austria's letters, *CODOIN* 28:127–30.
46 Núñez Muley 2007 [1567], 28.
47 On the looting and devastation that results immediately, see Hurtado de Mendoza 1970 [ca. 1570], 228–31. Population estimates appear in Cortes Peña and Vincent 1986, 56–61. Testimonies of profiteering fill the weighty dossier of a crown audit (*visita*), in AGS, Cámara de Castilla, legajo 2737. On how the expulsion undertaken supposedly to help suppress the rebellion actually strengthened the rebel cause, see Parker 2010, 534.
48 See the assessment of this final phase of the civil war by Domínguez Ortiz and Vincent 1978, 47–50.
49 The siege of La Galera is recounted in Mármol Carvajal 2015 [1600], 575–89; Hurtado de Mendoza 1970 [ca. 1570], 320–45; and Pérez de Hita 1998 [1619], 214–55. For an assessment of John of Austria's heavy-handed tactics and orders for the massacre of unarmed civilians, see Harvey 2005, 224–6.
50 The sight of the severed head on display is described in Hurtado de Mendoza 1970 [ca. 1570], 401–3; and Mármol Carvajal 2015 [1600], 728–9.
51 For statistics on the expulsion and deaths of Moriscos between 1569 and 1570, see Domínguez Ortiz and Vincent 1978, 52–6.
52 See Braudel 1966, 2:366.
53 On the immediate impact of slave auctions on the city population, see Martín Casares 2000, 207. Phillips 2014, 37–9, assesses the enslavement of Moriscos in the longer-term history of slavery in Iberia.
54 Deza himself would complain after the first group of settlers arrived that the landless peasants from Galicia lacked farming skills and even basic sustenance; see AGS Cámara de Castilla, legajo 2171. For a longer term assessment of resettlement, see Barrios Aguilera 1993.
55 The *visita* is preserved in the Archivo General de Simancas, Cámara de Castilla, legajo 2737.
56 Barrios Aguilera 1996.

3 A Black Poet and a Habsburg Phoenix

1 A complete transcription of the Venetian *avviso* that brought the first report of the battle to Holy League lands appears in Setton 1984, 1060n54; see also Fenlon 2007, 176–7.

2 See Paruta 1605, part 2, book 2, 163–231; and Cervantes, "The Captive's Tale," in *Don Quijote*, part 1, chapter 39, 476–8. The voluminous secondary-source bibliography on Lepanto can be approached with Guilmartin 2003, 235–68, and Capponi 2006, 253–86 as points of departure, supplemented with Bicheno 2003, 249–78. On the long-term geopolitical significance, see the seminal article by Hess (1972). Lepanto's resonance today is attested in the enthusiastic reception of recent studies targeted to generalist readers, including Barbero 2010, a resolutely old-fashioned chronicle, which has enjoyed multiple printings in Italy; and Crowley 2009, which details the maritime rivalry from the Fall of Constantinople in 1453 to Lepanto.

3 First-line reports of the battle include Benavides 1571; Diedo 1995 [1571], which draws on interviews with fighters returning from the battle; and the unsigned "Relación de lo que hizo la Armada de la Liga Cristiana" (1571), which John of Austria's command centre dispatched to Philip II. When I quote the latter, I follow the version preserved in AGS, Estado, legajo 1134, document 83, which was transcribed in *CODOIN* 3:216–23.

4 See, for example, the initial report from the Spanish command unit ("Relación de lo que hizo la Armada de la Liga Cristiana"; *CODOIN* 3:219), and Giovanni Pietro Contarini 1572, fol. 53r.

5 The original reads "cierto fue un trofeo extraño" (Benavides 1571, unnumbered folio).

6 Writing to Philip II just two weeks before the battle, John of Austria complained that his men were owed seven salary payments and lacked arms, adequate clothing, and in some cases, even went hungry. See AGS, Estado, legajo 1134, document 76. For examples of the tallies of slaves and other spoils in first-line reports, see the two Spanish reports of late October 1571, transcribed in *CODOIN* 3:227–36, as well as Giovanni Pietro Contarini 1572, fol. 55v.

7 "Relación de lo que hizo la Armada de la Liga Cristiana," in *CODOIN* 3:219. The passage reads, "fue Dios servido dar la victoria a la Real de su Magestad de la Real del Turco, degollando el Bassá con más de quinientos Turcos" (God willed the victory to the Royal Flagship of his majesty over that of the Turk, whereupon the pasha's throat was cut along with that of five hundred Turks). For examples of the tallies of slaves and other spoils in first-line reports, see the two Spanish reports of late October 1571, transcribed in *CODOIN* 3:227–36, as well as Giovanni Pietro Contarini (1572), fol. 55v.

8 The report from Don Juan de Austria's command element thus concludes that the clash was "la mayor batalla naval que ha habido muchos años ha, y aun se podría decir sin agraviar a nadie [que] jamás se vio ni oyó

habiendo venido a pelear no solo voluntariamente, pero de ambas partes con gran confianza de vencer cada una de ellas" (the largest naval battle seen for many years, and one could even say without slighting anyone that one has neither seen nor heard of two parts come to fight voluntarily with great confidence in victory) ("Relación de lo que hizo la Armada de la Liga Cristiana," in AGS, Estado, legajo 1134, document 83). See also Guilmartin 2003, 253.

9 For an example of early comparisons between Actium and Lepanto, see the chapbook that appeared in 1572 in Bologna, *Discorso sopra due grandi e memorabili battaglie navali fatte nel mondo*. Jenny Jordan (2004a and 2004b) illuminates the connections made between Lepanto and Actium in map books. On the literary connection between Actium and Lepanto, see Quint 1993, 21–49; Davis 2000, 70–8; Nicolopulos 2000, 103–6; and Blanco 2010, 493–7 and 2014.

10 On the expanded cult of Saint Giustina in Venice, see Fenlon 2007, 273–6. The Venetian ambassador's proposal for a Lepanto-anniversary strike against French Protestants is in the letter of Alvisse Contarini 1571.

11 See Panofsky 1969, 72–4, and Falomir Faus 2003, 288–9 for an analysis of the original composition and its seventeenth-century additions.

12 Parker (1998, 100–1) highlights the post-Lepanto amplification of Philip II's ambitions for eastward expansion. Archival work from García Hernán (1995, 67) documents the king's negotiations with the pope on this issue. On how Philip II sought genealogical affirmations of his eastern imperial ambitions, see Tanner 1993, 196–7. On the lasting literary imprint, see de Armas 2011, 40–2.

13 The original dispatch to officials in America dates from 26 December 1571 and calls Lepanto "cosa de grande importancia para la quietud y sosiego de toda cristiandad" (see "Aviso de la victoria de Lepanto," in AGI, Indiferente, legajo 427, libro 30, fols. 225–6).

14 Domínguez Ortiz and Vincent (1978, 58–9) describe the "panic" that shaped public attitudes towards Moriscos in the aftermath of the revolt and expulsion.

15 The royal secretary, Antonio de Eraso, signed his approbation 30 Oct 1572, suggesting the poet worked to finish by the battle's first anniversary (Latino 1573, 1st gathering, fol. 2). The volume appeared in print shortly after April 1573. It has two separately foliated sections: the first comprises two sections, one with epigrams in honour of the newborn crown prince along with an elegy in honour of Pius V; the second, with separately numbered gatherings and foliation, comprises the two books of the *Song of John of Austria*. Currently, the only complete Spanish translation of the

Song of John of Austria is José Sánchez Marín's 1981 Castilian version, which lacks footnotes to guide the reader through the dense topical and literary allusions. Fragments of the poem were published by Editorial Linkgua (Barcelona, 2007), in a series designed for popular readership. A facsimile edition of the entire 1573 volume of Lepanto poetry appeared in 1971 (Kraus reprints); it does not include any introductory or explanatory materials.

16 On Spanish "poets of Lepanto" in Spain, see López de Toro 1950, 24–5; and for Italy, Dionisotti 1974.

17 Bibliographies of Lepanto poetry are available in López de Toro 1950, 467–73; and Göllner 1968. Mammana 2007 catalogues Italian commemorations. Fenlon 2007 explores Lepanto's cultural impact in Venice. Though less frequently studied than poetry of Lepanto in the vernacular, examinations of neo-Latin poems of Lepanto are found in Silvio Barsi, introduction to Leo 2008 [1572]; and Miralles and Valsalobre 2010, 165. On poetry in Latin, see Vaccaluzzo 1909, as well as Wright, Spence, and Lemons 2014.

18 James Hankins 2001 and Peter Burke (1993, 34–65 and 2004, 43–60) have underscored Latin's continued relevance in international communications throughout the early modern era.

19 For an analysis of how such margin glosses worked in a schoolroom, see Kallendorf 2007b.

20 On the Aldus Manutius model of the un-annotated italic book as Spanish printers adopted it, see Griffin 1984, 80. To compare Latino's purposeful use of margin notes to the un-annotated literary publication mode that contemporaries favoured, consider his Lepanto volume (Latino 1573) in comparison to Gherardi 1572 or the Zaragoza 1578 edition of the second installment of Alonso de Ercilla's *Araucana*, whose Canto 24 narrates Lepanto. These three volumes are available on Google books (https://books.google.com/).

21 See the introduction to Wright, Spence, and Lemons 2014; and Vaccaluzzo 1909.

22 Fra Molinero 1995, 126.

23 Holt Parker, "Juan Latino," blog entry by Holt Parker, 5 April 2013. (http://renaissancelatinpoemoftheweek.blogspot.co.uk/2013/04/5-juan-latino-johannes-latinus-on-birth.html).

24 On Habsburg image making in relation to tranquility and moderation, see Río Barredo 2003, 112, and 2010. The broader dynastic patterns are explored in Coreth 2004, 1–12; and Elliott 1989, 142–61.

25 "On the Birth of Untroubled Times"; see Appendix 1, ll. 3–8; and Latino 1573, 1st gathering, fol. 9v. Appendix 1 provides a complete transcription and translation of this elegy addressed to Philip II. Subsequent citations

of the elegy will be from the appendix, with line numbers in parenthesis. I will also offer the corresponding folio numbers from the *princeps*, which as noted, has two separately foliated gatherings (noted here as 1st or 2nd gathering). See also Holt Parker 2013.

26 See Middlebrook 2009, 14.

27 See Relaño 2000, 9–10, on the idea of the "African puzzle" for Europeans. Citations from Gastaldi (1548) read: for the subtitle's advertisement, "infiniti nomi moderni, di Città, Provincie, Castella [...] il che in nissun altro Ptolomeo si ritrova," unnumbered folios; for the gloss to sub-Sahara Africa, fol. 129, "habitano intorno a questo Golfo gli Ethiopi Anthropophagi (cioe che mangiano gli homini)" and "quelli Etiopi, che comunamente si chiamano Hesperii (Regno di Senega, di Gambia, & di Ginea)."

28 See Mármol Carvajal 1573, fol. 15v (the uncharted geography) and fol. 44v (the people of black Africa, or lower Ethiopia). Mármol Carvajal's representation of Latino at court as a *procurador* is attested in AGS Expedientes de Hacienda legajo 734, document 4, and Registro General de Sello, legajo 1570 6–1.This veteran of the Alpujarras war submitted his African history for royal licensing in May 1572, just before Latino submitted his Lepanto volume (August 1572). Both were published in Granada in 1573, Mármol Carvajal with René Rabut and Latino with Hugo Mena. Rodríguez Mediano 2009, 251–4 assesses the influence here of the Gastaldi revisions to Ptolemy.

29 Bennassar (2000, 1–37) reconstructs the commander's childhood and frustrated aspirations to royal status. The Lepanto papers in the state archive attest to the slights John of Austria confronted. See AGS, Estado, legajo 1134, document 9 (complaints about back-stabbing advisors) and document 165 (hostile advisors subjecting him to humiliating financial restrictions). On how Philip's mistrustful micromanagement shaped John of Austria's battle plan, see Capponi 2006, 223. Smith 2015 contemplates the Juan Latino-Juan de Austria connection with reference to Gates's theory of signification.

30 For a brief consideration of how Latino's elegy references the trope of the phoenix, see Muñoz Martín and Sánchez Marín 1991, 283–4. Pliny's description appears in *Natural History* 10.2. Covarrubias, the foremost lexicographer of early modern Spain, registers the powerful resonance for Golden Age writers in his *Tesoro*'s entry for *fénix*. On Lope de Vega as the *fénix* of Spanish poets, see Wright 2001.

31 Kantorowicz 1997 [1957], 388–401 records how the phoenix signified the duality of royal power. Habsburg phoenix imagery is recorded in Bernat Vistarini and Cull 1999, 341.

32 Weber 2005.

33 On the black magus, see Snowden 1983, 107; Kaplan 1985, 79–80; and Koerner 2010, 16.
34 On the associations of Ethiopia and sub-Saharan Africa with Asia or the East, see Scafi 2006, 218–19; and Wey-Gómez 2008, 78–9.
35 On the transfer of the codex from Granada to the Escorial, see Alfonso X, 2010 [1283], 2:84. Constable (2007, 314) emphasizes the elite perspective of the entire volume and discusses the Castilian context in which the treatise emerged.
36 On the story of the Ethiopian eunuch as it reflected and shaped representations of black Africans, see Courtès 2010, 207–8; and Snowden 1970, 206 and 1983, 100–1.
37 The *Elogio de la casa de Velada, para el Marques don Gomez Davila,* BNE, mss. 3184, decries falsified family trees but also alleges that Hercules founded the city of Ávila, thus ascribing nobility from time immemorial to the marquises of Velada. On the Granada Venegas family, see Soria Mesa 1995. Lope de Vega satirizes this practice in numerous plays, as in *Los ramilletes de Madrid,* ll. 1384–6, in Vega Carpio 2012, 542: "Tan noble, hermano, nació, / que por su linaje todo / es hidalgo desde Adán" (his birth is so noble, brother, that his family has had hidalgo status since Adam). Bass (2008, 64–77) explores the cultural impact of this practice, with particular emphasis on theatrical reflections.
38 Núñez Muley 2007 [1567], 81 and 91, respectively.
39 On the importance of Las Casas's polemic as a foundational text for modern discourses of racial difference, see Greer, Mignolo, and Quilligan 2007, 1–26.
40 Fra Molinero (2005, 344) draws attention as well to how this eastward turn avoids Atlantic slave routes.
41 Bultman 2007, 181–206.
42 *Life of Domitian*, 23.2, in Suetonius, *Lives of the Caesars.*
43 The Renaissance reading technique that focused on extracting commonplaces is distilled in Kallendorf 2007a, 1–66; for Spain, see Bouza 2004, 42.
44 Particularly relevant sources with which to analyse Latino's *imitatio* include Pigman 1980, 6–11; Greene 1982; García Galiano 1992, 15–16; McLaughlin 1995, 22–48; and for the specific case of Lepanto as a focal point of *imitation,* Elizabeth B. Davis 2000, 61–97; and Nicolopulos 2000, 176–215.

4 Christians and Muslims on the Battle Lines

1 See Tasso 1587, fol. 3r. Armstrong-Roche (2009, esp. 10–16) explores the abiding interest among Spanish writers in an epic narration immersed in politics and history in their own time.

2 For early-modern reconfigurations of Fama, see Hardie 2012, 78–125, esp. 124–5. Another positive reconfiguration of Virgil's Fama in Lepanto poetry appears in Ottaviano Manini's "At Latio tandem pallentes dispulit umbras" (ll. 126–33, pp. 168–9), in Wright, Spence, and Lemons 2014. On the unusually fast delivery of letters with breaking news, see Braudel 1966 [1949], 1:335–8.

3 To facilitate consultation, parenthetical citations of the poem will refer to the Latin-English edition in Wright, Spence, and Lemons 2014, by line number and page, as well as to the folio number of the *princeps* as Latino 1573. The latter is available on Google books, where the Lepanto epic is in the second of two separate foliated gatherings of the volume, *Ad catholicum, pariter et invictissimum Philippum Dei gratia Hispaniarum regem, de felicissima serenissimi Ferdinandi Principis nativitate, epigrammatum liber … Austrias Carmen.*

4 Barrios Aguilera 2009, 824.

5 Prefatory "Epigramma" (Latino 1573, 1st gathering, fol. 5r, margin gloss): "Maiores Dezae Iudaeorum exactores" (Deza's ancestors [were] the scourge [expellers] of the Jews). The most prominent ancestor here is his uncle Diego de Deza; on this inquisitor, see Kamen 1997, 123. Pedro de Deza's prestige as an Old Christian also stemmed from his ability to prove blood purity to enter the prestigious Colegio Mayor de San Bartolomé (see Barrios Aguilera 2009).

6 John of Austria's criticisms of Deza appear in *CODOIN* 28:127–30. On the mutual hatred with the Counts of Tendilla, see Elliott 1990 [1963], 238–9. The *visita*, discussed in the final section of chapter 2, is the Archivo General de Simancas, Cámara de Castilla, legajo 2737.

7 Gracián Dantisco's Diurnal or daily log is transcribed by Andrés 1962, 47–8. In his elegy of *circa* 1576, Latino praises Gracián Dantisco for allowing the expeditious navigation of censorship channels (Latino 1576, Elegy "Ad illustrem Dominum Antonium Gratianum," unnumbered folios, Eiv–Eiiir).

8 See Vega Carpio 2007 [1598]. Consideration of how the adversary Drake dominates the epic appears in Wright 2001, 24–51, with further exploration in Wright 2008.

9 Vega Carpio 1989 [1941], 195.

10 Bouza 2012 details the bureaucratic steps for obtaining publication licence. For the additional obstacle of a work that narrates recent history, see Wright 2001, 24, which discusses the censorship of Lope de Vega's *Dragontea.*

11 The Bernardino de Villaldrando prologue praising Juan Latino's book of poems appears in Latino 1573, 1st gathering, fol. 4v.

12 As noted in chapter 2, Luis del Mármol Carvajal's 1573 *Primera parte de la descripción general de África* refers to his completed history of the Morisco

rebellion as forthcoming (fol. 278r), but that history only appeared in 1600 as *Historia de la rebelión y castigo de los moriscos del Reino de Granada.*

13 On the third Duke of Sessa's notorious indebtedness in these years, see Wright 2007, 255–6. On evidence Sessa's reputation suffered from controversial actions on the battlefield during the Morisco revolt, see Domínguez Ortiz and Vincent 1978, 38–9. Latino's tax litigation, pending since 1564, is documented in AGS, Expedientes de Hacienda legajo 734, document 4.

14 Spratlin 1938 registers the problems presented by the poem's religious dimension by noting: "The extent of Spain's devotion to the Catholic faith can be measured by the fanaticism of this imported Negro whose early gods were the antithesis of the God of the Hierarchy" (45). González Vázquez 1996 likewise laments the poem's excessive religiosity, suggesting it might be overcompensation for non-Christian origins.

15 For considerations of the opening passage, see Fra Molinero 2005, 335; and Seo 2011, 271.

16 The *Oxford Latin Dictionary* registers the association with Augustus.

17 On the disagreements that thwarted Philip II's aspirations to the imperial title, see Rodríguez-Salgado 1988, 34–40.

18 See Gregory 2006, 1–15.

19 See Sannazaro 2009, "De partu Virginis" (The Virgin Birth), Book 1, ll. 1–12.

20 Michael C.J. Putnam, introduction to Sannazaro 2009, xxii–xxiii.

21 See Panofsky (2005 [1943] 78–9) for analysis of the *sol iustitiae*; the influential explication of the image by Pierre Bersuire appears in *Repertorium Morale*, Book 5, ch. 28, "De sole" (Bersuire 1575, fol. 124r, section 15). For how Habsburg image making drew on Apollonian and solar images of Christ, see Tanner 1993, 223–48, esp 231.

22 Guilmartin (2003 [1974], 1–55) describes the interconnection between galley warfare, piracy, and commerce.

23 See, for instance, the battle orders printed in Giovanni Pietro Contarini 1572, fols. 43v–7v, which list the widely known Italian renegades Kara Hodja and Uluç Ali, as well as likely Jewish converts (David Iusuf). For brief biographical sketches of both Ottoman and Holy League commanders, see the appendix in Capponi 2006.

24 Casale (2007) notes the "challenge" of Ottoman meritocracy to Iberian notions of race-based inheritance. On the allure of Uluç Ali specifically, see Sola Castaño 2010, 148–9.

25 Hankins 1995, 135–44.

26 As noted in chapter 3, the ways Virgil's Actium shapes poems of Lepanto are detailed in Quint 1993, 21–49; Elizabeth B. Davis 2000, 70–8; Nicolopulos 2000, 103–6; and Blanco 2010, 493–7.

27 See Bicheno 2003, 78.

28 Menéndez y Pelayo (1927, 142) states that Latino's Virgilian hexameters show that "su negro autor estaba muy empapado de la lectura de Virgilio" (their black author was immersed in his reading of Virgil). González Vázquez (1983, 138) offers a list of Virgilian citations, but does not delve into the historical, narrative, or pedagogical context of the poem. His concluding remarks exclude Juan Latino from a heroic sphere of ostensibly "original" poets, as he avers that the freedman lacks the "fuerza de espíritu o inspiración" (force of spirit or inspiration) displayed by poets who are "vigorosamente originales y absolutamente individuales" (vigorously original and truly individual).

29 Ottoman historian Halil Inalcik (1974, 189) cites Sultan Selim II's orders. Philip II's parallel conception of a holy war is found in *CODOIN* 3:216; and in his "Instrucciones de Felipe II al marqués de Santa Cruz" (Instructions from Philip II to the Marquis de Santa Cruz). August 1571, in AGS, legajo 1134, document 43.

30 A reproduction of the battle standard now preserved in Spain's Armería Real (Madrid) is in Rodríguez Salgado, et al. 1988, 65 (image #2:34).

31 The captured Ottoman standard arrived in Spain with the first detailed report of Lepanto, as attested in Mármol Carvajal ca. 1571.

32 I explore the iconographic dimension here in Wright 2009, 79–80. On the role of devotional images in Granada's evangelization programs, see Pereda 2007, 249–387.

33 See Herrera 1572, 363–70; Rufo 1854 [1584],131–3; and Ercilla 1983 [1569–97], 662–90.

34 See the March 1573 "Memorial" in AGS, Castilla, legajo 2174.

35 Rigaux 2013, 51; the passage in Virgil is in 2.130.

36 Spanish reverence for Lucan on account of his birth in Córdoba and his historical accuracy within Latin verse registers in the influential translation of *De bellum civile* prepared by Martín Laso de Oropesa and then revised and expanded by Joan Baptista Bonello (see Lucan, 1588, prologue, unnumbered folios).

37 On Juan Latino's birth, see the Fernández de Córdoba (Abbot of Rute), ca. 1620, fol. 174r. Liang (2011, 25–35) explains how integral the frontier region of southern Córdoba was to the fortunes and identities of the Fernández de Córdoba family overall.

38 "La vida de Marco Anneo Lucano," in Lucan 1588, unnumbered folios. Though I cite from the 1578 edition that was revised and expanded by Joan Baptista Bonello, the same biography appeared in the original 1541 translation.

39 Lucan, *De bellum civile*, Book 1 (ll. 10–23) records the lost opportunity for empire building. The opening passage repeats forms of *scelus* (Book 1, l. 2 and l. 37) and nefas (Book 1, l. 6 and l. 37).

5 The Costs of Modern Warfare

1 Guilmartin 2003 [1974] describes the Venetian galleasses (245–6), and the amphibious nature of Mediterranean warfare at sea (73).
2 Giovanni Pietro Contarini 1572, fol. 51v.
3 See Murrin 1994, 138.
4 Latino's Lepanto volume reached the royal secretary Antonio Gracián Dantisco in August of 1572 (see Andrés 1962, 47–8), while Herrera's publication licence was granted 20 September 1572 (see Herrera 1572, front matter, unnumbered folios). Subsequent citations to Herrera's prose history of the battle will be to the transcription published in *CODOIN* 21:375–82.
5 Blanco (2010, 506–7). For analysis of Herrera's conception of the *canción* in relation to Italian models and the imprint in Spain of Garcilaso de la Vega, see Navarrete 1994, 160–4.
6 On the ironic reflections on "arms versus letters" in Cervantes, see Cruz 2002. Assessment of Herrera's fascination with artillery and its poetic implications appears in Gaylord 1971, 86. The historical comparison between ancient battles and modern clashes with artillery appears in Herrera, in *CODOIN* 21:374.
7 Middlebrook 2009, 146–7.
8 Kallendorf 2007b.
9 Complaints by John of Austria for his treatment in Granada appear in a letter to Ruy Gómez de Silva (undated, circa May 1570) in CODOIN 28:73; on the restrictions to his direct action at Lepanto, see Capponi 2006, 223.
10 Other poets who emulated the Trojan games of *Aeneid* 5 are found in Wright, Spence, and Lemons 2014: Davide Podavini (l. 80), Agostino Fortunio (ll. 4 and 10), and Giovanni Antonio Taglietti (l. 20). On the longer term impact of the funeral games in Spanish literature, see Armstrong-Roche 2009, 171–2, whose analysis of this theme in Cervantes helps understand the episode's imprint in Lepanto epics.
11 See Lucan's view of how anonymous soldiers suffer in *Civil War* 3.577 (naval battle); 4.48–120 (famine); and 5.237–99 (homesickness and mutiny).
12 The ranking of Virgil first and Lucan second appears in "La vida de Marco Anneo Lucano," in Lucan 1588 (translated by Martín Laso de Oropesa, unnumbered folios).
13 An analysis is provided in Hinds 1998, 2.

14 Benavides 1571, unnumbered folios.
15 The first Venetian report – mentioned at the beginning of chapter 3 – is transcribed in Setton 1984, 1060n54. The Spanish command unit report is in AGI, Estado, legajo 1134, document 83; a transcription was published in *CODOIN* 3:219.
16 On the summary execution of skilled fighters and expert artillerymen, see Guilmartin 2003 [1974], 263.
17 Diedo 1995 [1571], 207–8. On Philip II's prohibition against John of Austria engaging in direct combat and the supervisory arrangements he set up, see Capponi 2006, 223; and Bicheno 2003, 268.
18 Arcucci, "The Victory at Naupactus" (ll. 270–90; esp. ll. 272–3) in Wright, Spence, and Lemons 2014, 210–11. For the Pius V biography, see Catena 1587, 287.
19 On Barbarigo's complex manoeuver and its decisiveness in securing victory, see Guilmartin 2003 [1974], 215 and 258–60.
20 On how Renaissance schoolmasters embraced epic poetry to inculcate military valour, see Ong 1959, 114. An example of this application of epic at the highest level of society is recorded in the first complete Castilian translation of Virgil's *Aeneid*, whose prologue urges the future Philip II to scrutinize the epic (*escudriñar*) to learn about how to rule; see Virgil 1586 (translated by Gregorio Hernández de Velasco, prologue, unnumbered folios). Wilson-Okamura 2010 (203–6) analyses how the commentary and commonplace book traditions shaped interpretations of Virgil.
21 I build here on earlier discussions of this episode: see Anguita and Wright 2012 and Wright 2015. On the problems posed by the Nisus and Euryalus story in *Aeneid* 9, see Block 1982, 17–19; Horsfall 1995, 170–8; and Casali 2004.
22 Virgil's apostrophic promise of immorality is etched into the repository for unidentified remains at the National September 11 Museum in New York. Complaints about the inappropriateness of an allusion to the Nisus and Euryalus raid have informed public comment. See the compilation of scholarly opinions in Dunlap 2014 and the critique in Alexander 2011.
23 See Braund (1992, xlii–xliii) for analysis of Lucan's concern with the mistreatment of bodies.
24 Other poetic accounts of Ali Pasha's death mentioned are Herrera in *CODOIN* 21:362–3 for the prose history citations and *CODOIN* 21:380–1 for the "Canción"; and Juan Rufo, *La Austriada*, Canto 24 (in Rufo 1854, 131). Alonso de Ercilla, following Herrera, might have recounted Ali Pasha's death, but instead concludes his account, see *La Araucana*, Canto 24 (in Ercilla 1993, 690).

25 The overall circumstances of Ali Pasha's death do remain unclear (see Capponi 2006, 279). A shift in accounts comes in the seventeenth-century narrators who move away from earliest versions of a sword blow, to describe Ali Pasha's death by a bullet wound, after which his head was displayed as a trophy (see Cabrera de Córdoba 1998 [1619], 598; and Paruta 1605, 217). I have found no support in period documents for the assertion that John of Austria took "bitter offence" at the desecration of Ali Pasha's body, as reported, for example, in Bicheno 2003, 270; and Bennassar 2000, 137.

26 Albert Blaise's dictionary of patristic Latin (*Dictionnaire latin-français des auteurs chrétiens*) defines *bibo* as "s'imprègne du Christ dans l'intimité de son coeur" (to take Christ into the inner recesses of one's heart). Consultation through *DLD*, 24 June 2013.

27 Tovar's ca. 1586 account of the Aztec ruler's death six decades earlier reads: "dicen que pidió [Moctezuma] el baptismo y se convirtió a la verdad del Santo Evangelio, y aunque venía allí un clérigo sacerdote entienden que se ocupó más en buscar riquezas con los soldados que no en donde feneció el gran imperio y señorío de los famosos mexicanos" (they say he asked for baptism and accepted the truth of the Holy Gospel, and though an ordained priest did pass through, he focused more on seeking riches with the soldiers than on the place where the great emperor and lord of the renowned Mexicans lay dying); transcribed in Lafaye 1972, 83. See Todorov 1987, 56, for the implications of this myth in terms of the conceptions of Amerindians as Other. Bernal Díaz del Castillo (1982 [1560], chapter 95, 126–7) places heavy emphasis on this captivity and emphasizes the near conversion, but deflects any blame away from the Spanish captors.

28 Adorno 2007, 64.

29 See Adorno 2007, 206–13. On Cardinal Espinosa's role in the implantation of the Inquisition in the Americas and the repression in Granada during the same period, see Martínez Millán 1994.

30 Benavides 1571, unnumbered folios. Of the two sons, Saïd and Mohammed, only the former would survive captivity; see Bennassar 2000, 137–8. A French chapbook thus purported to be a copy of the letter from Saïd's mother, sister of the sultan Selim II, to John of Austria (see *Copie d'une lettre de La Rosse, mère de Sain Bej, prisonnier à Rome. Envoyée au Serenissime Don Jean d'Austria, et a lui presentée*).

31 Wardropper 1967.

32 On stereotypes of Turkishness in Spanish Golden Age literature, see Mas 1967, 190–211, who argues that Lepanto was a turning point in representations.

33 See Putnam 1965, 151–201; Parry 1989, 78–96, esp. 94–5; Lyne 1987, 103–13; and Kallendorf 2007a.

34 See John of Austria's memorandum of 27 September 1571, AGS, legajo 1134, document 76. This passage builds on Wright 2012, 148–9.

35 The poet records the role of "judge Nabbas" (l. 1309), which refers to the official named in state papers as Doctor Navas de Puebla; see AGS, legajo 1134, documents 76 and 182.

36 See Giovanni Pietro Contarini, 1572, fols. 53v–4r: "Poiche furono tutte le galee Turchesche ridotte in poter de Christiani, tutti, andorno bottinando et depreando le inimiche spoglie fino a notte restando il tutto in poter loro."

37 Leo 2008 [1572], *De bello turcico*, l. 603. The poem was completed in September 1572, and published in Rome in 1573.

38 Elizabeth Davis (2000, 70–3).

39 Guilmartin (2003 [1974], 19) emphasizes the lack of clear differentiation between merchant ships and warships in Mediterranean warfare at sea.

40 See Giovanni Battista Arcucci, "The Victory at Naupactus" (ll. 319–447, pp. 214–23 in Wright, Spence, and Lemons 2014); and Herrera, in *CODOIN* 21:372, which reads "pelearon con muy gran fortaleza la capitana del Colona, la de Saboya y la de Venecia, y se aventajó entre los venecianos el Canaleto."

41 See, for example, Pérez de Hita 1998 [1619], 15.

42 Sola Castaño (2010, 148–9) chronicles the extent to which Uluç Ali fascinated Spaniards, both for his skills as a mariner and his remarkable upward mobility.

43 See Guilmartin 2003 [1974], 262–3.

44 See the closing passage of the "Canción en alabanza de la Divina Majestad" in Herrera 1572 (*CODOIN* 21:382). On Algiers, both in terms of Spain's frustrated ambitions for domination and the literary career of Cervantes, see Garcés 2002, 15–123, and 2011, 1–78.

45 Indeed, Braudel (1966 [1949], 1:330) offered news of Lepanto as an example of the "battle against distance" that connected diverse Mediterranean realms. See also Barbarics and Pieper 2007, 65–78; and Fenlon 2007, 233–71. On Renaissance adaptions of Virgil's Fama, see Hardie 2012, 78–125, 411–38.

Conclusion: Song of the Black Swan

1 Scafi (2006, 218–19) and Wey-Gómez (2008, 78–9) explore how European cartographers conceived Ethiopia (sub-Saharan Africa) as part of the East. Relaño 2000 examines the emerging continental conception of Africa.

2 Francisco de Pedrosa sent Philip II his own epic poem in Latin on Lepanto, circa 1580, asking for print licence (*CODOIN* 3:289); that poem never appeared in print (see Pedrosa, ca. 1580). Mármol Carvajal's 1573 history of Africa describes his history of the Morisco rebellion as ready for publication (fol. 278r), though it only appeared in 1600; see also Castillo Fernández 2015, xxv.
3 Deza's own laments about landless Galician peasants flocking to Granada appear in AGS Cámara de Castilla, legajo 2171. See Barrios Aguilera 1996 for an analysis of the short-range desolation of the city's most emblematic Morisco neighbourhood, the Albaicín. Barrios Aguilera 1993 assesses the longer range impact of resettlement.
4 See Bermúdez de Pedraza 1638, 256v. On *advenedizo*, see Covarrubias, who records the most common sense of a lowly newcomer, but also notes its more specific application to denote converts from Islam to Catholicism.
5 Guerrero's intervention on Latino's behalf is cited in Marín Ocete 1924, 77–8. I could not locate this transcribed document in the city's municipal archive Marín Ocete cited nor find other copies in state archives. However, I was able to confirm the basic outlines of the space dispute and its direct focus on Latino's long-time classroom space in Archivo Universitario, Universidad de Granada, *Segundo libro de actas de Claustro y Grados, 1562–1600*, fol. 154.
6 In Silvestre 1582, the editor, poet Pedro de Cáceres y Espinosa, tells the story: "Hablando una vez a ciertos amigos, en compañía de Juan Latino, dicen que habló [Silvestre] a todos, y no a él, que no le vido, o se fue de industria, y quejándose Juan Latino delante de los mismos, dello, dicen que respondió, perdone señor maestro, que ente[n]di que era sombra de uno destos señores" (unnumbered folios).
7 Vickers 1988, 264.
8 For a brief account of the *Traslación* ceremony, see Siguënza 1986 [ca. 1602], 46–52. For the king's instructions, dated 30 November 1573, see AMG, legajo 1930, document 38; a scribe's acccount of the ceremony of appears in the same legajo, pieza 40–1.
9 I retain the orthography in the *princeps*, where Cygnus appears as a proper noun symbolizing the poet himself. I do, however, alter the spelling Cynus to Cygnus, following the widely accepted orthography. Indeed, a margin gloss to the passage spells the accusative form as Cygnum, suggesting the missing *g* in the passage may be a typesetting error.
10 Covarrubias's gloss on aging poets' swans songs reads: "Y así los [poetas] que en la vejez se han extremado en sus escritos, no sólo los poetas pero

los oradores, a los cuales no faltan sus números y sus cadencias, son comparados al cisne."

11 Taleb 2007 discusses the "black swan event" in terms of post-Enlightenment notions of the fragility of knowledge. Such unforeseen events include the terrorist attacks of 11 September 2001 and the civil war that ravaged Taleb's Lebanese homeland in the 1970s.

12 On the jesting built into the naming of his three black slaves, see Clénard (Clenardus) 1940, 1:114–15 and 3:67 (letter of 10 January 1537). Clenardus ponders selling Antonius in Granada; see Clénard (Clenardus) 1:205, 3:162.

13 Lida de Malkiel (1975, 80) explores how Garcilaso de la Vega's "Third Eclogue" adapts Virgil's simile. Covarrubias's note on the swan's whiteness reads: "Ella es un ave blanca de candidísimas plumas, sin mezclársele otra ninguna color; sólo el pico y los pies tiene colorados."

14 The frontispiece of *De Translatione* addresses the book "to the Catholic, and most invincible Philip, king of the realms of Hispania by grace of God." Latino is "poeta Catholicus" in a margin notation (Bviiii v, misfoliated as 19v).

15 Nebrija glosses the adjective *Catholicus* as "universalis"; Covarrubias registers *Catholicus* as "vale tanto como universal." "Universal," in turn, is "el que tiene noticia de muchas cosas diferentes y habla en ellas científicamente."

16 Dandelet 2001, 54, 70, 79.

17 On the clash at Navarino in August 1572 and the ensuing end of the Holy League Alliance, see Guilmartin 2003, 63 and Bennassar 2000, 156–68. On Uluç Ali's later years, enduring allure for Spanish adversaries, and how he embodied the Mediterranean "boundary crosser" (los que van y vienen), see Sola Castaño 2010, 65–6, 148–9.

18 See Bennassar (2000, 1–27) for an account of John of Austria's death.

19 MacKay 2012, 8–40 (King Sebastian's tragic emulation of John of Austria), and 46–61 (Philip II's machinations to claim the throne).

20 The symbolic centrality of the Escorial is discussed in Lazure 2007 and in political terms, in Gil Pujol 2004, 59.

21 Harris 2007, 26. On the transfer from the Capilla Real to the Escorial of a large number of the volumes from Isabel I's library, see Gallego Burín 1953, 67–74.

22 See AMG, legajo 1930 (document 71, 1572): "Real cédula para que se formen cofradías o hermandades de caballeros que ejerciten las armas," dated 6 September 1572. On the broader implications of jousting in relation to emerging early modernity, see Fallows 2010, esp. 1–19; for how

such displays of nobility played out during the city's economic and cultural recovery in the early seventeenth century, see Casey 2007, 31–53.

23 See Harris 2007, esp. xiv, 47–87; and García-Arenal and Rodríguez Mediano 2010b, esp. 13–16.

24 Archivo Universitario, Universidad de Granada, *Segundo libro de actas de Claustro y Grados, 1562–1600* (legajo 1450, fol. 331r).

25 Martínez Leiva and Rodríguez Rebollo 2007, 74, entry #89.

26 Henríquez de Jorquera (1987 [1643], 2:533) records a 1590 death, but bases his account of Latino on posthumous sources that include some inaccuracies. The parish archives of his Santa Ana neighbourhood do not record his death, prompting Antonio Marín Ocete (1924, 36) to propose Latino died between 1594 and 1597, years for which the death registry at Santa Ana is missing. Antonio (1996 [1783], 716) cites a lapidary inscription in the Santa Ana parish dated 1593. A newer plaque now on display in this church, dated 1990, gives 1597 as a date of death, following Marín Ocete.

27 I corroborated the baptismal records transcribed in Marín Ocete (1924, 74–6), which record two daughters and two sons born to Latino and Carlobal (Juana, Bernardino, Ana, and Juana). Records of a funeral for the burial of a daughter of Enrique Latino in 1602 suggest the couple may have had a fifth child. The special recognition of Latino's service to the university appears in the faculty senate minutes from 20 November 1599 (*Segundo libro de actas de Claustro y Grados, 1562–1600*, fol. 504r).

28 The passage in Antolínez de Burgos 1996 [ca. 1611, 365] reads: "'Mirad lo que pueden las letras que, a faltarnos éstas, ni vos saliérades de una caballeriza almohazando caballos, ni yo del campo, tras un arado.'" Bermúdez de Pedraza (1638, 260r) alters this anecdote, gesturing towards the idea of Latino as a witty court jester to the prelate.

29 Douglass 2014, 314. See also his account of the moment he finds his own power by speaking at an abolitionist meeting (287).

30 On Latino's emergence as a (fictional) character in the comedia *Juan Latino*, see Fra Molinero 1995; Beusterien 2006, 106–14; and Weissbourd 2013.

31 The fictionalized rape scene appears in Salazar 1623 [1615], 482–7. Fra Molinero (1995, 28) traces the expressions of this anxiety about interracial sex in Iberian theatre; Stella (2000, 129–47, esp. 139–40) analyses notarial evidence about the anxieties and obstacles to interracial marriages and families.

32 Cervantes, *Don Quijote*, I, p. 61. On the meaning of *esclavo bozal*, see Covarrubias. See also Beusterien 1999, for an analysis of the comic theatrical code of the "hablar de negros" (speech of blacks).

33 See Hankins 2001; and for Spain, Gil-Fernández 1981, 39–66.
34 Juan Tamayo Salazar (1658, 440–78) reprinted Latino's Lepanto epic, minus some of its margin glosses and the last sixteen verses, in a compilation of Spanish feast days.
35 Nicolás Antonio 1996, 716.

Epilogue: Juan Latino in the Harlem Renaissance

1 Schomburg 1996 [1927], 69. Documentation of the trip's preparation and financing is found in the Schomburg Papers. I thank Ashley Gibson, University of Georgia class of 2015, whose research paper titled, "Venciendo el prejuicio en el Siglo XVI: el éxito de Juan Latino" drew my attention to Schomburg's note and research trip. To my knowledge, her research was the first to recover this link to Schomburg that had been lost in studies from the 1930s through recent times. Even the monograph by Spratlin (1938) does not mention Schomburg's trip to Spain, despite the fact that he wrote to Schomburg at his New York Public Library office when seeking to hire new Spanish faculty for his department at Howard University.
2 Schomburg 1996 [1927], 69.
3 See Latino's declaration on 14 June 1572, signed Expedientes de Hacienda legajo 734, document 4.
4 See Johnson 1996 [1927], 11.
5 Johnson 1996 [1927], 4.
6 Johnson 1996 [1927], 78–9.

Appendix 1: Elegy for Philip II, "On the Birth of Untroubled Times"

1 This translation was prepared prior to the posting of Holt Parker's annotated prose translation, which includes useful notes on rhetorical devices and classical citations. See his blog entry of 5 April 2013 (http://renaissancelatinpoemoftheweek.blogspot.co.uk/2013/04/5-juan-latino-johannes-latinus-on-birth.html).
2 Margin: *A consequentibus* [argument based on outcome].
3 Margin: *Ab orbe condito inauditum* [without precedent since the world's creation]. / *Nigris parentibus catholicus floruit Dei misericordia* [with black parents, he prospered a Catholic by the mercy of God].
4 Margin: *Dominus Joannes ab Austria dux rarus* [Don Juan from Austria, singular leader]. / *A simili* [(argument) from likeness].

5 Margin: *Historia mirabilis* [wondrous history].
6 Margin: *Gentium primitiae Magi ab Oriente* [Magi from the East (bore the first offerings of mankind)]. The verses connect the birth of a royal heir to Anna of Austria (Aurora) to Christ's nativity that brought the Magi with offerings.
7 Margin: *Ubi tota cohors nigra* [where the whole court (is) black].
8 Margin: *Generationem eius quis enarrabit?* [who will tell of his offspring?].
9 Margin: *In actis Apostolorum historia nota* [a notable history in Acts of the Apostles]. / *Argumentorum nervi* [the strength of the argument]. Verses echo Acts 8. 27–39.
10 Margin: *Dominus Joannes ab Austria Garnatae poetam novit, et ad se familiariter admisit* [Don Juan de Austria met the poet of Granada and warmly welcomed him]. Even in a military mission like Granada, Don Juan had a structured, hierarchical entourage following the court protocols. The margin note distils the complex and often competitive negotiations for access in a court through the *ad se.*
11 Margin: *Mos regum* [custom of kings].
12 Margin: *Ex omni natione, quae sub caelo est* [(vows) from every nation that is under heaven]. In line 39 of the verse, *ecclesiae* abbreviated as *ecclesae. Filius ecclesiae,* from medieval jurisprudence, conceives the king as son and father of the church (*filius et pater ecclesiae*); see Kantorowicz 1997, 100.
13 Line 47 echoes a Virgilian formulation of the battle for Italy, "huc illuc; neque enim levia aut ludicra petuntur" (see *Aeneid* 12.764).
14 Margin: *Materia operis* [the substance of the work].
15 Margin: *Petitio honesta* [a worthy request]. In line 58, print technology is rendered in classical Latin, as a new kind of bas-relief (*typus novus*) on which words are stamped.
16 Margin: *Dotes regiae* [royal attributes]. / *Don Domini Joannis ab Austriae dotes mirabiles et Catholicae* [the wondrous and Catholic attributes of Don Juan of Austria]. / *Pugnat et ducit exercitum Caesar alter* [A new Caesar, he fights and leads the army]. In line 64 as elsewhere, *ecclesae* for *ecclesiae.* I render *dotes* as attributes or qualities, in light of John of Austria's well known and frustrated ambitions to be granted royal status by his brother King Philip II; see Bennassar 2000, 54. Holt Parker opts for the translation of *dotes* as gifts, an interpretation that would speak to notions of royal liberality that underpinned the image making of the Habsburgs and other *ancien régime* monarchies.
17 Margin: *Princeps magnus futurus patris similis* [the prince will be great like his father].

18 Margin: *Christianorum desiderium* [the hope of Christians]. In l. 76 and elsewhere, the poet uses *regibus* to convey the composite nature of the Spanish Monarchy, in which Philip II rules as king of diverse realms (Castile, Aragon, Navarre, Sicily, Naples, etc.), each considered in terms of its particular constitutional and juridical traditions. Pius V and other Catholic leaders voiced the hopes that Don Juan would follow the victory at Lepanto with a campaign to retake the Holy Land (here Christ's sepulchre) and Constantinople from the Ottoman empire.

19 Margin: *Allusio ad cornicem Tarpeiam* [allusion to the Tarpeian raven]. The prophecy of auspicious times ahead echoes Suetonius, *Life of Domitian* 23.2, with the *carmine cornix* echoing the *culmine cornix* (*Nuper Tarpeio quae sedet culmine cornix / 'Est bene' non potuit dicere, dixit: 'erit.'*).

Bibliography

Archives Consulted

Archivo General de Indias (AGI): "Aviso de la victoria de Lepanto." Indiferente, legajo 427, Libro 30. fols. 225–6.

Archivo General de Simancas (AGS)

Cámara de Castilla, Memoranda from the Second Revolt of the Alpujarras. Legajos 2171, 2174, 2737.

Estado, Documents from the Battle of Lepanto. Legajo 1134.

Expedientes de Hacienda. Legajo 734, doc. 4.

Registro General de Sello. Legajo 1570, pieza 6–1.

Archivo Municipal de Granada (AMG). Legajo 1930, pieza 40–1.

The Arthur A. Schomburg Papers (Schomburg Papers). Microfilm. Bethesda, MD: University Publications of America, 1991. [Originals in the New York Public Library, Schomburg Center for Research in Black Culture.]

Palace of Medina Sidonia (San Lucar de Barrameda, Spain). Legajo 2400.

Parroquia de Santa Ana (Granada). *Libro I.*

Universidad de Granada, Archivo Universitario. 2007. *Primer libro de actas de Claustro y Grados (1532–1560).* Edited and transcribed by María Amparo Moreno Trujillo and Juan María de la Obra Sierra. CD-rom. Granada: Universidad de Granada.

– *Segundo libro de actas de Claustro y Grados, 1562–1600.* Legajo 1450.

Print and Manuscript Sources

Adorno, Rolena. 2007. *The Polemics of Possession in Spanish American Narrative.* Yale: Yale University Press.

Africanus, Leo (al-Hassan al-Wazzan). 1563. *Della descrittione dell'Africa.* In *Delle navigationi et viaggi* by Giovanni Battista Ramusio, vol. 1, 3rd ed., fols. 1–195. Venice: Giunta.

Alexander, Caroline. 2011. "Out of Context." Editorial in *The New York Times.* 7 April 2011. http://www.nytimes.com/2011/04/07/opinion/07alexander.html.

Alfonso X., King of Castile. 2010 [1283]. *Libros de ajedrez, dados, y tablas.* Facsimile edition of Codex T.I.6 of the Biblioteca de El Escorial, edited by Manuel González Jiménez, et al. 2 vols. Lugo: Scriptorium Ediciones Limitadas.

Álvares, Francisco. 1557. *Historia de las cosas de Etiopia.* Translated by Thomas de Padilla. Antwerp: Johannes Steels.

Álvarez-Ossorio Alvariño, Antonio. 2001. *Milán y el legado de Felipe II: Gobernadores y corte provincial en la Lombardía de los Austrias.* Madrid: Sociedad Estatal para la Conmemoración de los Centenarios de Felip II y Carlos V.

Amelang, James S. 2011. *Historias paralelas: Judeoconversos y moriscos en la España moderna.* Madrid: Akal.

Andrés, Gregorio de, ed. 1962. "Diurnal de Antonio Gracián, Secretario de Felipe II." In *Documentos para la historia del Monasterio de San Lorenzo el Real de El Escorial,* 5:18–127. San Lorenzo del Escorial: Imprenta del Real Monasterio.

Anghiera, Pietro Martire de. See under Martyr, Peter.

Anguita, José María, and Elizabeth R. Wright. 2012. "Sombras de la *onorosa praeda*: un *exemplo* virgiliano para un aula granadina." *Criticón* 115:105–23.

Antolínez de Burgos, Justino. 1996 [ca. 1611]. *Historia eclesiástica de Granada.* Edited by Manuel Sotomayor. Granada: Universidad de Granada.

Antonio, Nicolás. 1996 [1783]. *Bibliotheca Hispana Nova.* Vol. 1 of 2. Madrid: Joaquín Ibarra. Rpt. Madrid: Visor.

Ares Queija, Berta, and Alessandro Stella, eds. 2000. *Negros, mulatos, zambaigos: derroteros africanos en los mundos ibéricos.* Seville: EEHA/CSIC.

Armstrong-Roche, Michael. 2009. *Cervantes' Epic Novel: Empire, Religion, and the Dream Life of Heroes in Persiles.* Toronto: University of Toronto Press.

Barbarics, Zsuzsa, and Renate Pieper. 2007. "Handwritten Newsletters as a Means of Communication in Early Modern Europe." In *Correspondence and Cultural Exchange in Europe, 1400–1700,* edited by Francisco Bethencourt and Florike Egmond. Vol. 3 of *Cultural Exchange in Early Modern Europe,* edited by Robert Muchembled and William Monter, 53–79. Cambridge: Cambridge University Press.

Barbero, Alessandro. 2010. *Lepanto: La battaglia dei tre imperi.* Bari: Laterza.

Barletta, Vincent. 2005. *Covert Gestures: Crypto-Islamic Literature as Cultural Practice in Early Modern Spain.* Minneapolis and London: University of Minnesota Press.

Barrios Aguilera, Manuel. 1993. *Moriscos y repoblación en las postrimerías de la Granada islámica*. Granada: Diputación Provincial de Granada.

Barrios Aguilera, Manuel. 1996. "El albaicín de Granada sin moriscos. Memoriales para su restauración." *Chronica Nova* 23:439–63.

Barrios Aguilera, Manuel. 2002. *Granada morisca, la convivencia negada*. Granada: Serie Granada.

Barrios Aguilera, Manuel. 2009. "Pedro de Deza y Guzmán." In *Diccionario biográfico español* 15 (8):821–5. Madrid: Real Academia de la Historia, 2009.

Bass, Laura R. 2008. *The Drama of the Portrait: Theater and Visual Culture in Early Modern Spain*. University Park, PA: Pennsylvania University Press.

Bass, Laura R. 2013. "Self-Fashioning." In *Lexikon of the Hispanic Baroque: Transatlantic Exchange and Transformation*, edited by Evonne Levy and Kenneth Mills, 301–3. Austin: University of Texas Press.

Beardsley, Theodore S., Jr. 1970. *Hispano-Classical Translations Printed between 1482 and 1699*. Duquesne Studies, Philological Series 12. Pittsburgh: Duquesne University Press.

Benavides, Nicolás Augusto. 1571. "Relación de la batalla de Lepanto de Nicolás Augusto de Benavides, dirigida a Lope de Acuña." 10 October 1571. Biblioteca Palacio Real (Madrid), II/2211, 56. http://avisos.realbiblioteca.es/?p=article&aviso=37&art=863. Accessed 11/25/2015.

Bennassar, Bartolomé. 2000. *Don Juan de Austria: Un héroe para un imperio*. Madrid: Ediciones Temas de Hoy.

Benzoni, Gino, ed. 1974. *Il Mediterraneo nella seconde metà del 500 alla luce di Lepanto*. Florence: Olschki.

Bermúdez de Pedraza, Franscisco. 1608. *Antigüedad y excelencias de Granada*. Madrid, Luis Sánchez.

Bermúdez de Pedraza, Franscisco. 1638. *Historia eclesiástica. Principios y progresos de la ciudad y religión católica de Granada. Corona de su poderoso reino y excelencias de su corona*. Granada: Andrés de Santiago.

Bernat Vistarini, Antonio, and John T. Cull. 1999. *Enciclopedia de emblemas españoles ilustrados*. Madrid: Akal.

Bersuire, Pierre. 1575. *Repertorium Morale*. Venice: Heir of Girolamo Scotto.

Betz, Richard L. 2007. *The Mapping of Africa: A Cartobibliography of Printed Maps of the African Continent to 1700*. 't Goy-Houten (The Netherlands): Hes & de Graaf.

Beusterien, John. 1999. "Talking Black in Spanish: An Unfinished Black Spanish Glossary." *Bulletin of the Comediantes* 51 (1–2):83–104. http://dx.doi.org/10.1353/boc.1999.0002.

Beusterien, John. 2006. *An Eye on Race: Perspectives from Theater in Imperial Spain*. Lewisburg: Bucknell University Press.

Bicheno, Hugh. 2003. *Crescent and Cross: The Battle of Lepanto 1571*. London: Cassell.

Bindman, David, and Henry Louis Gates, Jr, eds. 2010. *The Image of the Black in Western Art*. 1976. Rev. ed. 5 vols. Cambridge and London: Belknap Press of Harvard University Press.

Blanco, Mercedes. 2010. "Cantaste, Rufo, tan heroicamente: La batalla de Lepanto y la cuestión del poema heroico." In *Estudios sobre la Edad Media, el Renacimiento y la temprana Edad Moderna*, edited by Francisco Bautista Pérez and Jimena Gamba Corradine, 477–512. San Millán de la Cogolla (Spain): Seminario de Estudios Medievales y Renacentistas (SEMYR).

Blanco, Mercedes. 2014. "La Batalla de Lepanto y la cuestión del poema heroico." *Calíope* 19 (1):23–54.

Block, Elizabeth. 1982. "The Narrator Speaks: Apostrophes in Homer and Vergil." *Transactions of the American Philological Association* 112:7–22. http://dx.doi.org/10.2307/284067.

Blumenthal, Debra. 2009. *Enemies and Familiars: Slavery and Mastery in Fifteenth-Century Valencia*. Ithaca and London: Cornell University Press.

Bouza, Fernando. 2004. *Communication, Knowledge, and Memory in Early Modern Spain*. Translated by Sonia López and Michael Agnew. Foreword by Roger Chartier. Philadelphia: University of Pennsylvania Press.

Bouza, Fernando. 2012. *"Dásele licencia y privilegio": Don Quijote y la aprobación de los libros en el Siglo de Oro*. Madrid: Akal.

Braudel, Fernand. 1966 [1949]. *La Méditerranée et le monde méditerranéen a l'époque de Philippe II*. 2nd ed. Paris: Librairie Armand Colin.

Braun, Georg. 1593 [1581]. *Cities of the World, Book 3*. [*Civitates Orbis Terrarum. Liber Tertius*] Cologne: Bertram Buchholtz.

Braund, Susanna Morton, trans. 1992. *Civil War* by Lucan. Oxford: Clarendon Press.

Bultman, Dana. 2007. *Heretical Mixtures: Feminine and Poetic Opposition to Matter-Spirit Dualism in Spain, 1531–1631*. Valencia: Albatros-Hispanófila, Siglo XXI.

Burke, Peter. 1993. *The Art of Conversation*. Ithaca: Cornell University Press.

Burke, Peter. 2004. *Languages and Communities in Early Modern Europe*. Cambridge: Cambridge University Press. http://dx.doi.org/10.1017/CBO9780511617362.

Byrne, Susan. 2012. *Law and History in Cervantes'* Don Quixote. Toronto: University of Toronto Press.

Cabrera de Córdoba, Luis. 1998 [1619]. *Historia de Felipe II, Rey de España*. Edited by José Martínez Millán and Carlos Javiera de Carlos Morales. 2 vols. Salamanca: Junta de Castilla y León.

Calero Palacios, María del Carmen. 1978. *La enseñanza y educación en Granada bajo los Reyes Austrias*. Granada: Diputación Provincial.

Calero Palacios, María del Carmen. 1995. *La Universidad de Granada: Los documentos fundacionales*. Granada: Universidad de Granada.

Calero Palacios, María del Carmen. 1997. "La Universidad de Granada durante los siglos XVI y XVII." In Part I of *Historia de la Universidad de Granada*, edited by Caldero Palacios, María del Carmen, Inmaculada Arias de Saavedra, and Cristina Viñes Millet, 11–84. Granada: Universidad de Granada.

Callejón Peláez, Antonio Luis. 2008. *Primus inter heroes: Damas y guerreros en la decoración del Monasterio de San Jerónimo de Granada*. Granada: Mouliaá Map.

Cañizares-Esguerra, Jorge. 2013. "Self-Fashioning." In *Lexikon of the Hispanic Baroque: Transatlantic Exchange and Transformation*, edited by Evonne Levy and Kenneth Mills, 304–6. Austin: University of Texas Press.

Capponi, Niccolò. 2006. *Victory of the West: The Story of the Battle of Lepanto*. London: Macmillan.

Caro Baroja, Julio. 1979. *La estación de amor: Fiestas populares de mayo a San Juan*. Madrid: Taurus.

Caro Baroja, Julio. 2000 [1976]. *Los moriscos del Reino de Granada*. Madrid: Istmo.

Carretta, Vincent. 2005. *Equiano the African: Biography of a Self-Made Man*. Athens and London: University of Georgia Press.

Casale, Giancarlo. 2007. "The Ethnic Composition of Ottoman Ship Crews and the 'Rumi Challenge' to Portuguese Identity." *Medieval Encounters* 13 (1): 122–44. http://dx.doi.org/10.1163/157006707X174041.

Casali, Sergio. 2004. "Nisus and Euryalus: Exploiting the Contradictions in Virgil's 'Doloneia.'" *Harvard Studies in Classical Philology* 102:319–54. http://dx.doi.org/10.2307/4150045.

Casey, James. 2007. *Family and Community in Early Modern Spain: The Citizens of Granada, 1570–1739*. Cambridge: Cambridge University Press. http://dx.doi.org/10.1017/CBO9780511496707.

Casos notables de la ciudad de Córdoba. 2003 [ca. 1618]. Córdoba: Francisco Baena Altolaguirre.

Castillo Fernández, Javier. 2015. "Estudio introductorio." In Mármol Carvajal 2015, XXI–L.

Catena, Girolamo. 1587 [1586]. *Vita del gloriosissimo Papa Pio Quinto*. Rev. ed. Rome: Alessandro Gardano et Francesco Coattino.

Cervantes, Miguel de. 1978 [1605]. *Don Quijote*, I. Edited by Luis Andrés Murillo. Madrid: Castalia.

Checa, Fernando. 1994. *Tiziano y la Monarquía Hispánica: Usos y funciones de la pintura veneciana en España (siglos xvi y xvii)*. Madrid: Nerea.

Cicero. 1948. *De oratore*. Translated by E.W. Sutton and H. Rackham. LCL. Cambridge, MA: Harvard University Press.

Clénard, Nicolas (Clenardus or Cleynaerts). 1940. *Correspondance*. Edited and translated by Alphonse Roersch. 3 vols. Brussels: Palais des Académies.

CODOIN (Colección de documentos inéditos para la historia de España). Edited by Martín Fernández de Navarrete, et al. Vols. 2, 3, 21, and 28. Madrid: Viuda de Calero, 1843+.

Coleman, David. 2003. *Creating Christian Granada: Society and Religious Culture in an Old-World Frontier City, 1492–1600*. Ithaca and London: Cornell University Press.

Colón, Cristóbal. 1986 [1492]. "Diario del primer viaje (1492–1493)." In *Los cuatro viajes: Testamento*, edited by Consuelo Varela, 43–204. Madrid: Alianza.

Constable, Olivia Remie. 2007. "Chess and Courtly Culture in Medieval Castile: The *Libro de ajedrez* of Alfonso X, el Sabio." *Speculum* 82 (2):301–47. http://dx.doi.org/10.1017/S0038713400009404.

Contarini, Alvisse. 1571. Dispatch of 3 November 1571. In *Dépêches des ambassadeurs vénitiens par Gaston Raynaud*. Bibliothèque nationale de France (Paris), Microfilm 1727.

Contarini, Giovanni Pietro. 1572. *Historia delle cose successe dal principio della guerra mossa da Selim ottomano a venetiani fino al dì della gran giornata vittoriosa contra turchi*. Venice: Francesco Rampazetto.

Copie d'une lettre de La Rosse, mère de Sain Bej, prisonnier à Rome. Envoyée au Serenissime Don Jean d'Austria, et a lui presentée. 1572. Lyon: Rigaud.

Corazón de María, Ángeles del Purísimo. 2005. *Las carmelitas descalzas de San José de Granada*. Granada: Caja Granada.

Coreth, Anna. 2004 [1959, rev. ed. 1982]. *Pietas Austriaca*. Translated by William D. Bowman and Anna Maria Leitgeb. West Lafayette, IN: Purdue University Press.

Coroleu, Alejandro, Carlo Caruso, and Andrew Laird, eds. 2012. "The Role of Latin in the Early Modern World: Linguistic Identity and Nationalism 1350–1800." *Renæssanceforum* 8. http://renaessanceforum.dk/rf_8_2012.htm.

Cortés, Hernán. 1993 [1521]. "Segunda carta de relación." In *Cartas de relación*, edited by Ángel Delgado-Gómez, 159–309. Madrid: Castalia.

Cortes Peña, Antonio Luis, and Bernard Vincent. 1986. *La época moderna, siglos XVI, XVII, y XVIII*. Vol. 3 of *Historia de Granada*. Granada: Don Quijote.

Courtès, Jean Marie. 2010. "The Theme of 'Ethiopia' and 'Ethiopians' in Patristic Literature." In Bindman and Gates, 2.1:199–214.

Crowley, Roger. 2009. *Empires of the Sea: The Siege of Malta, the Battle of Lepanto, and the Contest for the Center of the World*. New York: Random House.

Cruz, Anne J. 1996. "Feminism, Psychoanalysis, and the Search for the M/Other in Early Modern Spain." *Indiana Journal of Hispanic Literatures* 9:31–54.

Cruz, Anne J. 2002. "Arms versus Letters: The Poetics of War and the Career of the Poet in Early Modern Spain." In *European Literary Careers: Classical Medieval and Renaissance*, edited by Patrick Cheney and Frederick de Armas, 186–205. Toronto: University of Toronto Press.

Curran, Andrew S. 2011. *The Anatomy of Blackness: Science and Slavery in an Age of Enlightenment*. Baltimore: Johns Hopkins University Press.

Dandelet, Thomas J. 2001. *Spanish Rome, 1500–1700*. New Haven: Yale University Press.

Davis, Elizabeth B. 2000. *Myth and Identity in the Epic of Imperial Spain*. Columbia and London: University of Missouri Press.

Davis, Natalie Zemon. 2006. *Trickster Travels: A Sixteenth-Century Muslim between Worlds*. New York: Hill and Wang.

de Armas, Frederick A. 2011. *Don Quixote among the Saracens: A Clash of Civilizations and Literary Genres*. Toronto: University of Toronto Press.

Devisse, Jean. 2010. "The Black and His Color: From Symbols to Realities." Translated by William Granger Ryan. In Bindman and Gates, 2.1:73–137.

Díaz del Castillo, Bernal. 1982. *Historia verdadera de la conquista de la Nueva España*. Edited by Carmelo Saenz de Santa María. Madrid: Instituto "Gonzalo Fernández de Oviedo," CSIC.

Diedo, Gerolamo. 1995. [1571]. "La Battaglia di Lepanto descritta da Gerolamo Diedo." In Onorato Caetani and Gerolamo Diedo, *La battaglia di Lepanto*, introduction by Salvatore Mazzarella, 177–224. Palermo: Sellerio Editore.

Dionisotti, Carlo. 1974. "Lepanto nella cultura italiana del tempo." In Benzoni, 127–51.

Discorso sopra due grandi e memorabili battaglie navali fatte nel mondo, l'una di Cesare Augusto con M. Antonio, altra delli sig. Venetiani, e della Santissima Lega con Sultan Selim, signor di Turchi. 1572. Bologna: A. Benaccio.

Domínguez Ortiz, Antonio. 2003 [1952]. "La esclavitud en Castilla durante la Edad Moderna." Rpt. in *La esclavitud en Castilla en la Edad Moderna y otros estudios de marginados*, 1–64. Granada: Editorial Comares, 2003.

Domínguez Ortiz, Antonio, and Bernard Vincent. 1978. *Historia de los moriscos: Vida y tragedia de una minoría*. Madrid: Biblioteca de la Revista de Occidente.

Dopico, Georgina, and Jacques Lezra. 2001. Introducción to Sebastián de Covarrubias. *Suplemento al tesoro de la lengua española castellana*, edited by Georgina Dopico and Jacques Lezra, ix–xx. Madrid: Ediciones Polifemo.

Douglass, Frederick. 2014 [1855]. *My Bondage and My Freedom*. Edited by David W. Blight. New Haven and London: Yale University Press.

Dunlap, David W. 2014. "Scholarly Perspectives on Inscription at the 9/11 Memorial Museum." *New York Times*. 2 April 2014. http://cityroom.blogs

.nytimes.com/2014/04/02/scholarly-perspectives-on-inscription-at-the-911-memorial-museum/.

Earle, Rebecca. 2012. *The Body of the Conquistador: Food, Race and the Colonial Experience in Spanish America, 1492–1700*. Cambridge: Cambridge University Press. http://dx.doi.org/10.1017/CBO9780511763359.

Elliot van Liere, Katherine. 2000. "Humanism and Scholasticism in Sixteenth-Century Academe: Five Student Orations from the University of Salamanca." *Renaissance Quarterly* 53 (1):57–107. http://dx.doi.org/10.2307/2901533.

Elliot van Liere, Katherine. 2003. "After Nebrija: Academic Reformers and the Teaching of Latin in Sixteenth-Century Salamanca." *Sixteenth Century Journal* 34 (4):1065–104. http://dx.doi.org/10.2307/20061645.

Elliott, J.H. 1989. *Spain and Its World: 1500–1700*. New Haven: Yale University Press.

Elliott, J.H. 1990 [1963]. *Imperial Spain: 1469–1716*. London: Penguin Books.

Elogio de la casa de Velada, para el Marques don Gomez Davila. BNE, Man. 3184.

Ercilla, Alonso de. 1993 [1589–97]. *La Araucana*. Edited by Isaías Lerner. Madrid: Cátedra.

Fagles, Robert, trans. 2006. *Virgil. The Aeneid*. New York: Penguin Books.

Fallows, Noel. 2010. *Jousting in Medieval and Renaissance Iberia*. Woodbridge, Suffolk: Boydell Press.

Falomir Faus, Miguel, ed. 2003. *Tiziano*. Madrid: Museo del Prado.

Feerick, Jean E. 2010. *Strangers in Blood: Relocating Race in the Renaissance*. Toronto: University of Toronto Press.

Fenlon, Iain. 2007. *The Ceremonial City: History, Memory and Myth in Renaissance Venice*. New Haven and London: Yale University Press.

Fernández Chaves, Manuel F., and Rafael M. Pérez García. 2005. "La esclavitud en la Sevilla del Quinientos: una propuesta metodológica en base a documentación parroquial (1568-1590)." In *Marginados y minorías sociales en la España moderna y otros estudios sobre Extremadura*, edited by Felipe Lorenzana de la Puente and Francisco J. Mateos Ascacíbar, 113–22. Proceedings of the VI Jornadas de Historia en Llerena. Llerena: Sociedad Extremeña de Historia.

Fernández de Córdoba, Francisco (Abbot of Rute). ca. 1620. *Casa de Córdoba, y origen de la fundación y antigüedad de esta ciudad*. Manuscript 3271. Biblioteca Nacional de España (Madrid).

Fra Molinero, Baltasar. 1995. *La imagen de los negros en el teatro del Siglo de Oro*. Madrid: Siglo XXI.

Fra Molinero, Baltasar. 2005. "Juan Latino and His Racial Difference." In *Black Africans in Renaissance Europe*, edited by T.F. Earle and K.J.P. Lowe, 326–44. Cambridge: Cambridge University Press.

Fuchs, Barbara. 2009. *Exotic Nation: Maurophilia and the Construction of Early Modern Spain*. Philadelphia: University of Pennsylvania Press. http://dx.doi.org/10.9783/9780812207354.

Gallego Burín, Antonio. 1953. "Nuevos datos sobre la Capilla Real de Granada." *Boletín de la Sociedad Española de Excursiones* 57:67–116.

Gallego Burín, Antonio. 1961. *Granada: Guiá artística e histórica de la ciudad*. Madrid: Fundación Rodríguez-Acosta.

Gallego Burín, Antonio, and Alfonso Gamir Sandoval. 1996 [1968]. *Los moriscos del Reino de Granada según el Sínodo de Guadix de 1554*. Facsimile edition with prefatory study by Bernard Vincent. Granada: Archivum.

Garcés, María Antonia. 2002. *Cervantes in Algiers: A Captive's Tale*. Nashville: Vanderbilt University Press.

Garcés, María Antonia. 2011. Introduction to *An Early Modern Dialogue with Islam: Antonio de Sosa's* Topography of Algiers *(1612)*, translated by Diana de Armas Wilson. Notre Dame, IN: University of Notre Dame Press.

García-Arenal, Mercedes, and Fernando Rodríguez Mediano. 2010a. "Los libros de los moriscos y los eruditos orientales." *al-Qantara* 31 (2):611–46. http://dx.doi.org/10.3989/alqantara.2010.v31.i2.244.

García-Arenal, Mercedes, and Fernando Rodríguez Mediano. 2010b. *Un oriente español: Los moriscos y el Sacromonte en los tiempos de Contrarreforma*. Madrid: Marcial Pons.

García Ballester, Luis. 1984. *Los moriscos y la medicina: Un capítulo de la medicina y la ciencia marginadas en la España del siglo XVI*. Barcelona: Labor Universitaria.

García Galiano, Ángel. 1992. *La imitación poética en el Renacimiento*. Kassel: Reichenberger.

García Hernán, Enrique. 1995. *La Armada española en la monarquía de Felip II y la defensa del Mediterráneo*. Madrid: Tempo.

García Mercadal, José, ed. 1999 [1951]. *Viajes de extranjeros por España y Portugal, desde los tiempos más remotos hasta comienzos del Siglo XX*. Vol. 1. Rev. ed. Agustín García Simón. Salamanca: Junta de Castilla y León, 1999.

Garrad, K. 1956. "La industria sedera granadina en el siglo XVI y su conexión con el levantamiento de las Alpujarras (1568–1571)." *Miscelanea de Estudios Arabes y Hebraicos* 7:73–104.

Gastaldi, Giacomo (Jacopo Gastaldo), ed. 1548. *La Geografia di Claudio Ptolomeo alessandrino: con alcuni comenti et aggiunte …* Venice: Giovanni Baptista Pedrezano.

Gates Jr, Henry Louis, 2014 [1988]. *The Signifying Monkey: A Theory of African-American Literary Criticism. 25th-Anniversary Edition*. New York and Oxford: Oxford University Press.

Gates, Jr, Henry Louis, and Maria Wolff. 1998. "An Overview of Sources on the Life and Work of Juan Latino, the 'Ethiopian Humanist.'" *Research in African Literatures: The African Diaspora and Its Origins* 29 (4):14–51.

Gaylord [Randel], Mary M. 1971. *The Historical Prose of Fernando de Herrera*. London: Tamesis.

Gherardi, Pietro. 1572. *In Foedus et Victoriam contra Turcas iuxta Sinum Corinthiacum*. Venice: Guerraea.

Gil Fernández, Luis. 1981. *Panorama social del humanismo español (1500–1800)*. Madrid: Alhambra.

Gil Pujol, Xavier. 2004. "Un rey, una fe, muchas naciones: Patria y nación en la España de los siglos XVI y XVII." In *La Monarquía de las naciones: Patria, nación y naturaleza en la Monarquía de España*, edited by Antonio Álvarez-Ossorio Alvariño and Bernardo J. García García, 39–76. Madrid: Fundación Carlos Amberes.

Gilroy, Paul. 1993. *The Black Atlantic: Modernity and Double Consciousness*. Cambridge, MA: Harvard University Press.

Göllner, Carl von. 1968. *Turcica: Die europäischen Türkendurcke des XVI. Jahrhunderts*. Vol. 2 (1551 to 1600). Bibliotheca Bibliographica Aureliana 23. Bucharest: Editura Academiei.

González Vázquez, José. 1983. "Juan Latino, imitador de Virgilio." *Estudios de Filología Latina* 3:129–38.

González Vázquez, José. 1996. "Valoración de la producción latina del Renacimiento granadino." In *Clasicismo y humanismo en el Renacimiento granadino*, edited by José González Vázquez, Manuel López Múñoz, and Juan Jesús Valverde Abril, 317–41. Granada: Universidad de Granada.

A Greek-English Lexicon. 1996. Edited by Henry George Liddell and Robert Scott. Revised by Henry Stuart Jones. Oxford: Clarendon Press.

Greenblatt, Stephen. 1980. *Renaissance Self-Fashioning*. Chicago: University of Chicago Press.

Greene, Thomas M. 1982. *The Light in Troy: Imitation and Discovery in Renaissance Poetry*. New Haven and London: Yale University Press.

Greer, Margaret R., Walter D. Mignolo, and Maureen Quilligan. 2007. *Rereading the Black Legend: The Discourses of Religious and Racial Difference in the Renaissance Empires*. Chicago: University of Chicago Press.

Gregory, Tobias. 2006. *From Many Gods to One: Divine Action in Renaissance Epic*. Chicago and London: University of Chicago Press. http://dx.doi.org/10.7208/chicago/9780226307565.001.0001.

Griffin, Clive. 1984. "The Crombergers of Seville and the First Italic Book Printed in Spain." In *Palaestra Typographica: Aspects de la production du livre humaniste et religieux au XVIe siècle*, edited by Jean-François Gilmont, 57–96. Aubel (Belgium): P.M. Gason.

Griffin, Clive. 1988. *The Crombergers of Seville: The History of a Printing and Merchant Dynasty*. Oxford: Clarendon Press.

Guilmartin, John Francis, Jr. 2003 [1974]. *Gunpowder and Galleys: Changing Technology and Mediterranean Warfare at Sea in the 16th Century*. Rev. ed. London: Conway Maritime Press.

Hankins, James. 1995. "Renaissance Crusaders: Humanist Crusade Literature in the Age of Mehmed II." *Dunbarton Oaks Papers* 49, Symposium on Byzantium and the Italians, 13th–15th Centuries, 111–207. http://dx.doi .org/10.2307/1291712.

Hankins, James. 2001. "A Lost Continent of Literature." In *The Lost Continent: Neo-Latin Literature and the Rise of Modern European Literatures. Harvard Library Bulletin* ns 12 (1–2):21–8.

Hardie, Philip. 2012. *Rumour and Renown: Representations of Fama in Western Literature*. Cambridge: Cambridge University Press.

Harris, A. Katie. 2007. *From Muslim to Christian Granada: Inventing a City's Past in Early Modern Spain*. Baltimore: Johns Hopkins University Press.

Harvey, L.P. 1990. *Islamic Spain, 1250 to 1500*. Chicago and London: University of Chicago Press.

Harvey, L.P. 2005. *Muslims in Spain: 1500–1614*. Chicago and London: University of Chicago Press.

Henríquez de Jorquera, Francisco. 1987 [1643]. *Anales de Granada: Descripción del Reino y Ciudad de Granada. Crónica de la Reconquista (1482–1492). Sucesos de los años 1588–1546*. Vol. 2. Edited by Antonio Marín Ocete. 1934. Rev. ed. Pedro Gan Giménez. Granada: University of Granada.

Herodotus. 1971. *The Histories*. In *Herodotus*. Translated by A.D. Godley. LCL. London: William Heinemann.

Herrera, Fernando de. 1572. *Relación de la guerra de Chipre y suceso de la Batalla Naval de Lepanto*. Seville: Alonso Picardo. Rpt. in *CODOIN* 21:243–382.

Hess, Andrew C. 1968. "The Moriscos: An Ottoman Fifth Column in Sixteenth-Century Spain." *American Historical Review* 74 (1):1–25. http://dx.doi.org/ 10.2307/1857627.

Hess, Andrew C. 1972. "The Battle of Lepanto and Its Place in Mediterranean History." *Past & Present* 57 (1):53–73. http://dx.doi.org/10.1093/past/ 57.1.53.

Hinds, Stephen. 1998. *Allusion and Intertext: Dynamics of Appropriation in Roman Poetry*. Cambridge: Cambridge University Press.

Horsfall, Nicholas, ed. 1995. *A Companion to the Study of Virgil*. Leiden: E.J. Brill.

Hurtado de Mendoza, Diego. 1970 [ca. 1570]. *Guerra de Granada.* Edited by B. Blanco-González. Madrid: Castalia.

Inalcik, Halil. 1974. "Lepanto in the Ottoman Documents." In Benzoni, 185–92.

Irigoyen-García, Javier. 2014. *The Spanish Arcadia: Sheep Herding, Pastoral Discourse, and Ethnicity in Early Modern Spain.* Toronto: University of Toronto Press.

Johnson, Charles S., ed. 1996 [1927]. *Ebony and Topaz: A Collectanea.* Rpt. *The Politics and Aesthetics of 'New Negro' Literature,* edited by Cary D. Wintz. Vol. 2 of *The Harlem Renaissance, 1920–1940.* New York and London: Garland.

Jordan, Jenny. 2004a. "Galley Warfare in Renaissance Intellectual Layering: Lepanto through Actium." *Viator* 35:563–80. http://dx.doi.org/10.1484/J.VIATOR.2.300210.

Jordan, Jenny. 2004b. "Imagined Lepanto: Turks, Mapbooks, Intrigue, and Spectacular in the Sixteenth Century Construction of 1571." Dissertation. UCLA.

Juvenal. 2004. *Satires.* In *Juvenal and Persius,* translated by Susanna Morton Braund, 128–511. LCL 91. Cambridge, MA: Harvard University Press.

Kagan, Richard L. 1974. *Students and Society in Early Modern Spain.* Baltimore: Johns Hopkins University Press.

Kagan, Richard L. 1981. *Lawsuits and Litigants in Castile 1500–1700.* Chapel Hill: University of North Carolina Press.

Kallendorf, Craig. 2007a. *The Other Virgil: "Pessimistic" Readings of the Aeneid in Early Modern Culture.* Oxford: Oxford University Press. http://dx.doi.org/10.1093/acprof:oso/9780199212361.001.0001.

Kallendorf, Craig. 2007b. *The Virgilian Tradition: Book History and the History of Reading in Early Modern Europe.* Aldershot, UK: Ashgate.

Kamen, Henry. 1997. *The Spanish Inquisition: A Historical Revision.* New Haven and London: Yale University Press.

Kantorowicz, Ernst H. 1997 [1957]. *The King's Two Bodies: A Study in Mediaeval Political Theology.* Rev. ed. Preface by William Chester Jordan. Princeton: Princeton University Press.

Kaplan, Paul H.D. 1985. *The Rise of the Black Magus in Western Art.* Ann Arbor: UMI Research Press.

Kaplan, Paul H.D. 2010. "Italy, 1490–1700." In Bindman and Gates, 3.1:93–190.

Koerner, Joseph Leo. 2010. "The Epiphany of the Black Magus circa 1500." In Bindman and Gates, 3.1:16–92.

Lafaye, Jacues, ed. 1972. *Manuscrit Tovar: Origines et croyances des Indiens du Mexique.* Graz: Akademische Druck.

Latino, Juan (Joannes Latinus). 1573. *Ad catholicum, pariter et invictissimum Philippum Dei gratia Hispaniarum regem, de felicissima serenissimi Ferdinandi*

Principis nativitate, epigrammatum liber … Austrias Carmen. Granada: Hugo Mena.

Latino, Juan (Joannes Latinus). 1576 (?). *De augusta et catholica regalium corporum translatione per Catholicum Philippum […] Epigrammatum sive Epitaphiorum, libri duo* (abbrev. *De Translatione*). Granada: Hugo de Mena.

Latino, Juan (Joannes Latinus). 2014 [1573]. *The Song of John of Austria (SJA)*. In Wright, Spence, and Lemons, 288–405.

Lazure, Guy. 2007. "Possessing the Sacred: Monarchy and Identity in Philip II's Relic Collection at the Escorial." *Renaissance Quarterly* 60 (1):58–93. http://dx.doi.org/10.1353/ren.2007.0076.

Lemons, Andrew. Forthcoming. "Juan Latino's Worldly Poetics: Lepanto, Lucretius and Literary Tradition." *Calíope* 21.

Leo, Bernardino. 2008. "De bello turcico." In *La battaglia di Lepanto e il De bello turcico di Bernardino Leo*, edited by Silvio Barsi, 171–297. Milan: Bruno Mondadori.

Lewis, Martin W., and Kären E. Wigen. 1997. *The Myth of Continents: A Critique of Metageography*. Berkeley and London: University of California Press.

Liang, Yuen-Gen. 2011. *Family and Empire: The Fernández de Córdoba and the Spanish Realm*. Philadelphia: University of Pennsylvania Press.

Lida de Malkiel, María Rosa. 1975. *La tradición clásica en España*. Barcelona: Ariel.

López, Miguel A. 1982. *Maestros y graduados (1532–1542)*. Granada: Universidad de Granada.

López de Toro, José. 1950. *Los poetas de Lepanto*. Madrid: Instituto Histórico de Marina.

Lowe, Kate. 2012. "The Lives of African Slaves and People of African Descent in Renaissance Europe." In Spicer, 13–33.

Lucan. 1588. *De bellum civile*. Translated by Martín Laso de Oropesa. Revised and expanded by Joan Baptista Bonello. Burgos: Felipe de Junta.

Lucan. 1950. *De bellum civile*. Edited by A.E. Housman. Oxford: Blackwell.

Lyne, R.O.A.M. 1987. *Further Voices in Vergil's Aeneid*. Oxford: Clarendon Press.

MacKay, Ruth. 2012. *The Baker who Pretended to be King of Portugal*. Chicago and London: University of Chicago Press. http://dx.doi.org/10.7208/chicago/9780226501109.001.0001.

Mammana, Simona. 2007. *Lèpanto: Rime per la vittoria sul Turco. Regesto (1571–1573) e studio critico*. Rome: Bulzoni Editore.

Marín Ocete, A[ntonio]. 1923. "El negro Juan Latino: Ensayo de un estudio biográfico y crítico." Part 1. *Revista del Centro de Estudios Históricos de Granada y su Reino*. 13 (1–2):97–120.

Marín Ocete, A[ntonio]. 1924. "El negro Juan Latino: Ensayo de un estudio biográfico y crítico." Part 2. *Revista del Centro de Estudios Históricos de Granada y su Reino* 14 (1–2):25–82.

Marineo Sículo, Lucio. 1533. *Las cosas memorables de España (*full title: *Obra compuesta por Lucio Marineo Sículo coronista de sus Majestades de las cosas memorables de España)*. Alcalá: Miguel de Eguía.

Mármol Carvajal, Luis del. ca. 1571. "Relación hecha por Luis del Marmol del estandarte que se tomó á los turcos en la batalla naval de Lepanto." In *CODOIN* 3:270–3.

Mármol Carvajal, Luis del. 1573. *Primera parte de la descripción general de África*. Granada: Rene Rabut.

Mármol Carvajal, Luis del. 2015 [1600]. *Historia del [sic] rebelión y castigo de los moriscos del Reino de Granada*. Edited by Javier Castillo Fernández. Granada: Universidad de Granada / Tres Fronteras Ediciones.

Márquez de la Plata, and Vicenta Ferrándiz. 2005. *Mujeres renacentistas en la corte de Isabel la Católica*. Madrid: Castalia.

Martial. 1993. *Epigrams*. Translated by D.R. Shackelton Baily. Vol. 2. LCL 95. Cambridge, MA: Harvard University Press.

Martín Casares, Aurelia. 2000. *La esclavitud en la Granada del siglo XVI: Género, raza y religión*. Granada: Universidad de Granada.

Martín Casares, Aurelia, ed. 2014a. *Esclavitudes hispánicas (siglos XV al XXI): Horizontes socioculturales*. Granada: Editorial Universidad de Granada.

Martín Casares, Aurelia. 2014b. "Evolution of the Origin of Slaves Sold in Spain from the Late Middle Ages till the 18th Century" In *Schiavitù e servaggio nell'economia europea. Secc. XI–XVIII*. Selected Conference Proceedings of the Quarantecinquesima settimana di studi, 14–18 April 2013. Edited by Simonetta Cavaciocchi, 409–30. Florence: Firenze University Press.

Martínez, María Elena. 2008. *Genealogical Fictions: Limpieza de Sangre, Religion, and Gender in Colonial Mexico*. Stanford: Stanford University Press.

Martínez Hernández, Santiago. 2004. *El Marqués de Velada y la corte en los reinados de Felipe II y Felipe III: Nobleza cortesana y cultura política en la España del Siglo de Oro*. Salamanca: Junta de Castilla y León.

Martínez Leiva, Gloria, and Ángel Rodríguez Rebollo, eds. 2007. *Qvadros y otras cosas que tienen su Magestad Felipe IV en este Alcázar de Madrid. Año de 1636*. Madrid: Fundación Universitaria Española.

Martínez Millán, José. 1994. "En busca de la ortodoxia: El Inquisidor General Diego de Espinosa." In *La corte de Felipe II*, edited by José Martínez Millán, 189–228. Madrid: Alianza.

Martínez Millán, José, and Carlos J. de Carlos Morales, eds. 1998. *Felipe II (1527–1598): La configuración de la Monarquía Hispánica*. Salamanca: Junta de Castilla y León.

Martyr, Peter (Pietro Martire de Anghiera). 1530 [1492]. "Letter to Pedro González de Mendoza, Archbishop of Toledo (30 March 1492)." In *Opus epistolarum Petri Martyris Anglerii Mediolanensis*, fols. 23v–4r. Alcalá: Miguel de Eguía.

Mas, Albert. 1967. *Les turcs dans la littérature espagnole du Siècle d'Or*. Vol. 1. Paris: Centre de Recherches Hispaniques.

Masó, Calixto C. 1973. *Juan Latino: Gloria de España y de su raza*. Chicago: Northeastern Illinois University.

Maurer, Christopher. 1993. "Un monarca, un imperio y una espada: Juan Latino y el soneto de Hernando de Acuña sobre Lepanto." *Hispanic Review* 61 (1):35–51. http://dx.doi.org/10.2307/473285.

McLaughlin, Martin L. 1995. *Literary Imitation in the Italian Renaissance: The Theory and Practice of Literary Imitation in Italy from Dante to Bembo*. Oxford: Clarendon Press.

Mela, Pomponius. 1498. *Opus preclarissimus Pomponii Mellae cosmographi cum introductionibus et aliis tantopere necessariis*. Salamanca: n.p.

Méndez Rodríguez, Luis. 2011. *Esclavos en la pintura sevillana de los Siglos de Oro*. Seville: Universidad de Sevilla.

Menéndez y Pelayo, Marcelino. 1927. *Estudios sobre el teatro de Lope de Vega*. Edited by Miguel Artigas. Vol. 6. Madrid: Librería General de Victoriano Suárez.

Mercado, Tomás. 1571. *Suma de tratos, y contratos*. Seville: Hernando Díaz.

Middlebrook, Leah. 2009. *Imperial Lyric: New Poetry and New Subjects in Early Modern Spain*. University Park: Pennsylvania State University Press.

Miralles, Eulàlia, and Pep Valsalobre. 2010. "From Lluís Joan Vileta to Joan Pujol: Latin and Vernacular Poetry on the Battle of Lepanto in Catalonia." In *Humanism and Christian Letters in Early Modern Iberia (1480–1630)*, edited by Barry Taylor and Alejandro Coroleu, 159–72. Newcastle upon Tyne: Cambridge Scholars Publishing.

Montells y Nadal, Francisco de Paula. 2000 [1870]. *Historia del origen y fundación de la Universidad de Granada*. Ed. facs. Cristina Viñees Millet. Granada: Universidad de Granada.

Morell y Terry, Luis. 1997 [1892]. *Efemérides granadinas*. Ed. facs. Prologue by Antonio Gallego Morell. Granada: Gráficas Alhambra.

Muñoz-Fernández, Ángela. 2000. "Relaciones femininas y activación de los mecanismos del privilegio y la merced: La casa de Isabel I de Castilla." In *Las mujeres y el poder: representaciones y prácticas de vida*, edited by Ana I. Cerrada Jiménez and Cristina Seguar Graíño, 115–33. Madrid: Al-Mudayna.

Muñoz Martín, María Nieves, and José Antonio Sánchez Marín, 1991. "Las elegías de Juan Latino." In *Humanismo renacentista y mundo clásico*, edited by José Antonio Sánchez Marín and Manuel López Muñoz, 281–300. Madrid: Ediciones Clásicas.

Münzer, Hieronymous (Jerónimo). 1920 [1494–5]. "Itinerarium Hispanicum Hieronymi Monetarii," edited by Ludwig Pfandl. *Revue Hispanique* 48 (113): 1–179.

Murrin, Michael. 1994. *History and Warfare in Renaissance Epic*. Chicago and London: University of Chicago Press.

Nader, Helen. 1979. *The Mendoza Family in the Spanish Renaissance, 1350–1550*. New Brunswick: Rutgers University Press.

Navagero, Andrea. 1754 [1563]. *Viaggio in Ispagna del magnifico M. Andrea Navagero, eletto oratore a Carlo V, imperadore*. In *Opera omnia*, 302–71. Venice: Typographia Remondiniana.

Navarrete, Ignacio. 1994. *Orphans of Petrarch: Poetry and Theory in the Spanish Renaissance*. Berkeley and Los Angeles: University of California Press.

Nicolopulos, James. 2000. *The Poetics of Empire in the Indies: Prophecy and Imitation in La Araucana and Os Lusíades*. University Park: Pennsylvania State University Press.

Nirenberg, David. 2002. "Mass Conversion and Genealogical Mentalities: Jews and Christians in Fifteenth-Century Spain." *Past & Present* 174 (1):3–41. http://dx.doi.org/10.1093/past/174.1.3.

Núñez Muley, Francisco. 2007 [1567]. *A Memorandum for the President of the Royal Audiencia and Chancery Court of the City and Kingdom of Granada (1567)*. Edited and translated by Vincent Barletta. Chicago: University of Chicago Press. http://dx.doi.org/10.7208/chicago/9780226547282.001.0001.

Ong, Walter. 1959. "Latin Language Study as a Renaissance Puberty Rite." *Studies in Philology* 66 (2):103–24.

Orozco Díaz, Emilio, and Jesús Bermúdez Pareja. 1958. "La Universidad de Granada desde su fundación hasta la rebelión de los moriscos (1532–1568)." In *Carlos V (1500–1558): Homenaje de la Universidad de Granada*, 563–93. Granada: Universidad de Granada.

Ortelius, Abraham. 1570. *Theatrum orbis terrarum,* Antwerp: Aegid. Coppenium Diesth (on line http://www.loc.gov/item/98687183/).

Padrón, Ricardo. 2004. *The Spacious Word: Cartography, Literature, and Empire in Early Modern Spain*. Chicago: University of Chicago Press.

Panofsky, Erwin. 1969. *Problems in Titian, Mostly Iconographic*. The Wrightsman Lectures, New York University Institute of Fine Arts. New York: Phaidon.

Panofsky, Erwin. 2005 [1943]. *The Life and Art of Albrecht Dürer*. Rev. ed. Introduction by Jeffrey Chipps Smith. Princeton: Princeton University Press.

Parker, Geoffrey. 1998. *The Grand Strategy of Philip II*. New Haven and London: Yale University Press.

Parker, Geoffrey. 2010. *Felipe II: La biografía definitiva*. Translated by Victoria E. Gordo del Rey. Barcelona: Planeta.

Parker, Holt. 2013. "Juan Latino," blog entry by Holt Parker, 5 April 2013. (http://renaissancelatinpoemoftheweek.blogspot.co.uk/2013/04/5-juan-latino-johannes-latinus-on-birth.html).

Parry, Adam M. 1989. *The Language of Achilles and Other Papers,* Oxford: Clarendon Press.

Paruta, Paolo. 1605. *Historia vinetiana.* Venice: Domenico Nicolini.

Pedrosa, Francisco de. ca 1580. *Naumachia.* BNE. Manuscript 3960.

Pereda, Felipe. 2007. *Las imágenes de la discordia:Politica y poética de la imagen sagrada en la España del 400.* Madrid: Marcial Pons.

Pérez de Hita, Ginés. 1998 [1619]. *La guerra de los moriscos* (*Segunda parte de las guerras civiles de Granada*). Edited by Paula Blanchard-Demouge [1915]. Fac. ed. Edited by Joaquín Gil Sanjuán. Granada: Archivum.

Phillips, William D., Jr. 2014. *Slavery in Medieval and Early Modern Iberia.* Philadelphia: University of Pennsylvania Press. http://dx.doi.org/10.9783/9780812209174.

Pigman, G.W., III. 1980. "Versions of Imitation in the Renaissance." *Renaissance Quarterly* 33 (1):1–32. http://dx.doi.org/10.2307/2861533.

Pike, Ruth. 1967. "Sevillian Society in the Sixteenth Century: Slaves and Freedmen." *Hispanic American Historical Review* 47 (3): 344–59. http://dx.doi.org/10.2307/2511025.

Pliny. 1938. *Natural History.* Translated by H. Rackham. LCL, vol. 1 and 3 of 10. Cambridge, MA: Harvard University Press.

Pregmáticas [sic] *y provisiones de su M. el Rey don Felipe nuestro señor, sobre la lengua y vestidos, y otras cosas que han de hacer los naturales de este reino de Granada.* 1567. Granada: Hugo Mena.

Puglisi, Anthony Mark. 2008. "Escritura y ambición: *La Historia del rebelión y castigo de los moriscos* de Luis del Mármol Carvajal." *Investigaciones Históricas* 28:141–56.

Putnam, Michael C. J. 1965. *The Poetry of the Aeneid: Four Studies in Imaginative Unity and Design.* Cambridge, MA: Harvard University Press.

Quinn, Mary B. 2013. *The Moor and the Novel: Narrating Absence in Early Modern Spain.* Hampshire, NY: Palgrave Macmillan. http://dx.doi.org/10.1057/9781137299932.

Quint, David. 1993. *Epic and Empire: Politics and Generic Form from Virgil to Milton.* Princeton: Princeton University Press.

Quintanilla Raso, María Concepción. 1980. "La biblioteca del marqués de Priego (1518)." *En la España Medieval* 1:347–82.

Quintilian. 2001. *The Orator's Education (Institutiones Oratoriae).* Translated by D.A. Russell. Vol. 1 of 5. Cambridge: Harvard University Press.

Raccolta di varii poemi Latini, Greci, e Volgari. 1572. Venice: Sebastiano Ventura.

Randel, Mary Gaylord. See Gaylord, Mary.

"Relación de lo que hizo la Armada de la Liga Cristiana desde los treinta de Setiembre de 1571 años hasta diez de octubre después de la victoria que hubo de los 7 de este de la Armada del Turco." In AGS, Estado, legajo 1134, document 83. Transcribed in *CODOIN* 3:216–23.

Relaño, Francesc. 2000. *La emergencia de África como continente: un nuevo mundo a partir del viejo*. Lleida: Universitat de Lleida.

Rigaux, Maxim. 2013. "Cultura e identidad en el *Austrias carmen* de Juan Latino (Joannes Latinus)." Masters thesis. Ghent University. Ghent, Belgium.

Río Barredo, María José del. 2003. "De Madrid a Turín: el ceremonial de las reinas españolas en la corte ducal de Catalina Micaela de Saboya." *Cuadernos de Historia Moderna Añejo* 2:97–122.

Río Barredo, María José del. 2010. "Rituals of the Viaticum. Dynasty and Community in Habsburg Madrid." In *Exploring Cultural History: Essays in Honour of Peter Burke*, edited by M. Calaresu, F. de Vivo, and J.P. Rubiés, 55–76. Aldershot, UK: Ashgate.

Rodríguez Marín, Francisco. 1903. *Luis Barahona de Soto: Estudio biográfico, bibliográfico y crítico*. Madrid: Sucesores de Rivadeneyra.

Rodríguez Mediano, Fernando. 2009. "Luis del Mármol, lecteur de León: Une appréhension espagnole de l'Afrique." In *Léon l'Africain*, edited by François Pouillon, with Alain Messaoudi, Dietrich Rauchenberger, and Oumelbanine Zhiri, 239–67. Paris: Karthala.

Rodríguez-Salgado, M.J. 1988. *The Changing Face of Empire: Charles V, Philip II and Habsburg Authority, 1551–1559*. Cambridge: Cambridge University Press.

Rodríguez Salgado, M.J., et al., eds. 1988. *Armada 1588–1988: An International Exhibition to Commemorate the Spanish Armada*. London: Penguin.

Ronsard, Pierre de. 2010 [1572]. *The Franciad (1572)*. Translated, annotated, and with an introduction by Phillip John Usher. New York: AMS Press.

Rubio, David. 1934. *Classical Scholarship in Spain*. Washington, DC: Mimeoform Press.

Rufo, Juan. 1854 [1584]. *La Austriada*. Edited by Cayetano Rosell. BAE, vol. 29. Madrid: Rivadeneyra.

Rute, Abbot of. See Fernández de Córdoba, Francisco.

Salazar, Ambrosio. 1623 [1615]. *Espejo general de gramática en diálogos para saber perfectamente la lengua castellana*. Rouen: Adrian Morront.

Sánchez Marín, José A. 1981. Introducción to *La Austriada* de Juan Latino, edited and translated by José A. Sánchez Marín, 17–38. Granada: Instituto de Historia del Derecho.

Sánchez Marín, José Antonio, and María Nieves Muñoz Martín. 2009. "El maestro Juan Latino en la Granada renacentista: Su ciudad, su vida, sus protectores." *Florentia iliberritana* 20: 227–60.

Sandoval, Prudencio de. 1955 [ca. 1603]. *Historia de la vida y hechos del emperador Carlos V*. Edited by Carlos Seco Serrano. BAE, vols. 80–2. Madrid: Atlas.

Sannazaro, Jacopo. 2009. *Latin Poetry*. Translated by Michael C.J. Putnam. Cambridge, MA: I Tatti Renaissance Library / Harvard University Press.

Saunders, A.C. de C.M. 1982. *A Social History of Black Slaves and Freedmen in Portugal, 1441–1555*. Cambridge: Cambridge University Press.

Scafi, Alessandro. 2006. *Mapping Paradise: A History of Heaven on Earth*. London: The British Library.

Schomburg, Arthur A. [Arturo Alonso]. 1996 [1927]. "Juan Latino, Magister Latinus." In Johnson 1996 [1927], 67–73.

Scott, Rebecca J., and Jean M. Hébrard. 2012. *Freedom Papers: An Atlantic Odyssey in the Age of Emancipation*. Cambridge, MA, and London: Harvard University Press. http://dx.doi.org/10.4159/harvard.9780674065161.

Seijas, Tatiana. 2014. *Asian Slaves in Colonial Mexico: From Chinos to Indians*. Cambridge: Cambridge University Press. http://dx.doi.org/10.1017/CBO9781107477841.

Seo, J. Mira. 2011. "Identifying Authority: Juan Latino, an African Ex-Slave, Professor, and Poet in Sixteenth-Century Granada." In *African Athena: New Agendas*, edited by Daniel Orrells, Gurminder K. Bhambra, and Tessa Roynon, 258–76. New York: Oxford University Press. http://dx.doi.org/10.1093/acprof:oso/9780199595006.003.0016.

Seo, J. Mira. 2012. "Juan Latino (1518–ca. 1594/1596)." In *Dictionary of African Biography*, edited by Emmanuel K. Akyeampong and Henry Louis Gates, Jr, 3:470–2. Oxford: Oxford University Press.

Setton, Kenneth M. 1984. *The Papacy and the Levant (1204–1571): The Sixteenth Century from Julius III to Pious V*. Vol. 4. Philadelphia: The American Philosophical Society.

Siguënza, José de. 1986 [ca. 1602]. *La fundación del Monasterio del Escorial*. Madrid: Turner.

Silvestre, Gregorio. 1582. *Las obras del famoso poeta Gregorio Silvestre*. Edited by Pedro de Cáceres y Espinosa. Granada: Fernando de Aguilar.

Smith, Chantell. 2015. "From Juan to Juan: The Triumph of Poet and Subject in Juan Latino's *Austrias carmen*." In *Slavery, Migrations, and Transformations: Connecting Old and New Diasporas to the Homeland*. Edited by Toyin Falola and Danielle Porter Sanchez, 231–49. Amherst, NY: Cambria Press.

Snowden Jr, Frank M. 1970. *Blacks in Antiquity: Ethiopians in the Greco-Roman Experience*. Cambridge, MA: Belknap Press of Harvard University Press.

Snowden Jr, Frank M. 1983. *Before Color Prejudice: The Ancient View of Blacks*. Cambridge, MA: Harvard University Press.

Sola Castaño, Emilio. 2010. *Uchalí: El Calabrés Tiñoso, o el mito del corsario muladí en la frontera*. Barcelona: Edicions Bellaterra.

Soler Fiérrez, Eduardo. 2014. *Juan Latino, el esclavo catedrático*. Madrid: Eirene Editorial.

Soria Mesa, Enrique. 1995. "Una versión genealógica del ansia integradora de la élite morisca: El origen de la Casa de Granada." *Sharq al-Andalus* 12:213–21.

Spicer, Joaneath, ed. 2012. *Revealing the African Presence in Renaissance Europe*. Exhibition Catalogue, Walters Art Museum, Baltimore, MD (14 October 2012 to 21 January 2013). Baltimore: Walters Art Museum.

Spivakovsky, Erika. 1970. *Son of the Alhambra: Don Diego Hurtado de Mendoza, 1504–1575*. Austin and London: University of Texas Press.

Spratlin, V.B. 1938. *Juan Latino, Slave and Humanist*. New York: Spinner Press.

Stella, Alessandro. 2000. *Histoires d'esclaves dans la péninsule Ibérique*. Paris: École des Hautes Études en Sciences Sociales.

Stoichita, Victor. 2010. "The Image of the Black in Spanish Art: Sixteenth and Seventeenth Centuries." In Bindman and Gates, 3.1:191–234.

Suetonius. 1997. *Lives of the Caesars*. Translated by J.C. Rolfe. LCL 38. London: William Heinemann.

Sweet, James H. 1997. "The Iberian Roots of American Racist Thought." *William and Mary Quarterly* 54 (1):143–66. http://dx.doi.org/10.2307/2953315.

Taleb, Nassim Nicholas. 2007. *The Black Swan: The Impact of the Highly Improbable*. New York: Random House.

Tamayo Salazar, Juan. 1658. *Anamnesis sive Commemorationis Sanctorum Hispanorum*. Lyon: Philippe Borde, Laurent Arnaud, and Cl. Rigaud.

Tanner, Marie. 1993. *The Last Descendant of Aeneas: The Hapsburgs and the Mythic Image of the Emperor*. New Haven and London: Yale University Press.

Tasso, Torquato. 1587. *Discorsi del signor Torquato Tasso dell'arte poetica; et in particolare del Poema Heroico*. Venice: Giulio Vassalini.

Todorov, Tzvetan. 1987. *The Conquest of America: The Question of the Other*. Translated by Richard Howard. New York: Harper Torchbooks.

Vaccaluzzo, Nunzio. 1909. "Dei poeti latini della battaglia di Lepanto." *Archivio storico per la Sicilia orientale* 6 (2–3):197–226.

Valentino, Cesare. 1571. "Proyecto de puente conmemorativo en Mesina." Engraving in *Estampas varias* (Colección Gondomar). Real Biblioteca (Madrid), Manuscript IX/M/113 (106). Rome.

Van den Broecke, Marcel P.R. 1998. "Introduction to the Life and Works of Abraham Ortelius (1527–1598)." In *Abraham Ortelius and the First Atlas*, edited by Marcel Van den Broecke, Peter van der Krogt, and Peter Meurer, 29–54. Houten, The Netherlands: HES Publishers.

Vecindario de Granada. 1561. Manuscript. AGS, Cámara de Castilla, legajo 2,150.

Vega Carpio, Lope de. 1989 [1941]. *Epistolario de Lope de Vega Carpio*. Edited by Agustín González de Amezúa. Madrid: Artes gráficas Aldus, Vol. 3. Rpt: Madrid: Real Academia Española and Arco/Libros.

Vega Carpio, Lope de. 2007 [1598]. *La Dragontea*. Edited by Antonio Sánchez-Jiménez. Madrid: Cátedra.

Vega Carpio, Lope de. 2012. *Los ramilletes de Madrid*, edited by Elizabeth R. Wright. In *Comedias de Lope de Vega*, Parte XI, coordinated by Laura Fernández and Gonzalo Pontón, 1:467–610. Madrid: Gredos.

Velázquez, Luis José. 1797. *Orígenes de la poesía castellana*. Málaga: Herederos de D. Francisco Martínez de Aguilar.

Vickers, Brian. 1988. *In Defence of Rhetoric*. Oxford: Clarendon Press.

Vilches, Elvira. 2010. *New World Gold: Cultural Anxiety and Monetary Disorder in Early Modern Spain*. Chicago: University of Chicago Press.

Virgil. 1586. *La Eneida de Virgilio*. Rev. ed. Translated by Gregorio Hernández de Velasco. Zaragoza: Lorenzo y Diego Robles.

Virgil. 1969. *Aeneid*. In *Opera*, ed. R.A.B. Mynors. Oxford: Clarendon Press.

Voyages: The Trans-Atlantic Slave Trade Database (accessed 1 December 2015, http://www.slavevoyages.org/).

Wallace, Andrew. 2010. *Virgil's Schoolboys: The Poetics of Pedagogy in Renaissance England*. Oxford: Oxford University Press. http://dx.doi.org/10.1093/acprof:oso/9780199591244.001.0001.

Wardropper, Bruce W. 1967. *Poesía elegíaca española*. Salamanca: Anaya.

Weber, Alison. 2005. "Lope de Vega's *Rimas sacras*: Conversion, Clientage, and the Performance of Masculinity." *PMLA* 120 (2):404–21. http://dx.doi.org/10.1632/003081205X52400.

Weissbourd, Emily. 2013. "'I Have Done the State Some Service': Reading Slavery in *Othello* through *Juan Latino*." *Comparative Drama* 47 (4):529–51. http://dx.doi.org/10.1353/cdr.2013.0057.

Wey-Gómez, Nicolás. 2008. *The Tropics of Empire: Why Columbus Sailed South to the Indies*. Cambridge, MA, and London: MIT Press.

Wilson-Okamura, David Scott. 2010. *Virgil in the Renaissance*. Cambridge: Cambridge University Press. http://dx.doi.org/10.1017/CBO9780511762581.

Wright, Elizabeth R. 2001. *Pilgrimage to Patronage: Lope de Vega and the Court of Philip III, 1598–1621*. Lewisburg, PA: Bucknell University Press.

Wright, Elizabeth R. 2007. "Los Duques de Sessa, sus deudas y disputas: El mecenazgo como patrimonio familiar." In *Dramaturgia festiva y cultura nobiliaria en el Siglo de Oro*, edited by Bernardo J. García and María Luisa Lobato, 249–67. Madrid: Iberoamericana.

Wright, Elizabeth R. 2008. "From Drake to Draque: A Spanish Hero with an English Accent." In *Material and Symbolic Circulation between Spain and*

England, 1554–1604, edited by Anne J. Cruz, 29–38. Aldershot (England) and Burlington (VT): Ashgate.

Wright, Elizabeth R. 2009. "Narrating the Ineffable Lepanto: The *Austrias Carmen* of Joannes Latinus (Juan Latino)." *Hispanic Review* 77 (1):71–92. http://dx.doi.org/10.1353/hir.0.0042.

Wright, Elizabeth R. 2012. "Scrutinizing Early Modern Warfare in Latin Hexameters: The *Austrias Carmen* of Joannes Latinus (Juan Latino)." In *Poiesis and Modernity in the Old and New Worlds*, edited by Anthony J. Cascardi and Leah Middlebrook, 139–58. Nashville: Vanderbilt University Press.

Wright, Elizabeth R. 2015. "Modern War, Ancient Form: Lessons from Lepanto for a Latin Seminar in post-Bellum Granada." In *Representing Imperial Rivalry in the Early Modern Mediterranean*, edited by Barbara Fuchs and Emily Weissbourd, 126–44. Toronto: University of Toronto Press.

Wright, Elizabeth R., Sarah Spence, and Andrew Lemons. 2014. *The Battle of Lepanto*. I Tatti Renaissance Library 61. Cambridge, MA: Harvard University Press.

Ximénez de Enciso, Diego. 1951. *Juan Latino*. In *El Encubierto y Juan Latino*, edited by Eduardo Juliá Martínez, 141–356. Madrid: Artes Gráficas.

Zamora, Margarita. 1993. *Reading Columbus*. Berkeley and Los Angeles: University of California Press.

Index

Page numbers in italics indicate figures.

TORONTO IBERIC

1 Anthony J. Cascardi, *Cervantes, Literature, and the Discourse of Politics*
2 Jessica A. Boon, *The Mystical Science of the Soul: Medieval Cognition in Bernardino de Laredo's Recollection Method*
3 Susan Byrne, *Law and History in Cervantes'* Don Quixote
4 Mary E. Barnard and Frederick A. de Armas (eds), *Objects of Culture in the Literature of Imperial Spain*
5 Nil Santiáñez, *Topographies of Fascism: Habitus, Space, and Writing in Twentieth-Century Spain*
6 Nelson Orringer, *Lorca in Tune with Falla: Literary and Musical Interludes*
7 Ana M. Gómez-Bravo, *Textual Agency: Writing Culture and Social Networks in Fifteenth-Century Spain*
8 Javier Irigoyen-García, *The Spanish Arcadia: Sheep Herding, Pastoral Discourse, and Ethnicity in Early Modern Spain*
9 Stephanie Sieburth, *Survival Songs: Conchita Piquer's* Coplas *and Franco's Regime of Terror*
10 Christine Arkinstall, *Spanish Female Writers and the Freethinking Press, 1879–1926*
11 Margaret Boyle, *Unruly Women: Performance, Penitence, and Punishment in Early Modern Spain*

12 Evelina Gužauskytė, *Christopher Columbus's Naming in the* diarios *of the Four Voyages (1492–1504): A Discourse of Negotiation*
13 Mary E. Barnard, *Garcilaso de la Vega and the Material Culture of Renaissance Europe*
14 William Viestenz, *By the Grace of God: Francoist Spain and the Sacred Roots of Political Imagination*
15 Michael Scham, *Lector Ludens: The Representation of Games and Play in Cervantes*
16 Stephen Rupp, *Heroic Forms: Cervantes and the Literature of War*
17 Enrique Fernandez, *Anxieties of Interiority and Dissection in Early Modern Spain*
18 Susan Byrne, *Ficino in Spain*
19 Patricia M. Keller, *Ghostly Landscapes: Film, Photography, and the Aesthetics of Haunting in Contemporary Spanish Culture*
20 Carolyn A. Nadeau, *Food Matters: Alonso Quijano's Diet and the Discourse of Food in Early Modern Spain*
21 Cristian Berco, *From Body to Community: Venereal Disease and Society in Baroque Spain*
22 Elizabeth R. Wright, *The Epic of Juan Latino: Dilemmas of Race and Religion in Renaissance Spain*

www.ingramcontent.com/pod-product-compliance
Lightning Source LLC
LaVergne TN
LVHW090153080826
844660LV00013B/796/J

* 9 7 8 1 4 4 2 6 3 7 5 2 8 *